# EXILE FROM EXILE
## Israeli Writers from Iraq

SUNY Series in Israeli Studies
Russell Stone, editor

# EXILE FROM EXILE

## Israeli Writers from Iraq

Nancy E. Berg



STATE UNIVERSITY OF NEW YORK PRESS

Published by
State University of New York Press



Printed in the United States of America



For information, address the State University of New York Press, State University Plaza, Albany, NY 12246

Production by Bernadine Dawes • Marketing by Nancy Farrell

**Library of Congress Cataloging-in-Publication Data**

Berg, Nancy E.
Exile from exile : Israeli writers from Iraq / Nancy E. Berg.
p. cm. — (SUNY series in Israeli studies)
Includes bibliographical references and index.
ISBN 0-7914-2979-2 (hc : acid-free). — ISBN 0-7914-2980-6 (pb : acid-free)
1. Israeli fiction—history and criticism. 2. Arabic literature—Jewish authors—History and criticism. 3. Arabic literature—Iraq—History and criticism. 4. Jews, Iraqi—Israel—Intellectual life.
I. Title. II. Series
PJ5029.B47 1996
892.4'3609920694—dc20 95-44136
CIP

1 2 3 4 5 6 7 8 9 10

*Dedicated with love to my parents,*
*Shirley and Dave Berg*

# Contents

# Acknowledgments


Many people helped me in the writing of this book and I would like to express my gratitude and thank those who helped me the most.

My interest in this topic began years ago, when Professor Edna Amir Coffin introducted me to Sami Michael through his novel *Ḥasut* in a Hebrew literature course. A few years later Gaby and Raḥel Warburg, then directors of the Israeli Academic Center in Cairo, introduced me to the author himself on one of his first visits to Egypt. By then I had already serendipitously bought Shmuel Moreh's anthology *Short Stories by Jewish Writers from Iraq* (and shelved it until I had the necessary language ability). Later I benefitted from his generosity with time and materials. Through the Association for Israeli Academics from Iraq he supplied me with many of the books otherwise unavailable in the bookstores.

Roger Allen read multiple drafts beginning with the initial proposal. Yael Zerubavel exhibited similar patience and encouraged me with her enthusiasm. Their close readings, constructive criticisms, and hours of consultation helped me from getting lost in the detail. Without their comments, and those of others who read the manuscript—in whole or in part—it would be a different book. I am grateful to Dan Laor and Walter Zenner who encouraged me with their comments and gifts of relevant publications, Dick Davis for his feedback on style, and Peter Heath and Robert Hegel for their suggestions on content and form. Anonymous reviewers have helped me to clarify and improve the original manuscript; I am particularly grateful to Ammiel Alcalay for his careful reading and generosity in sharing his views.

Many in Israel helped me by sharing their homes, friendship, enthusiasm, contacts, and personal archives. Nitza Ben Dov introduced me to Sasson Somekh who probably knows more about this topic than anyone else, both on the personal and academic level. He gave me much of his valuable time while taking a sabbatical at the Annenberg Institute; and since then he has made himself available whether in the States, in Tel Aviv, in Jerusalem, or in Cairo. In addition to his direct help, he also made many opportunities available to me, from access to the excellent library at the Annenberg to providing me with an introduction to the writer Samīr Naqqāsh.

Alex Zehavi helped me formulate some of the ideas about literary exile that underlie this study as well as introduced me to members of the Iraqi Jewish community. These included David Sagiv and Nissim Rejwan, who offered a personal perspective on the history and literature of the Jewish community in Iraq. I look forward to the day Nissim publishes his memoirs.

The writers Eli Amir, Shimon Ballas, Yitzhak Bar-Moshe, Shalom Darwīsh, Yaakov (Bilbul) Lev, Sami Michael, and Samīr Naqqāsh (as prolific in his correspondence as in his writing) and David (Rabi) Rabeeya (in the US) were wonderfully forthcoming—and patient—to a novice interviewer.

During the process of revision I had several opportunities to discuss different sections of this work. The most fruitful of these were at Beit Berl College and the University of Haifa. I am especially thankful to David Semach, Shimon Ballas, and Reuven Snir for their continuing support, interest, and feedback.

Many of my friends and colleagues, especially Rosanna Perotti Al-Busaidi, Chris Ruane, and the late Nancy Grant, have been helpful in many ways. Marc Saperstein was the first to recognize a book in the penultimate draft, tracked down bibliographic details, smoothed over infelicities of language, and kept me from committing more egregious errors than might be found. My thanks are also due to Yossi Galron for prompt and precise bibliographic aid. Any errors or oversights in this area or others, however, are fully my responsibility.

The largesse of the Mellon Foundation and the Lady Davis Fund supported me during the research phases; the Yad HaNadiv/Barecha Foundation was truly generous and a blessing for the final states of writing.

I am grateful to the staff members of the Annenberg Research Institute library, the Museum of Babylonian Jewry in Or Yehudah, the

Jewish National Library, the Van Pelt library at the University of Pennsalvania, and the archives of the Tchernikhovsky Bet HaSofer in Tel Aviv.

For kindly granting permission to reprint from their publications, thanks to the following:

From the essay "Exile and European Thought: Heine, Marx and Michiewicz in July Monarcy Paris" by Lloyd S. Kramer. *Historical Reflections / Reflexions Historique* 11, no. 1 (Spring 1984), p. 48. Used by permission of the publishers.

From the article "Immigrant Absorption and Social Tension in Israel" by Samuel Z. Klausner. *The Middle East Journal* 9, no. 3 (1955), p. 283. Used by permission of the Middle East Institute.

From the essay "Notes on Exile" by Czeslaw Milosz. *Books Abroad* (Spring 1976), p. 284. Used by permission of World Literature Today.

Grateful appreciation also to the Jewish Museum for the cover. Credit is due to the Jewish Museum/Art Resource, NY. Janco, Marcel, Ma'abarot in Grey, c. 1950. Oil on Canvas, 31 5/8 inches. Gift of Allan Stroock, JM28-63. Photo credit: Geoffrey Clements, Jewish Museum, New York, U.S.A.

I am indebted to Mara and Sa'adia Cohen, Hannah and Simon Naveh, and Ami and Osnat Elad for their unlimited support, friendship, and hospitality. Many other friends, in addition to teachers, old classmates, new colleagues, and family members, helped in innumerable ways throughout the process from proposal to page proofs. I am grateful to them all and especially to Stan, who picked up my slack, walked the dogs, typed my first draft, and never seemed to tire of hearing about these writers from Iraq.

# Preface

This book examines the literature of a particular group of writers. They belong to a community of Jews who moved from Iraq to Israel during the period of mass immigration (1948–51).

Their departure from Iraq signaled the end of the oldest Jewish community in the Diaspora; their arrival in Israel came at the beginning of a new nation. While the movement of the Babylonian Jewish community to Israel was seen as partial fulfillment of the Zionist dream, the separation from home created the condition of exile for individuals.

In this study I focus on those who write narratives. All of the writers under discussion are experienced in short stories as well as longer works of fiction. However, I do not limit myself to the purely fictional genres, but include memoirs and stories that verge on the autobiographical.

In part 1, I attempt to establish a context for this study, first by examining the theoretical underpinnings to the study of exile in both the literary and Jewish contexts and then by detailing the historical and literary milieu within which these writers have created their works.

The plight of the exile generally, and the exiled writer specifically, is not unique to these few individuals. Questions of language, culture, and identity, balancing the past and present, are shared by all transplanted artists. The experience of exile is central to the individual. Exile writing tends to be autobiographical in nature, and thus gives expression to the major issues of life in exile, such as mediating the tension between past and present. Writing is the main strategy used to deal with the exile's difficulty of being understood (and of understanding) and the need to mediate between past and present. For both the writers and their character counterparts, memory—the past—can be controlled by the act of telling.

In part 2, I examine the narrative fiction of these Iraqi Israeli writers against the background of exile literature. I begin by looking at the exiled writer's dilemma: the choice of language. How does a writer choose which language to use and how does this choice affect what is written (and what is read)? These particular writers were confronted with the choice between Arabic or Hebrew as their literary medium; with all due respect to the political and cultural implications of these choices, the decision is ultimately that of an individual.

In analyzing the works themselves, I asked, what expression does the experience of exile find in the writing of the Iraqi Jews who came to Israel during the mass immigration? Which strategies do the writers use to deal with the experience and which strategies are incorporated in the process and product of their writing? Here are three main areas of interest: (1) issues of language within the narrative and external to it; (2) the portrayal of the past in Iraq and the present in Israel, as well as the conflict between the two; (3) the response to the literature, including the evaluation of individual works and authors, and the position of the writing within a larger context.

These works explore the polar opposites of home and exile. Home is reconstructed in some of these narratives as secure shelter for long-lost childhood. Home means family and friends, shared customs and affection. Exile is the alienation both from the past—the home left behind—and the present surroundings; it means discontinuity in time and space.

The literature of transition portrays the process by which exile becomes home, not by a return to the past but by reconciliation with the present. Complementary narratives reveal the process by which home became not-home and led to the mass exodus of the Iraqi Jewish community.

Despite the centrality of the experiences portrayed to Israeli society—those of the uprooted and ingathered—the literature of these writers has been virtually ignored. The Israeli literary establishment is dominated by writers of Ashkenazi (European) background, and more and more by those native to Israel (sabras). In the standard surveys of modern Hebrew and Israeli literature, few of the Iraqi exiles or their works are even mentioned. Literary scholarship from outside of the

Iraqi Jewish community has given little attention to these works until recently.

In the past few years, Israeli society has evinced greater awareness of some of the issues raised by this literature, and has shown greater acceptance of non-European "ethnicity." The Museum of Babylonian Jewry opened April 1988 in Or Yehudah (outside of Tel Aviv). It has permanent displays, changing exhibits, and a small library. With the Association of Jewish Academics from Iraq (established in 1980), it has been active in sponsoring conferences dedicated to the exploration and preservation of the heritage of Iraqi Jewry with a more specific focus. The Institute to Study the Zionist-Ḥalutz Movement in Iraq was recently established in Gilo. Studies, symposia, and conferences proliferate.

Many other Jewish communities from Arab and Islamic lands are represented among the Israeli population. I have been asked any number of times, why the Iraqi Jews? A combination of several factors have led to the visibility, if not the prominence, of the Iraqi Jewish community in Israel. They were among the largest groups to arrive in Israel during the first few years of its existence, were among the most urbanized and well educated of communities stemming from Arab countries, and were among the most intact. Unlike other communities, most of the Iraqi elite did not have the option to settle in the West and relatively few chose not to emigrate. The Iraqi Jews were traditionally well educated in Arabic and Arab culture, as reflected in their important contributions to the development of modern Iraqi literature before their exodus.

This study has enabled me the to explore their continued participation in the field of literature. It presents voices and perspectives that contribute to the diversity in Israeli, and indeed exile, literatures. I begin with a discussion of exile in general, its place in literature, and in Jewish tradition. In chapter 2 I present a brief historical survey of Iraqi Jewry. Understanding the depth and strength of the roots that the community grew in modern Iraq emphasizes the enormity of its uprooting. I explore the "push-pull" factors leading up to the mass exodus of 1949–51. While Zionists may have been inclined to see the immigration of more than 120,000 Iraqi Jews as a validation of their ideological aims, it is not clearly so. The move of the Iraqi Jews to Israel was not voluntary; Israel offered sanctuary to those forced to seek it. Before the exile Jews were important participants in Iraqi society, and especially in its rich cultural life. This is the topic of chapter 3, which focuses on the cultural background of the Iraqi Jewish community and, in particular, on their contribution to modern Iraqi literature. The literary figures of that time are the direct predecessors of the authors under discussion in this study. Exploring the unique position of Iraqi Jewish writers in Baghdad enables us to appreciate what happened in Israel. The choices facing these writers are examined in chapter 4. The question of language as the medium of literary expression—whether to write in Arabic or in Hebrew—is central in this chapter, as is the connection between the choice of language and the subjective experience of migration.

The following chapters study narrative works by these authors and the relationship between these works and the language in which they are written. I look at the move from Iraq to Israel from the writer's perspective and its literary expression, exploring the meaning of "home" and "exile" within their works. The authors writing in Hebrew reach out to the Israeli audience. They depict the crises faced by new arrivals to Israel in the early days of the state. This literature of the transit camps (and of transition) is discussed in chapter 5. These camps were intended as a temporary measure to house the vast number of immigrants pouring into the new country. The novels about these camps use the metaphor of adolescence as a symbol of the transition from one society to the other. In contrast, the works written in Arabic are nostalgic looks at home and childhood. I "return" to Iraq in chapter 6 by way of the authors' remembrances and reconstructions of the past. Those writing in Arabic focus on the past as the source of their inspiration. A different perspective on the past in Iraq is presented in chapter 7 through the fiction of the Hebrew authors. These works serve as a counterpoint to the former, representing the past without nostalgia. The last chapter places these authors and their writing within the contexts of Israeli, Jewish, and world literature.

# PART ONE

## The Literature of Exile and Iraqi Jewish Writing

# 1

# Exile, Literature, and Jewish Writers

> I don't exist in this country, not as a writer, a citizen nor human being. I don't feel that I belong anywhere, not since my roots were torn from the ground.
>
> —Samīr Naqqāsh

THE ACT OF MOVING FROM ONE PLACE TO ANOTHER, OF LEAVING ONE country and settling in a different state, gains a specific set of connotations and has definite emotional significance once it is labeled with the term "exile." The word itself requires some response, some engagement on the part of the speaker, the listener, the reader. It holds a special position in literature and literary studies, as well as in the experience of the Jewish people.

Paul Tabori, author of *The Anatomy of Exile,* offers the following definition of exile:

> An exile is a person compelled to leave or remain outside his country of origin on account of well-founded fear of persecution or for reasons of race, religion, nationality, or political opinion; a person who considers his exile temporary (even though it may last a lifetime), hoping to return to his fatherland when circumstances permit—but unable or unwilling to so as long as the factors that made him an exile persist.[1]

The term *exile* refers to a person who has been separated involuntarily from home or country, as well as to the act and state of being separated, the circumstance(s), and period of time of separation.[2] The same word refers to both the person and the condition.

Involuntary exiles include those people who leave seemingly of their own accord but really because of circumstances beyond their control. The exile is reluctant to leave, and only does so when "leaving is only just better than staying."[3] The involuntary and individual nature of the condition of exile distinguishes it from the condition of the expatriate or the refugee. The expatriate voluntarily departs from his or her native land without the yearning to be reunited. The expatriate has been characterized as the reverse of the exile; his "main aim is never to go back to his native land or, failing that, to stay away as long as possible."[4] Though similar to the refugee in lacking control over his or her departure, the exile is seen as more of an individual, less passive, and more capable of creativity and decision-making.[5]

The chronological or psychological aspect of the situation reinforces the geographical or physical dimension. "Distance in space reinforces the effect of distance in time."[6] The exile is deprived of the homeland, the setting for times past. This leads to the development of certain mental structures, ways of attempting to bridge the distance. The exile is subject to bouts of nostalgia, in which memories of the past are richer than the actual present. The loss of home creates the desire to regain it whether through return or recollection. Home becomes more precious for having been lost, and most precious by having been lost forever.

The condition of exile has both temporary and permanent qualities. While colored by the hopelessness of permanence, it is dynamic and subject to change. This change does not necessarily occur through a change of the conditions leading to the exile but can happen on the part of the exiled. The period of exile may come to an end not by the return home, but by a change in the exiled one's perception of home. Once the exile stops thinking of returning home and begins to put down roots, the state of exile has come to an end. At that point the exile can be redefined as an immigrant.

In contrast to exiles, immigrants move to a new place with the explicit goal of settling there. If "exile" implies separation *from* one's home and impermanence, "immigration" transforms the notion of home. The main issue for the immigrant is resettling, not return. The problems and processes related to integrating into one's new home, and indeed making it home, are foremost. In practice some distinctions between exile and immigrant become blurred. The very early stages of immigration may be experienced as a variation of exile. Immigrants may remember their previous home with longing and occasionally wish to return. Exiles may begin to adapt—however slightly or reluctantly—to their temporary home. Whether one is an immigrant or an exile may lie in one's perception of the situation rather than in the situation itself.

The condition of exile, "a discontinuous state of being"[7] leads to a crisis of identity. Changes in the environment have led to changes in the frame of reference by which personal identity is formed and maintained. In his discussion of the experience of foreign intellectuals in nineteenth-century Paris, Lloyd Kramer writes:

> Exile challenges more than the social and intellectual identities, however, for it often brings about major psychological adjustments as well. The experience of living among alien people, languages, and institutions can alter the individual's sense of self about as significantly as any of the traumas known to psychologists. The referents by which people understand themselves change dramatically when they are separated from networks of family, friends, work, and nationality.[8]

In trying to adapt to the new setting, the exile may become estranged from his or her own self. The discontinuity on the outside mirrors the discontinuity inside. Robert Edwards traces the sense of self-alienation from classical and medieval thought on exile.[9] Exiled people no longer feel themselves to be the same persons as they were in the past,[10] nor do they fit into their present. "The exile is always an alien at one stage or another of his destiny."[11] The exile remains on the outside, looking in, whether critically or longingly.

It is this search for identity, at least in part, and the dual existence of living here and there that gives rise to exile literature. Exile is considered both a defining and an excluding condition for the writer. The former view, that "any major artist and truly creative mind [is] a foreigner in his own country,"[12] presents the artist as outsider. Ovid serves as the classic example of the connection between exile and poetic creation.[13] In more modern times, a great number of well-known and highly regarded writers have experienced exile. As Maria-Ines Lagos-Pope states, "It is significant and not coincidental that among the most recent Nobel prize winners for literature one finds several exiles."[14] The exile status of writers in this century has become "a commonplace thing."[15] On the other hand, David Williams places the exile outside of community and social intercourse (word exchange, he suggests, is a metaphor for community) and asserts "the exile is a man without the opportunity of dialogue, [a man who] lacks speech."[16] If literature is communication, then the one who remains outside of the community cannot create.

These two opposing views are not irreconcilable, for it is in the very nature of writing that outsiders may try to transcend the condition of exile and join their new community.[17] The literature of exile—writing by the exiled and about the state of exile—is the result of this attempt.

The writer exiled to a different linguistic environment is faced with the choice of holding onto the familiar or venturing forth to a new language. Some of the former are writers who continue to write in their mother tongues because of the (real or perceived) inability to learn another language,[18] while some of the latter are those who feel "the language has chosen them."[19] Writers who consciously choose the language of their writing necessarily weigh several factors.

In his study *Transcending Exile* Milbauer asks,

> Why . . . would a foreigner undertake such a painful and exhaustive endeavour as mastering a new language in order to eventually make it into a medium of his art, a means to reach an audience, an instrument of intellectual survival?[20]

One Iranian writer in exile in the United States discounted marketability as irrelevant and love for language as insufficient; the writer considered only the international status (of English) as decisive.[21]

There are those who choose not to undertake this "painful and exhaustive endeavor." They keep their mother tongue as their first language to avoid this difficulty. Further reasons include keeping their link to their past,[22] contributing to their national culture,[23] or avoiding a (perceived) state of (linguistic) exile.[24] Continuing to write in one's mother tongue even when one is removed from its native environment does not necessarily lead to linguistic stagnation. Ewa Thompson proposes the possibility of "linguistic cross-fertilization" and enrichment of the literary *koine*.[25] According to the exiled writer Czeslaw Milosz:

> A writer living among people who speak a language different from his own discovers after a while that he senses his native tongue in a new manner. . . . new aspects and tonalities of the native tongue are discovered, for they stand out against the background of the lan-

> guage spoken in the new milieu. Thus the narrowing down in some areas (street idioms, slang) is compensated for by a widening in others (purity of vocabulary, rhythmic expressiveness, syntactic balance).[26]

Those who do learn and use a new language are often aware of the difficulties involved in the adjustment. Nabokov describes the switch to English (from Russian) as "exceedingly painful—like learning anew to handle things after losing seven or eight fingers in an explosion."[27] Another writer speaks of always writing with an accent.[28] This accent is sometimes noted by the reader. Conrad's "adoption by English" is deemed as less than thorough by some of his critics: "But grammatical quirks, indigenous to French rather than English, continued to plague that convoluted style we associate with Conrad."[29] Personal style may be differently interpreted as linguistic incompetence. A writer sensitive to this danger may compensate with showy displays of linguistic virtuosity or conscious avoidance of experimentation.[30]

The disadvantages of writing in a second language can often be compensated for—at least in part—by a greater sensitivity to the meanings and sounds of words that non-native speakers bring to their writing. Compensation may also be found in the chosen language's perceived advantages over the writer's mother tongue. Conrad favored English over his native Polish because of his belief in the former's greater linguistic variety.[31] Nabokov switched to English in order to obtain a new audience.[32] The reasons for writing in one language or another are as different as the writers' situations. Whatever the motivation, the linguistic medium does have its impact on the writing and reading of the exile literature.

Exile literature has been alternately defined as literature that uses the experience of exile as subject and theme,[33] or literature that is written in exile.[34] The latter category views "the writers' expression as a reaction to [the exile situation]; the artistic greatness into which their suffering and pain, their fear and desperation have been sublimated and transformed."[35] Claudio Guillén distinguishes between the literature of exile in which "exile becomes its own subject matter" and what he calls the literature of counterexile. This literature is inspired by (but transcends the actual condition of) exile in a shift toward universalism. In other words, the literature of counterexile draws inspiration from the writer's particular experience of exile but is not limited by this experience.[36] In the modern era, the experience of exile is also generalized into a metaphor for the alienation of the individual.[37]

At the heart of the condition of exile is the state of homelessness, which implies both the loss of a home and the need for one. The writer in exile may attempt to mediate this lack through the creative process—that is, by recreating home through art. The actual childhood homes of the writers under discussion here are recorded in their writing and presented to the reader.

Much of exile writing is autobiographical, rooted in the experience of the alienated individual. The literature is an expression of the state of exile, and a strategy to resolve this state. Seidel defines the exile's task to be transforming "the figure of rupture back into a 'figure of connection.'"[38] Through art the writer mediates between the past and the present. In her autobiographical *Lost in Translation* Eva Hoffman discusses some of the issues involved in this act of balancing:

> The conservatives of the sentiments believe that recovering their own forgotten history is an antidote to shallowness. The ideologues of the future see attachment to the past as that most awful of all monsters, the agent of reaction. . . . Only certain East European writers, forced to march into the future too often, know the regressive dangers of both forgetfulness and clinging to the past. But then, they are among our world's experts of mourning, having lost not an archeological but a living history. And so they praise the virtues of a true memory. Nabokov unashamedly reinvokes and revives his childhood colors in the glorious colors of *teşknota* [nostalgia]. Milan Kundera knows that a person who forgets easily is a Don Juan of experience, promiscuous and repetitive, suffering from the unbearable lightness of being. Czeslaw Milosz remembers the people and places of his youth with the special tenderness reserved for objects of love that are no longer cherished by others.[39]

The ideal therapeutic process by which the "exiled writer" ceases to be an exile is through communicative writing. By coming to terms with the present and remembering the past, the writer succeeds in integrating the experience of transition, and through communicating this experience joins the community without being negated by it.

To understand the meaning of exile for the Iraqi Jewish writers in Israel, one needs to explore the special connotations of this concept within the Jewish tradition. Arnold Eisen states that "to write a history of Jewish exile is to write the history of the Jews."[40] The Hebrew term *galut* (exile) expresses the "Jewish conception of the condition and feelings of a nation uprooted from its homeland and subject to alien rule."[41] It refers to both the condition of being uprooted and the community of the uprooted. The word has come to designate the Jewish communities in exile, which are also known collectively as the Diaspora.[42]

While the theological significance of the concept *galut* cannot be explored within the constraints of this study, it is important to point out certain ideas and themes that are relevant to our understanding of its meaning for the Iraqi Jewish writers. The literature deals with *galut* on both the symbolic-mythic and the actual-historical levels. The shifting between these two levels adds to the difficulty in trying to encapsulate ideas about the meaning and cause of exile. Theories of *galut* include responses to questions of causality and characterization within religious, national, and political frameworks.

The beginning of Genesis offers three prototypes of the exile experience: the narratives of the *banishment* of Adam and Eve from the Garden of Eden, the forced *wanderings* of Cain, and the *dispersal* of the builders of the Tower of Babel.[43] Moreover, these biblical stories reflect the progression toward noncommunicability in exile from the interspecial communication between Eve and the serpent to the creation of different languages at Babel. "Come, let us go down and confuse their language there, so that they can no longer understand one another."[44] Exile here is of universal nature: forced separation from home, continual rootlessness, and the impossibility of communication.

Historically, the first exile of the Jewish people resulted from the destruction of the Holy Temple by the Babylonians in 586 B.C.E. Over time, Jews became dispersed due to natural catastrophes and political oppressions, as well as through seeking the possibility of economic and social betterment.[45] From the beginning, exile created a state of crisis. The severance of the Jewish people from their home caused a break in the historical continuity of national life, brought an end to those practices of the Israelite religion which were associated with the Temple, and put into question the belief in the Jews as God's chosen people. The theological and philosophical responses to the crisis changed over time; however, certain themes and patterns recur. At the core is an attempt to reconcile faith with disaster.

The concept of *galut* has certain Jewish connotations and symbolic dimensions when it is specified as exile from the Land of Israel. Judaism had to be redefined outside of Zion. The destruction of the Second Temple and, later, the exile from the land, necessitated radical changes in practice if the Jewish religion were to survive. No longer could the Jews make pilgrimages to the Holy Temple and offer sacrifices upon its altar. Nor did the laws concerning the land apply to the lands of exile. The absence of the Holy Temple and the banishment of the Jews from the site led to modifications in religious practice. These modifications, such as the substitution of liturgy for animal sacrifices, the founding of synagogues and establishment of alternate celebrations for the pilgrimage festivals, allowed Judaism to flourish in exile. Major adaptations in the practice of the Jewish religion led to more emphasis on sacred time than on sacred space.[46] This change enhanced the ability of Judaism to survive this state of exile.

The exile of the Jews involved not only the expulsion from the Land of Israel, but a series of expulsions from temporary "homes" and the scattering of the Jews throughout the Diaspora. The displacement and dispersal of the Jews among other peoples caused a crisis of religious, national, and political identity. Minority status endangered the autonomy and integrity of Jews as a nation. The subjugation of the dispersed Jewish communities to foreign rule outside of their own land, first to "pagans" and later to the Christian and Islamic empires, posed a challenge to their ability to maintain a distinct political identity. It was this loss of the political-ethnic center, according to H. H. Ben-Sasson, which turned the Diaspora into *galut*.[47] At the same time, the Jews' self-definition as "exiles" helped preserve the concept of nationhood in these circumstances.[48]

For the religious identity of the nation, the condition of *galut* was highly problematic. The quality that makes Jews unique—the election of Israel as God's chosen people—is thrown into question by their exile. If Jews are the chosen, how could God have permitted them to be banished, dispersed, and subjugated by the nonchosen? Outsiders challenged the status of the Jews on this basis. Medieval Christian thought viewed the extended exile(s) of the Jews as proof that they were no longer God's elected ones. The Christians believed that the Jews had fallen into disfavor over the sin of the crucifixion.

One of the answers to the question of chosenness was to interpret exile as a collective punishment, building on the biblical idea of banishment as a punitive measure for transgressions. Jews sinned and needed purification; the land spewed out its inhabitants because of defilement through idolatry.[49] This expression of divine displeasure was recast by Yehudah HaLevi and others as proof of Israel's chosenness.[50] Powerlessness was seen as necessary for spiritual growth.[51] The waiting mode of exile may be reinterpreted as a *prozdor* (corridor) to renewal.[52]

Alternatively, *galut* is seen as part of the Jews' universal mission to atone for others' sins. The *galut* thus becomes a normative Jewish condition to allow the Jews to fulfill their role as God's eternal people and to serve as *or lagoyim* (light unto the nations)[53] which they can do only through exile and dispersal, living among those in need of enlightenment. Exile becomes a missionary opportunity for *tikkun olam* (reforming the universe).[54] Returning to the Land of Israel would mean giving up the mission and the meaning of life.[55] Exile, according to Maimonides, is therefore a condition of order and not chaos, part of God's sublime (and incomprehensible) plan at Creation. It is unnecessary to look for natural causes for the exile, because history is different for the Jews.[55] Extended exile thus proves the election of Israel rather than its banishment. The fact that Jews were neither assimilated nor annihilated demonstrated God's protective intervention.

Just as loss presents the possibility for recovery, exile (*galut*) offers the hope of redemption *(ge'ulah)*. Jacob Neusner discusses the coupling of return with exile and the primacy of this pattern in the historic consciousness of the Jews in his book *Self-Fulfilling Prophecy*.[57] The first return from the Babylonian Exile, c. 450 B.C.E., established the pattern that has assumed a significance out of proportion to the actual number of Jews who fulfilled it. Returns from subsequent places of exile reinforced this pattern. Neusner argues that this bipartite structure, exile and return, is fundamental to the religion that unites the Jews and shapes their world.[58]

Longing for the return to Zion has inspired great literature over the two thousand years of the Diaspora, odes to Jerusalem, and the annual invocation of *L'shanah HaBa'ah B'Yerushalayim* (Next year in Jerusalem) at the conclusion of the Passover seder.[59] "Jews cultivate a sense of exile as a condition of authentic Jewishness."[60] The experiences—actual, historical, and mythical—unite the Jews as a people and set them apart from others.

In his study tracing the development of the concept of exile and land in Jewish thought, Arnold Eisen describes the mystification of the land (and therefore of exile) in the Genesis narratives, the spiritualization of homelessness in Deuteronomy, and the particularization of *galut* in rabbinic times. Exile became the "political estate of a particular people," i.e., the Jews.[61]

The Zionist movement was a relatively recent response to the experience of exile. It was a variation on both the traditional conception of exile and modern European nationalism, made possible—if not necessary[62]—in part by the complementary developments of Emancipation and the Enlightenment.[63] The ideology of Zionism called for a radical reassessment of the *galut* and the condemnation of anything that hints of "*galut* mentality" *(galutiyut)*.

> There is hardly a single blemish to be found on our body and soul that Zionist thought and its literature does not "diagnose" as a product of *galut*. Everything in our life and existence that is displeasing to the thinker or writer, every complaint that the nations of the world make against us, all stem from *galut*.[64]

The motif of sickness and ill health[65] is recalled and embodied in the image of the Diaspora Jew, the weak, pale, defenseless shtetl dweller.[66] Critical to the Zionist interpretation of history is the condemnation of the Jews' politically powerless condition in the Diaspora.

The Zionists agreed that the very lack of Jewish sovereignty was an "unnatural" condition. Every other nation had its state; and the Jews were powerless and despised because they had no land, no sovereignty.[67] A Jewish polity was seen as necessary to restore the Jews to normalcy.[68]

Furthermore, the Zionist movement emphasized the geopolitical and national over religious significance of *galut*. While the Bible endowed the geographical site of the Land of Israel with symbolic importance, the religious interpretation of its uniqueness was not enough. Paradoxically, Zionism was a secular movement calling for the return to the land made holy by the Jewish religion.[69] It focused on a place sanctified by the past and the future.

Modern Zionism shifted from a symbolic reading of exile to one more political, from a focus on homelessness to a definition of statelessness. For political Zionists, modern Zionism was a variation of eighteenth- and nineteenth-century nationalist movements. The movement therefore called for *shlilat hagolah* (the negation of the Diaspora) and an ingathering of the exiles. For religious Zionists this meant preparation for, or a hastening of,[70] the messianic era. *Galut* compromised Jewish national life and the possibility of becoming a nation among others.

According to the Zionist conception the meaning of return is imbued with secular holiness. Moving to Israel and leaving the *galut* is an act of *aliyah* (ascension). Immigration is so central to Israeli society that the history of the prestate settlement is divided into *aliyot* (waves of immigration). "Each immigrant is considered a victory of sorts, a kind of bodily enhancement of the [Zionist] vision. . . ."[71]

It is ironic that the success of Zionism in establishing a state caused a rupture in the Jews' experience, similar to that caused by exile. The Zionist dream of the ingathering of the exiles has in effect made exiles of many of the ingathered. The heart of the paradox is the clash between the Jewish notion of exile, which functions on the national level, and the universal notion, which concerns the individual. To leave one's personal home, even for one's ancestral land, may be for some more of a shock than a cure. The realization of the symbolic national dream can be experienced as an exile from one's homeland.

Such sentiments are particularly true for many members of the Babylonian Jewish community, the community established by the first Jewish exile in 586 B.C.E. This community was deeply rooted in Iraq—well integrated, although not assimilated. Many of the Jews were proud Iraqi nationalists, considering themselves first and foremost Iraqis.[72] Only a small minority were active Zionists at the time of the mass exodus from Iraq (1949–51).[73] Most left Iraq due to worsening sociopolitical conditions in their homeland; as they said "leaving was just better than staying."[74] Yet coming from a traditional Jewish background their expectations were, at least in part, shaped by this tradition. The irony that the realization of the Zionist dream created exiles arises from the dual identity of the Iraqi/Diaspora Jew in the twentieth century.

For centuries Jewish literature has been written in exile. Whether written in a Jewish language or the local vernacular, marginality has been an almost inherent quality of the literature.[75] Yudkin speaks of the "persistent sense of orphanhood in modern Hebrew literature" and a sense of dislocation: this literature is separated from the past much the same way as the Land of Israel is separated from the land(s) of the Diaspora.[76] The bilingual (and multilingual) tradition of the Jews generated by the fact of the Diaspora lies at the very foundation of modern Hebrew literature and has been referred to as "belletristic multilingualism" in recent studies.[77]

The title of this book, *Exile from Exile,* presents the tension between the two poles of interpretation; the move to Israel from Iraq is an end to the national state of exile and the beginning of a personal exile from one's homeland. The imposition of the national paradigm on the individual experience results in ambivalence and confusion. National redemption and personal exile are played out in the experience of the individual. There are two sides of the "double exile":

intensification and negation. In the first case, the writer as double exile is exiled not only from the homeland but also from its language and culture,[78] from an established audience, and from the literary markets and partnerships.[79] In the second sense, the double exile functions as a double negative and cancels out. Those exiled (metaphorically) or marginalized in their own homeland are often demarginalized by the second exile. This is, of course, the fulfillment of the Zionist vision. Qualities that they developed in response to the first exile or marginalization—such as adapting to the majority culture—serve them well in (adapting to) their new setting. The marginalized who are forced to develop an independent sense of self, are less likely to be shaken by the crisis of identity. In fact, both of these possibilities—intensification and negation—exist at opposite ends of a continuum that folds back on itself, a Möbius strip of return and exile.

The writers under discussion have chosen different strategies with which to resolve their banishment from Iraq. This book explores these strategies, examining the question of language choice, representation of the present (exile), memories of the past (home) and the (re)construction of home. Underlying the study is the perception that their writing belongs to the category of exile literature. I offer a reading of this body of work within the dual concepts of exile and Israeli literature. In the next chapter I look at the history leading up to this exile.

# 2

# The Jewish Community in Iraq

FROM ITS FOUNDING, THE JEWISH COMMUNITY OF IRAQ HAS PRESENTED a special case study because of a combination of several factors: its antiquity, size, level of educational achievement, and the extent of integration (without assimilation). The Iraqi Jews were in general more educated and more urbanized than their Yemenite and Moroccan counterparts, and more immersed in Arabic-Islamic culture than the Jews of Egypt.[1] The community shared many of the traditions, superstitions, and customs of their non-Jewish neighbors. "In fact," concludes one scholar, "the Jewish community of Iraq was thoroughly Arab, or if you prefer, Arabized."[2] Landschut describes the cultural affinity:

> Middle-class Jews in Iraq took to European dress at about the same time as the Muslims. Likewise, in their daily habits, their houses, and, last but not least, in their language, there was no marked difference between the two communities.[3]

He perhaps overstates the similarities because of a comparison with other Jewries of the Middle East. While dress was not generally a distinguishing characteristic by this century (although headdress was at times maintained as an ethnic marker),[4] language certainly was, especially in the larger cities where Jews lived in their own neighborhoods until the thirties and forties. Otherwise the Jews were more similar to their neighbors than not. At the same time the community preserved its own separate identity with its autonomous infrastructure (governing councils and institutions), observance of religious customs, and historic ties.

The Jewish community of Iraq traced its roots back to the first Jewish exile. Nebuchadnezzar's conquest of Judah, the smaller of the two Hebrew kingdoms, in 586 B.C.E. destroyed the Holy Temple and exiled the Judeans to Babylon to join the descendents of the Israelites who had been exiled by the Assyrians in 719 B.C.E. The exile led to the development of an adaptive Judaism that enabled the religion to exist outside the Land of Israel. The Judeans established themselves rather quickly in Babylon; as evidence, when Cyrus issued a declaration welcoming them back to Jerusalem in 538 B.C.E., there was great resistance to return to rebuild the Temple.[5]

The Babylonian Exile is considered to have lasted only seventy years (until the rebuilding of the Second Temple), and yet many of the Judeans stayed in Babylon, adopting it as their new home. Over the years the community grew and developed into the center for world Jewry. Babylon became home of the world-famous *yeshivot* (religious learning academies) of Nehardea, Sura, and later (after the capture of Nehardea ca. 261 C.E.), Pumbedita. The greatest achievement of these academies was the Babylonian Talmud, the foundation of medieval Jewish civilization.

With the advent of Islam (635 C.E.) the Jews were accorded the official status of *dhimmī*, the non-Muslim subjects of a Muslim state. Bernard Lewis describes the arrangement as a contractual relationship with the community[6] whereby the *dhimmī* accepted certain restrictions in exchange for the tolerance and protection of the state.[7] Most of these restrictions, such as imposing certain dress and mount regulations, asserted the social superiority of Muslims over the protected peoples. Financial obligations included the *jizya* (poll tax) and *badal-al-ʿaskar* (dispensation from military duty). The "symbolic expression[s] of subordination"[8] were periodically renewed by decree, something which suggests that they were not continuously enforced. "In general dhimmīs were allowed to practice their religions, pursue their avocations and live their own lives, so long as they were willing to abide by the rules."[9]

The ruling government depended on the Exilarch, the head of the Jewish community in exile, to collect taxes and maintain order among his coreligionists. His authority was especially enhanced during the Abbasid period. Whereas his duties were primarily administrative and judicial (he would also represent members of the Jewish community as needed), the *geonim* were the heads of the *yeshivot* and tended to *halakhic* (religious law) and academic matters. For centuries they were considered the rabbinical leadership of world Jewry; they helped disseminate, clarify and privilege the Babylonian Talmud as the central halakhic text.[10] The most famous holder of the office was Rabbi Sa'adia Gaon.[11]

Relations between the Jews and their majority neighbors went through different phases, mostly dependent on the level of tolerance afforded by the rulers. The famed traveler Benjamin of Tudela visited Babylon in the twelfth century during a period of high tolerance. In his description, he seems particularly impressed by the role and the wealth of the Exilarch, translated here as the Prince of Captivity.

> Baghdad is inhabited by about one thousand Jews, who enjoy peace, comfort and much honor under the government of the great king. Among them are very wise men and presidents of the colleges, whose occupation is the study of mosaic law [p. 100/60.1]. . . . The principal of all these however, is R. Daniel Ben Chisdai, who bears the titles of: Prince of Captivity [*rosh galut*] and Lord [*adonenu*] and who possesses a pedigree, which proves his descent from King David. [p. 101/ 61.2]. . . . The Prince of Captivity possesses hostelries, gardens and orchards in Babylonia and extensive landed property inherited from forefathers, of which nobody dares deprive him. [p. 103/63.1]. . . .
>
> At the time of installation of the Prince of the Captivity he spends considerable sums in presents to the king, or *Khalif*, his princes and nobles [(p. 104/ 63.2]. . . . Many of the Jews of Bagdad are good scholars and very rich . . . the city contains twenty-eight jewish synagogues, situated partly in Bagdad and partly in al-Khorkh [p. 104/64.1]. . . .[12]

Islamic rulers depended on *dhimmīs* for their medical and financial needs; successful Jewish merchants took advantage of such opportunities to build trading houses into banking firms from the beginning of the tenth century. The emergence of a flourishing mercantile class was a major contributing factor to the growing importance of Babylonian Jewry.[13] The Mongol conquest of Baghdad in 1258 ushered in an era of relative harmony, as did the alternating reigns of the Ottomans, the Al-Kuyunlu (1470–1508, 1534–1623, 1638–1917), and the Persians (1508–34, 1623–38). During these periods the Jewish community continued to thrive. Most of the Ottoman Turkish pashas of the eighteenth and nineteenth centuries were less forbearing. Iraqi Jews left for India and elsewhere particularly during the oppressive regime of Da'ud Pasha (1817–31),[14] thus paving the way for Jewish involvement in international trade and commerce in the following generations.

## MODERN TIMES

### *Urbanization*

The Jewish population was concentrated in the cities, especially Baghdad. The rule of Midhat Pasha (1869–72) as the Ottoman *wālī* and the opening of the Suez Canal in 1869 created conditions favorable for Jews to move south from the mountains and to urban areas (primarily Baghdad and Basra).

Midhat Pasha's policies included land reforms, modernizing the educational system, controlling the Bedouin tribes to the south, and offering the cities protection from these tribes and other marauders.[15] The opening of the Suez Canal established a sea route for European–Far Eastern trade. Basra in the south became an important port at the expense of Mosul and other northern cities along the overland route.[16] Business and economic opportunities also encouraged the move to the cities. Few Jews were landowners,[17] thus they were more easily mobile than their landowning neighbors. In the mid-nineteenth century most Jews were engaged in "crafts, hawking and small commercial businesses."[18]

The opening of the Suez Canal enabled the Iraqi Jews to capitalize on the "Jewish advantage" in trade and commerce, based in part on an international network that extended to India, the Far East, and England. The British occupation and mandate (1917–32) and foreign language training in the Jewish schools also contributed to economic development in the community. The British administration offered many opportunities for Iraqis who knew both English and Arabic. Jews joined the civil service, the transport sector (railways and the port of Basra), banks, the Iraqi petroleum company, and other foreign companies.[19]

The move to urban areas contributed to improvements in the educational, economic, and social status of the Jews. Because of different social expectations, Jews of the cities married later and had fewer children. Their higher life expectancy has been attributed to differences in lifestyle and sanitation.[20] The establishment of Jewish hospitals, first in

Basra and in Baghdad, joined the better sanitary conditions already present in the cities and towns in decreasing rates of infant mortality, infection, and contagion.[21]

Contemporary researchers considered the Jewish communities of Baghdad and Basra to be among the wealthiest of Jewish communities in the Middle East on the eve of the mass exodus.[22]

> The Jewish control of Iraqi commercial life was an essential factor in the adherence of the Iraqi Jewish leadership to Iraq. The control was almost total for many generations and did not arouse any envy worth mentioning. Keeping the Sabbath and Jewish holidays, which stopped most of the commerce in the capital, had been accepted by the majority of Baghdad's Moslems for many generations. The Jewish involvement in Iraqi trade, especially imports, during the thirties was almost absolute, with the Jews controlling 95% of the total imports.[23]

By the end of the first World War[24] the Jews were the largest single ethnic or religious group in the capital.[25] As of 1950, the 120,000 Jews constituted 2.5 percent of the total population; an estimated ninety thousand to one hundred thousand lived in Baghdad,[26] a city of almost three hundred thousand.

### *Secularization*

Until the turn of this century the Jews of Iraq tended to maintain strict observance of Jewish law and tradition: holiday celebrations, synagogue attendance, endogamous marriages.[27] Conversion was rare.[28] "[There were] no known cases of educated Jews who converted voluntarily to the dominant religion."[29]

> The few cases of conversion to Islam—there were scarcely any cases of conversion to Christianity—were the result of family disputes. Jewish girls, and a lesser number of married women, generally adopted the Muslim religion if they had been seduced before marriage or had betrayed their husbands. If a man converted, he did so because he did not succeed in obtaining a divorce from his wife. But certainly there must have also have been individual cases of conversion out of hope of material benefit—money, a job, or the like.[30]

Yet many of the Jews were already less religiously observant in the generation prior to the mass *aliyah* (immigration to Israel). Opportunities and policies accounted in large part for the secularizing trend. Modern education, and especially attendance in the state schools, which were open on Saturday, encouraged less strict observance. In addition the Young Turk reforms of 1908 (and the constitution of 1909, which guaranteed equal rights and full citizenship to the Jews), the British occupation (1917–21) and mandate (1922–32) led to greater laxity in religious observance.[31] Taking advantage of the new equality sometimes demanded compromises on restrictive religious practices. Employment opportunities in the British administration required working on Saturdays, thereby breaking the Sabbath laws.

Observances that were based in the home rather than in public life were generally maintained. For example, dietary laws were followed; those who were self-employed did not work on the Sabbath; and life-cycle rituals were celebrated according to Jewish rites. Several accounts suggest that observance continued more out of respect for the old ways or by force of habit than from fervent belief. Cohen claims, "In the mid 1900s there were only a few who were religious out of conviction."[32] This statement may tell us more about western (Jewish) expectations than about Iraqi Jews, however their participation in modern education and commerce supports the possibility of less than rigid observance.

Under the British occupation and mandate, the Jews flourished, enjoying unusual prosperity and feelings of security. The Jews were an integral part of Iraqi society. Most considered themselves first and foremost Iraqis. The Arab education they received in the free-tuition state schools and in the state-controlled part of the curriculum in the Jewish schools contributed to the "Iraqization" of the Jews. The realization of the impending end to British rule reinforced the Iraqi orientation prevalent among the leaders of the Jewish community.[33]

## THE BEGINNING OF THE END

Iraq was one of the first countries in the Arab world to gain independence from Great Britain (1932). It subsequently became a popular sanctuary for Arab nationalists from other countries attempting a similar achievement, especially Palestinians[34] and Syrians,[35] as well as a repository for anti-British sentiment. This antagonism toward the former colonizers fostered an atmosphere hospitable to support for Germany, Britain's enemy. Pro-Nazi sentiment was ably fueled by the German envoy Grobba's propaganda machine.[36] With the death of King Faisal I, the reins of power were handed to his son Ghāzī. By most accounts, Ghāzī was a weak ruler incapable of maintaining the tenuous balance among the various factions of the population.[37] His lack of leadership afforded minorities little protection.

In addition, the governments formed in this period leading up to the Second World War were generally unstable and easily toppled by coups d'état. It was not long before the Jews, one of the most prominent minority groups in Iraq and the most populous in the capital city, became targets for the discontent.

In 1934, non-Muslim employees of the Ministry of Economics and Transportation were fired in one of the first efforts to "nationalize" (i.e., Arabize) the government. The majority of those fired were Jews. Unlike their Christian coworkers, they were not reinstated shortly thereafter.[38]

The next year laws were passed restricting the teaching of Hebrew[39] and forbidding the public use of tobacco during Ramadan by Jews and Christians.[40] An unstated quota, limiting the entrance of Jews to institutions of higher learning took effect.[41]

Violence erupted in September 1936 with the murder of two Jews leaving a social club on Erev Rosh Hashanah (the eve of the Jewish New Year), three days after Sa'id Thabit had published a manifesto against the Jews in the name of the Committee for the Defense of Palestine. Another Jew was killed the following day; a bomb that exploded on Yom Kippur (The Day of Atonement) miraculously claimed no victims.[42] Yet these remained almost isolated incidents. After recovering from the initial shock, the Jewish community continued as usual; its leadership attempted to appease the anti-Zionists by statements of dissociation. The famous statesman Ezra Menaḥem Daniel proclaimed: "Nahnu 'Arab qabla an nakun Yahudan" (We are Arabs before we are Jews).[43]

## THE FARHŪD

The Farhūd[44] has been written about extensively elsewhere.[45] While the actual statistics—numbers of victims and extent of property damage—vary widely according to the accounts, the conditions leading up to the pogrom are fairly well established.

The formation of a power vacuum at the end of May 1941 coincided with preparations for the Jewish holiday of Shavuot (The Feast of Weeks). Prime Minister Rashīd 'Alī had fled the capital just as the British army was at the city gates (according to rumor), leaving his minister of economics Yūnus Al-Sabawī with free rein to incite his pro-Nazi youth groups.[46] Jewish leaders going out to greet the British army met the Iraqi army instead. Angry soldiers, frustrated at their defeat and agitated by the deteriorating economic condition (felt most deeply by the poor) and the sight of Jews setting out to celebrate Shavuot in the finest clothing created the potential for riots.

Two days of looting and pillaging followed, unchecked by the Iraqi army and the local police. Rioters were joined by throngs of "Arabs" and "Bedouins" (inhabitants of the poorest neighborhoods). By the time the British entered the city to take control, 150 to 180 Jews had been killed, 450 to 2,000 wounded, and up to £3.5 million in property stolen or destroyed. A panel of inquiry set up by the government led to the arrest of Rashid Alī's supporters.[47]

The Farhūd was limited to the confines of Baghdad. Not only was (and is) Baghdad the largest city of Iraq, but also the greatest number of Jews resided there. A well-established Jewish infrastructure of neighborhoods and institutions had kept Jews more separate from their Muslim neighbors than their coreligionists in smaller cities and towns. The anonymity of the city in comparison with the smaller communities was perhaps the key to understanding why the pogrom did not spread. The Jewish victims in Baghdad, having less contact with their Muslim neighbors, could not as easily seek their protection from the angry hordes.

## REACTIONS TO THE FARHŪD

On the whole, the Jewish community recovered quickly from the trauma of the Farhūd. The government's stance was reflected in the results of the official inquiry, and the policy of compensating the victims helped to reassure the Jews. A booming wartime economy and a shift in the political atmosphere also encouraged the "Jewish talent for forgetting and adapting."[48] The majority dismissed the Farhūd as a freak incident. Yet there were those who felt it was impossible to continue life as usual. Two of the most popular reactions to the situtation, particularly among the youth, were the embracing of Communism and Zionism.

The Zionists believed that there was no future for Jews in Iraq; they believed that they had to join with other Jewish communities in establishing a state in Palestine and encouraging Jewish settlement there. The Communists blamed the pogrom on the political system. The Jews among them preferred to ensure a future by changing the structure of Iraqi society. The two movements represented different reactions to the same factors; both were diametrically opposed to those who were ready to forget and adapt.

The Communists and Zionists were prosecuted under the same law. In 1938 Article 5 of the Criminal Code stipulated that adherence to Communism was a crime punishable by death or lengthy imprisonment.[49] Zionism was viewed as a byproduct of Communism.[50] An amendment in 1948 added Zionism to the list of capital offenses. The charge of one did not necessarily preclude the other, as in the famous case of Shafiq Addas. Addas, a wealthy businessman well connected in Iraqi society, was arrested and charged with being a Communist and a Zionist. The trial was little more than a farce; the defense counsel was dismissed after the prosecution presented a score of witnesses.[51] Shafiq Addas's hanging in September 1948 sent a strong message to Jews and non-Jews alike. Jews realized that no member of their community was safe, no matter how assimilated, rich, or well connected. Others understood that no Jew, not even a successful, well-accepted businessman, was above suspicion.[52]

The Communist Party attracted many Jewish members for various reasons: the platform of progressive social thinking; the opportunities it offered for leadership positions (unavailable in the other political parties of the day); and its anti-Zionist stance.[53] In 1946, the Iraqi Communist Party (ICP) was denied a license as a political party. A segment of the party re-formed as the Anti-Zionist League (AZL) ('Uṣbat Mukāfaḥat Al-Ṣahyūniyyah). Jews formed the core of the membership.[54] The league printed a daily paper, *Al-'Uṣba*(circulation about six thousand).[55] The paper was banned in June 1946 shortly after its founding. The league itself was disbanded; members were arrested and charged with the crime of Zionism.[56] Yiẓḥak Bar-Moshe concludes: "They were charged as Communists . . . and sentenced as Jews."[57] The Communist Party continued to function as an underground movement, continuing to attract Jewish members and government persecution.

Ultimately both Zionists and Communists alike found refuge in the state of Israel. The Zionists immigrated in fulfillment of their ideological aspirations, the Communists "because only in Israel [could] they be Communists to their hearts' content"[58] and because they had no where else to go.

The Zionist activity that began in the shadow of the Farhūd had ties to an earlier indigenous organization. The Zionist League of

Mesopotamia (Agudah Ẓiyonit LeAram Naharayim), established in Baghdad in 1921 and officially recognized by the Iraqi government, was rooted in Zionist-related activity from earlier times.[59] By the turn of the century, Aharon Sassoon, known as "HaMoreh" (The Teacher), had begun to spread Zionist doctrine and the Hebrew language. Zionism was expressed by locally initiated[60] donations to the Jewish National Fund (JNF);[61] some families bought land in Palestine. Several Zionist associations were founded in 1921: the Israeli Literature Association (Jam'iyyah Isrā'īliyyah Adabiyyah) in July;[62] a clubhouse and library (August); and the Zionist *Yeshurun* newspaper (November). The organization Aḥi'ever was founded to foster Jewish and Zionist culture; several sports leagues were organized as well.

The Iraqi Law of Associations (July 1922) limited Zionist activity by not renewing the licenses of any of the organizations. A compromise was reached that allowed the activities to continue as long as they did not attract notice. The next year King Faisal received the JNF representative and personally gave him permission to solicit funds.[63]

Anti-Jewish clubs and societies were on the rise from 1929 onward. Bowing to pressure, the authorities further restricted Zionist activity in 1929[64] and forbade all such activity (including the teaching of Hebrew) in 1935. "HaMoreh" had been forced to leave the Jewish community-sponsored school in 1923 and had subsequently established his own. Others were forced to leave Iraq.

There was little Zionist activity between 1936 and 1941, although the connection with Ereẓ Yisrael was maintained. The Farhūd led more directly to the establishment of the Babylonian Pioneer Movement (HaTenuah), the promotion of education, self-defense (HaShurah), and emigration (Aliyah Bet). Shlomo Hillel describes this "Zionism of the Cellars" in his personal account.[65] There were ten to fifteen members per cell; only first names were used; and the emissaries from Palestine (Enzo Sereni et al.) were in contact only with the leaders at highest level. He offers an estimate of two thousand members.[66] The underground's major achievement was the planning and implementation of the mass exodus, first by carrying out illegal clandestine operations and later by organizing the legal emigration.

As the situation worsened for the Jews of Iraq, more and more tried to leave despite the hardships involved. An almost contemporary account declared that "the right of the Jews to leave Iraq—either to emigrate or as tourists—has always been restricted."[67] These restrictions ranged from financial extortion to outright prohibition. When permitted to leave the country, Jews were required to leave a monetary guarantee of their intent to return. In 1947 the security deposit was 1,500 Iraqi dinars (1,500 pounds sterling); the day after the declaration of the State of Israel, it was doubled.[68]

Many Jews chose to emigrate illegally despite the threat of five to seven years of hard labor if caught.[69] Popular escape routes included the Shatt al-ʿArab waterway to the south and the physically demanding Khanekin-Qasr Shirin routes to the north. A sudden enforcement of border security by the Iranian border patrol, as part of Teheran's attempt to foster better relations with Baghdad, was only a temporary setback. Perhaps the financial incentives were too powerful. Local Arabs were often hired as "guides"; border guards were not always above accepting bribes.[70] The Kurds in the north are also credited with helping Jews cross to relative safety.[71]

The Zionist underground organized parties of illegal immigrants by forging passports, forming families from previously unrelated individuals, and raising funds to pay for the expenses incurred. They even arranged for clandestine air transport.

Shlomo Hillel describes "Operation Michaelberg" (1947), by which three planeloads of Jews from Iraq were smuggled to Israel. "Empty" Iranian Airways jets were flown to Cairo and Beirut with "emergency" landings in Haifa to deposit their secret cargo.[72] Of course, such subterfuge could not continue indefinitely.

In May 1948 the risks suddenly increased. The government took advantage of the declaration of the State of Israel to redirect protests away from local problems of unemployment, corruption, and shortages.[73] Emigration was declared a capital offense; many Jews were arrested simply on the suspicion of helping others to escape.[74] These waves of arrests, suspended in September 1948, were renewed in the fall of the next year. One particular incident led to the imprisonment of many. Sa'id Khalaschi, a young (disaffected) Zionist-turned-Communist, was caught and informed on his former colleagues, nearly crippling the underground.[75]

Martial law was declared in December 1949, and the situation worsened for the Jews. Bar-Moshe recounts the persecutions suffered and the travesties of justice permitted by the military courts, of which the execution of Shafiq Addas was only one example.[76] Illegal emigration continued almost unabated.

There was a gradual change in the government's attitude vis-à-vis the Jewish exodus. Top officials realized the impossibility of stopping covert emigration, something that was becoming more of an embarrassment every day. Another factor in the changing attitude was the worsening economy, due in large part to the burden of supporting troops in Palestine-Israel, a decreased export market for oil, and an ever-increasing trade deficit.[77] The Iraqi government was also influenced by world sentiment, especially British and American pressure.[78]

A transfer plan was proposed by which Jewish citizens would be exchanged for Palestinian refugees. It was thought that allowing the free movement of Jews would remove the subversive elements (particularly Zionists and Communists) and restore calm among those remaining. It has also been suggested that the Iraqis decided to legalize emigration in order to sabotage Israel by overburdening the limited resources of the fledgling state. In his personal account, Shlomo Hillel quotes Levi Eshkol, the treasurer of the Jewish Agency (the organization in charge of the absorption of immigrants):

> Tell your good Jews that we'll be delighted to have them all, but they mustn't rush. Right now we lack the ability to absorb them. We don't even have tents. They'll have to live in the streets. . . . I don't want them protesting outside my window.[79]

Yet the magnitude of the underestimates (by the Israelis as well as the Iraqis) casts doubt on the idea of sabotage as strategy. The estimates (Iraqis: seven thousand to ten thousand; Israelis: ten thousand to twenty thousand) fell far short of the actual numbers.[80]

On 9 March 1950 the Law of Denaturalization was declared, allowing Jews to emigrate to Israel upon the forfeiture of their citizenship.[81] In addition to the reasons suggested above, financial gain may have persuaded the government to change its policy. The Jewish Agency agreed to pay a certain fee per head.[82] The difficulties of the prospective emigrants did not come to an end with the legislation of Law 1/1950. The wealthier Jews had trouble disposing of their property; the disadvantage of a flooded market was further compounded by an anti-Jewish boycott. Government policy made it almost impossible to transfer money. Transportation was another factor in the bottleneck: sea routes were closed by Iraq's refusal to recognize Israel; overland routes were necessarily abandoned because of Syria and Lebanon's hostility. Eventually flights were arranged from Iraq to Israel by providing for a per capita fee to be paid and an intermediary stop in a "neutral" country. The Jews weathered these logistical impediments, and still suffered indignities at the hands of officials at the airport in Baghdad. During "Operation Ezra and Nehemiah" up to 1,400 Iraqi Jews were transported per day via Cyprus. In all, 121,512 Jews were brought to Israel between 15 May 1948 and 5 August 1951 (the conclusion of the operation). Small-scale immigration continued by way of Iran and Turkey.[83]

It is generally agreed that Zionism was not the primary motive in this massive immigration. In Shiblak's discussion of the "push-pull factors," he focuses on the feelings of insecurity and anxiety plaguing the Jewish community.[84] While it is debatable just how effective Zionist propaganda was in encouraging the exodus, the worsening situation of the Jews in Iraq, the uncertainty, and the failing economy surely contributed. The effect of the financial strain was twofold. Not only were Jewish businessmen and traders unable to make a profit, but also the nationwide depression fueled anti-Jewish sentiment among the populace. There is even evidence to show that the government manipulated the Palestinian conflict to divert attention from the various food and goods shortages.[85]

The Law of Denaturalization was legislated for a period of one year. The very day after it lapsed (emigration was allowed to continue until August 1951 for those who signed up by 9 May 1951) the Law for the Control and Management of the Assets of Denaturalized Iraqi Jews froze over $200 million and "presented" it to the Iraqi government. This law made overnight paupers of many of the estimated twenty-five hundred[86] Jews who stayed. The government acknowledged that the timing of this law was carefully planned.[87]

Very few Jews stayed in Iraq after the mass exodus of 1948–51. Those who remained behind faced more difficult times ahead.[88] A small number emigrated to countries east and west, joining family members already established in trade and commerce, seeking educational and occupational opportunities. The vast majority emigrated to Israel, joining Jews from other countries during the period of mass emigration. Ironically, the Communists joined the Zionists, and the secular joined the religious in "the promised land." Most left Iraq because they saw no future in the place that had been home for twenty-six hundred years.

# 3

# Jewish Writers of Modern Iraqi Fiction

> The Jews are the life and soul of the citizenship of Iraq.
>
> —King Faisal I

THE JEWS OF IRAQ MADE A CONTRIBUTION NOT ONLY IN POLITICS, HEALTH, trade, and commerce, but in the cultural sphere as well. The extent of Jewish participation in the Iraqi literary scene was unprecedented in the Arab world. Cohen writes that the process of the Jews' Iraqization was "evidenced in the emergence of the first Jewish poets and writers [in modern times] writing in the Arabic language as Iraqis."[1] According to Shmuel Moreh, eleven out of fourteen novels and thirteen out of fifteen short-story collections by Jews written in Arabic and published in the Arab world were written by Iraqi Jews. (The remainder were by Egyptian Jews.) In no other Arab country, it appears, did Jews reach such a high level of literary creativity in Arabic.[2]

Jews were among the pioneers of the short-story genre in Iraq. According to Reuven Snir[3] three quarters of the literary pioneers were Jews. Murād Mīkhā'īl (1909–86) is considered to have written the first "artistic" Iraqi short story to be published.[4] Jewish writers were among the first to use realism and local color, setting their stories in contemporary Iraq.[5]

The reasons for Jewish literary activity were many. The eclipse of the traditional religious school system by the Western-oriented Alliance school and others encouraged an openness to the West that included the appreciation of Western literary forms. Jewish attendance at free state schools, and the patriotic attitude of many of Iraq's Jews, effected the acceptance of the Arabic-Islamic heritage as part of their own. They felt the need for a modern indigenous literature and had the tools to help establish it.[6]

In the mid-nineteenth century a variety of factors led to the formation of the middle class. "A new mercantile bourgeois class arose, due to European capital, efforts of the Turkish military to eliminate some of the feudal kingdoms during their third period of occupation (beginning in 1831), and the reforms of Midhat Pasha in the 1860s."[7]

The rising literacy rate created a potential audience,[8] and the proliferation of newspapers offered an easy venue for literary creations. It is no coincidence that 1909, the year after the Young Turk revolution, marks the "beginning of Jewish writing in literary Arabic."[9] The first book by a Jew in literary Arabic (*The Ottoman Revolution* by Selim Yiẓḥak) and two Jewish newspapers (Nissim Yusif Somekh's Arabic and Turkish language *Al-Zuhur* and Yiẓḥak Yeḥezkel Menaḥem 'Ānī's *Bayn al-Nahrayn*) appeared that year.[10] Many more Jewish-owned and -sponsored journals followed, taking advantage of the new freedom and equality granted to the Jews.

Most of the literary pioneers were in their youth. The older generation was less likely to participate to the same extent for several reasons. Having been educated during the period of Ottoman Turkish rule, members of this generation were in general less fluent in literary Arabic than their younger counterparts. Literature was not a financially rewarding field. Monetary considerations were more likely to influence someone who was expected to support a family than someone who did not yet bear such responsibility. Additionally, the social disapproval accorded literary endeavors—especially the writing of fiction—had greater effect on someone who had already worked to establish a good reputation. The differences in educational, financial, and social status help explain the dominance of younger writers in the Iraqi literary renaissance. According to another view, the young had both the time to write and the boldness to try to publish.[11]

## THE SHORT STORY AND ITS WRITERS

The development of the modern Iraqi short story follows that of its Syrian-Lebanese and Egyptian counterparts.[12] In the beginning stages, works were translated and adapted from Western languages. The proliferation of newspapers and journals offered a forum for these translations, and then for the original works. These first original works were rather dry and didactic, presumably in reaction to the romances and adventure stories that comprised the majority of the published translations. Moreover, the indigenous form of the anecdotal tale with its accompanying moral did not easily graft onto the European model of romance and adventure. Iraqi writers reworked the Western genres of the novel (often serialized in local newspapers) and the short story to treat local issues.

These pioneers were faced with several challenges in adapting the European models for domestic themes, issues, and settings. They needed to develop a new literary idiom, one that simplified the elaborate rhetoric of the classical language and eliminated deliberate obscurity. The question of respectability dogged the genre and was compensated in part by financial rewards to the writers and in part by the highly didactic tone taken by many in the beginning. In these areas and others, the Iraqi pioneers of fiction were influenced by their Arab predecessors from Egypt and the Levant. We see the origins of the Arabic school of social realism in many of these early works, a style that remains popular in the Arab world to this day.

As mentioned, the first short story published in Iraq was written by Murād Mīkhā'īl;[13] the second,[14] "Al-Shābb al-Makhdū'" was published unsigned.[15] Mīkhā'īl's contribution was greater in the field of poetry than in prose. Along with Ja'far al-Khalīlī and Dhū al-Nūn Ayyūb, there were several important Jewish pioneers of the short-story form: Anwar Shā'ūl, Ya'qūb Bilbūl, and Shalom Darwīsh.

## ANWAR SHĀ'ŪL

Anwar Shā'ūl was among the first short-story writers in Iraq, and certainly one of the most important. He was born in 1904 in the town of Ḥilla to the Abū Rubin branch of the famous Sassoon family.[16] Shā'ūl moved to Baghdad with his family in 1916.[17] His studies at the Alliance school were interrupted by the need to work because of the war. He taught Arabic[18] at the Ahliyyah school which was run by the Jewish community.[19] He graduated in 1927 from secondary school[20] and finished law school four years later.[21] He served as secretary of Jewish community for three years.[22] In 1937, he joined many other leaders of the Jewish community in signing an anti-Zionist declaration.[23] As a lawyer he was the legal advisor to the private treasury of the royal household from 1935 to 1949; he defended Jews arrested on charges of Communism[24] as well as Shalom Darwīsh.[25]

Anwar Shā'ūl was among the first to publish short stories,[26] and perhaps the first to publish a short-story collection. His influence is especially strong because of his encouragement of other writers and his role in the development of the short-story genre. He was involved in many facets of the literary world: writing, editing, translation, and publishing. The most influential of all of his literary activities was his contribution to the Iraqi periodicals of the twenties and thirties.

He was coeditor of Salmān Shīnah's[27] Zionist Arabic-language weekly *Al-Miṣbāh* (The lamp) from 1924 to 1927.[28] In 1927, *al-ʿĀlam al-ʿArabī* (The Arab world) started publishing a weekly story feature; Shā'ūl was a frequent contributor.[29]

Even more significant was his establishment of the literary weekly *al-Ḥaṣīd*[30] in 1929[31] in order to offer space for literary creations. He instituted a weekly short-story feature, and two years later, in an unprecedented move, announced the paper's intention to pay for stories.

> To encourage the Iraqi story and to stimulate developing Iraqi writers or those who are ready to develop, *al-Ḥaṣīd* is pleased to announce that it is prepared to pay for each Iraqi story published a sum between three and ten rubiyat.[32]

Many Jewish and non- Jewish short-story writers got their start in the pages (and for the coffers) of *al-Ḥaṣīd*.

In addition to his prose, poetry, and editing, he also translated a number of works, including Schiller's play *Wilhelm Tell*[33] and two collections of short stories.[34] He also founded a publishing house, *Sharikat al-tijārah wa-al-Ṭibāʿah*, and served as its director (1945–60).[35] He made *aliyah* in 1971 and continued to write up to his death in 1984.

His short stories were collected in two volumes: *Al-Ḥiṣād Al-Awwal* (The first harvest)[36] and *Fī Ziḥām al-Madīnah* (In the turmoil of the city).[37] He was among the first to view the short story as an agent for social change. Most of his stories deal with social problems and show an interest in the underclass. They record a social reality, at times offering cautionary tales against the evils of gambling, drinking, and other addictions. He argued against human excesses and presented thought-provoking scenes of poverty and despair. Many of the evils he depicted, he claims, are rooted in the British occupation of Baghdad, and Western decadence: the proliferation of houses of prostitution, bars, nightclubs, dancing, drinking, gambling, and consorting. His stories describe the struggles of the impoverished: a mother caught stealing in order to provide her daughter with a new dress for the holiday; a beggar sleeping in the street; a woman driven to murder her fifth child by her poverty and at her husband's urging. The stories are divided by the author himself into the following categories: social, political, literary, love, fantasy, and "other." He also supported the cause of women. In "Banafsajah" (Violette), for example, he champions the right of a young woman to choose her own partner in marriage.

The stories of *Al-Ḥiṣād Al-Awwal* are not artistically successful. They fail to hold together, straining the reader's "suspension of disbelief" with implausible turns of plot and unbelievable coincidences. Most were written when he was a student, and under the pressure of producing a weekly story (twenty-four were first published in *al-ʿĀlam al-ʿArabī;* five in *al-Ḥaṣīd,* two in *al-Bilād*). One critic offers the judgment that the language he used was superior to that used in the works of other writers, but he concedes that this does not necessarily add to the artistic value of his stories.[38]

In general, the stories have received mixed critical attention. Some have been singled out for praise even years after their publication: "Mashāhid Laylah" (Night scenes) is praised for its "clear social realism";[39] and "Al-Ḥubb al-Mabtūr" (Unrequited love) "succeeds artistically."[40] Suhayl Idrīs describes "Al-Darwīsh" (The dervish) as "tasty" and "humorous," and he declares "Sukr wa-Majnūn" (Drunk and crazy) to be "a true description of society."[41] The author has been criticized for naïveté, for lack of artistry, maturity, and depth of thought,[42] for ineffective language, unfocused stories, and carelessness, and for common ordinariness,[43] superficiality,[44] and improbability.[45] Anwar Shā'ūl himself was not unaware of his shortcomings at the time of publication:

> This first harvest of mine is not without flaws or difficulties because I am only one of the Iraqi short story writers to try to create the Iraqi story out of nothing; I am merely the explorer on the path of a mature literature . . .[46]

Despite all such criticisms, scholars in general agree about Shā'ūl's historic role. His collection has also been judged to be of sociological value[47] because of his ability to describe scenes of poverty in an effective manner. He was among the first to use social realism as a means of serving society and advocating the correction of social ills,[48] despite being "satisfied with merely sketching the problems of the era" [49] in a style considered more journalistic than literary.[50]

Despite his criticism of Shā'ūl, Yūsuf 'Izz Al-Dīn regards the writer as indisputably one of the pioneers of the short-story genre. He credits the writer with preparing the way for the writing and the acceptance of the genre, and ranks him with the non-Jewish pioneers Muḥammad Aḥmad al-Sayyid and Ja'far al-Khalīlī.[51]

Anwar Shā'ūl was less influential in the formal and thematic aspects of the short story than in his encouragement of the development of the genre by familiarizing readers and writers with the modern Western short story through translation and original works.[52] 'Abd al-Ilāh credits him with being one of the first to take an interest in the short story, though not one of its founders, like al-Sayyid.

> [Shā'ūl's efforts] were indeed a first step, but did not succeed in establishing the modern Iraqi short story, as did the efforts of al-Sayyid. However, he was a key factor in motivating a number of educated people to make their contribution by practicing storywriting. He established this genre and secured a place for this art in Iraqi society. He set the story in its appropriate place in the world of literature.[53]

Suhayl Idrīs raises a dissenting voice about Shā'ūl's actual influence on the genre.

> It has become customary to consider Anwar Shā'ūl one of the pioneers of the Iraqi short story alongside Muḥammud al-Sayyid. But we would prefer to compare him with Al-Manfalūṭī in Egypt. Despite the appearance of each in the generation of pioneers, their influence in creating narrative literature is weak.[54]

One tends to agree with the above-mentioned critics that Anwar Shā'ūl was not a very good short-story writer. Shā'ūl's short stories show a number of obvious shortcomings: lack of focus, improbable surprise endings, simplistic and naïve treatment of themes, a journalistic style, and a failure to generate and sustain the reader's interest. In fairness it should be added that they are not all evident simultaneously. A few of his stories rise above the rest, such as "Nafnūf al-'Īd" (The holiday dress) and "Mushāhid Laylah" (Night scene). Despite his failures, Shā'ūl remains a significant figure and is mentioned by all of the literary historians of the era. While perhaps he is not one of the foremost pioneers, he is certainly important, both for his direct and indirect contributions. He was one of the first to practice the art and encouraged other writers by offering a forum for their works (as coeditor of *Al-Miṣbāḥ*, then in his own *Al-Ḥaṣīd*), by awarding payment, by helping to create a readership through translation, by installing a weekly story feature, and by contributing to the same feature in *Al-'Ālam Al-Arabī.*[55]

YA'QŪB BILBŪL

Another pioneer, Ya'qūb (Lev) Bilbūl, was born in 1920, and educated at the Shammāsh and Alliance schools, where English was the language of instruction.[56] In 1938, he graduated from the Alliance school and published his first book. He went on to study economics and business, and became a clerk in the chamber of commerce, then presided over by the businessman and poet Me'īr Baṣrī. During the years 1945–51, he edited the monthly journal of the chamber; he also did the annual report and wrote business, economics, and literary articles that were published in Iraq and in Egypt. He emigrated to Israel in 1951 and five years later graduated as a major in law and economics at Tel Aviv University.[57]

He published his first book, *Al-Jamrah al-'Ūlā* (The first coal), in 1938, and he claims it was the only belletristic book published in Iraq that year.[58] He also composed Shakespearean sonnets (as did Me'īr Baṣrī) that were influenced by the philosophy of Henri Bergson. He did not write for a specifically Jewish audience. Only in retrospect did he realize that a number of features disclosed his Jewish identity: vocabulary (e.g., the use of words such as *sutra* to mean jacket), plot elements (inviting singers to perform on happy occasions—he claims that only the Jews did so), and subject matter (the problem of *mahr*, the dowry—only Jews required that it be paid by the bride's father).[59] These unintentional "ethnic markers" indicate that differences, however slight, were maintained between the Jewish and majority populations.

In general, Bilbūl has been praised for both his commitment to social realism and his short-story technique. His stories show an understanding of the genre (focus and unity) and an awareness of narrative devices.[60] While others fault him for his naïveté,[61] lack of originality or credible plotting,[62] and weakness in characterization,[63] he is generally regarded as a literary pioneer.[64] Even the most critical of modern scholars sees fit to list him among the twenty-one most important writers of the novel and short story between 1920 and 1955.[65] In their anthology of modern Arabic literature, the Makariuses state: "Il peut être considéré comme un des premiers écrivains irakiens modernes et comme un courageux chef du file de l'école réaliste."[66]

His most anthologized story, "Ṣūrat Ṭibq al-Aṣl," expands on Shā'ūl's initial expressions of social realism. It tells of a midwife hired to affirm the pregnant state of a young unmarried girl before her brothers act to erase the shame. The story is clearly critical of the traditions that require the men to murder their sister in order to restore honor to their family.

Bilbūl furthered the development of the realistic school, tightening the structure, refining descriptive technique, and adding a level of analysis (not only presenting social ills but attempting to uncover their sources). Perhaps most significantly, Bilbūl wrote some of his dialogue in colloquial Arabic; he used it for greater authenticity rather than out of desire to reach the masses.[67]

## SHALOM DARWĪSH

Shalom Darwīsh was born in 1912 or 1913.[68] For his first eight years, he lived in western Iraq (Amarrah). He began his studies in the more traditional Talmud Torah and transferred to the Rahīl Shahmoun School (formerly known as al-Ta'āwun) after the family's move to the capital.[69] Upon graduating from the Shahmoun School in 1928, he went to work for the Jewish community and was appointed secretary after Anwar Shā'ūl resigned in the following year. In 1933, he finished secondary school at Al-madrasah al-thānawiyah al-markaziyyah al-masā'iyya, (Evening Division of the Central Secondary School). He began law school in 1935, first in night classes, and then, after the night sessions were canceled, obtained permission from the Jewish community council to attend during the day.[70] He resigned his post in 1944 to begin practicing law.[71] He continued to be active in politics and literature. He was a member of the National Democratic Party and was nearly elected as the Jewish delegate from Baghdad when he ran for parliament.[72]

He emigrated to Israel by way of Iran in 1950. In Israel, he worked for some time in the Ministry of Religious Affairs and obtained law certification in 1954. For many years, he contributed a weekly column on legal matters to one of the Israeli papers. Until recently he continued to practice law in Haifa and to write.

Darwīsh began publishing his stories and literary criticism in Shā'ūl's *Al-Ḥaṣīd* in 1929.[73] His stories were collected in two volumes while he lived in Iraq: *Al-Aḥrār wa-al-ʿAbīd* (Free men and slaves, 1941); and *Baʿḍ al-Nās* (Some people, 1948), which were well received by the reading public. In addition, he participated in *al-Bilād,* whose importance lay not only in its prose and poetry (original and translated works), but also in its service as a forum for ideas about literature.[74] He was a frequent contributor to the *qiṣṣat al-yawm* (story of the day) feature.

Even the ever-critical Da'ūd Sallūm concedes that among Iraqi writers of the short story Darwīsh is an important name because of his talent for description and his ability to focus and analyze character.[75] These praises are echoed by many of the other critics.[76] His use of colloquial language, as well as his humorous and at times satirical style,[77] distinguishes him from many of his peers and has earned him the nickname "Voltaire of Iraq." [78]

In his survey of the modern Iraqi short story, the contemporary critic Suhayl Idrīs highlights Darwīsh's "Qāfilah Min al-Rīf" (Caravan from the countryside)[79] as "one of the best [works] of narrative fiction," comparing it to the great Russian stories. He concludes: "Thus despite his limited story output, Shalom Darwīsh shows one of the brightest faces of short-story writers in modern Iraqi literature."[80] The story is indeed worthy of such attention. It is based on experiences of the writer's own life, such as his family's poverty and its move to Baghdad upon the death of his father. "Qāfilah Min al-Rīf" is a deceptively simple story that effectively describes the characters and their sufferings. Despite the wretchedness of their situation, the story is pervaded by an air of nobility[81] and an atmosphere of hope.[82] The sophistication evident in his writing represents a new stage in the development of Iraqi fiction.

## CONTRIBUTION OF THE JEWISH WRITERS TO MODERN IRAQI FICTION

The Jewish writers of Iraq in the thirties and forties were virtually indistinguishable from their non-Jewish counterparts by their works and their goals. They sought a wide audience in establishing a modern

Iraqi narrative tradition. They tried to avoid ethnic markers: characters' names, specific neighborhoods, parochial themes.

> Jews are not mentioned throughout their works. The neutral names bestowed on most of their characters are those popular among Jews, Christians and Muslims in the more developed Arab lands between the wars. Religion [was] of a similar undenominational variety. . . .[83]

The Western and Islamic heritages fed their art in almost equal fashion. They wrote not as Jews, but as Iraqis. In his introduction to *Al-Jamrah Al-'Ūlā* Ya'qūb Bilbūl declares his desire for "Iraq to unfurl the banner of literature" [84] with every intention of being a part of the Arab literary renaissance.

On the other hand, the writers did not seem to make any attempt to hide their own Jewish identity, generally shunning the use of neutral or Islamicized pseudonyms.[85] Marmorstein declares: "The Jewish origins of these writers are apparent only from their names."[86] Yet the astute reader may well discover additional clues. The critic 'Abd al-Ilāh seems especially sensitive to Anwar Shā'ūl's religious background:

> Like these stories, their author is judged to be Jewish. They have described the Jewish environment in Iraq: its milieu, its physical existence, its psychology, and its problems in a naïve and superficial fashion. In that way these stories are distinguished from others—if there is distinction in this—and attract [the reader's] attention. Only among some stories of other Iraqi Jewish writers do we find this Jewish atmosphere described in a way similar to what we find here in Anwar Shā'ūl's collection. The most prominent, Ya'qūb Bilbūl, does so in his collection *Al-Jamrah Al-'Ūlā*. The number one Jewish problem described in the collection *Al-Ḥiṣād al-Awwal* is one that concerns the Jews of Iraq and especially the poor among them who have many daughters. The Jewish girl is a heavy burden on her family because the Jews of Iraq, like other Jews, pay a large sum to their daughters when they marry.[87]

In a related review Yūsuf 'Izz al-Dīn also points out the inclusion of the dowry question in one of Ya'qūb Bilbūl's stories in order to identify it as a Jewish story.[88] 'Izz al-Dīn relates Bilbūl's treatment of the Jewish comunity to Anwar Shā'ūl's, which he commends on its success in describing what he considers to be an otherwise incomprehensible and closed society. [89]

In general, the Jewish writers in Iraq who wrote in Arabic worked toward creating a nonsectarian literature for Iraq. On the whole they succeeded. Nir Shoḥet quotes Yehoshua ben Hanania (Ya'akov Yehoshua):

> The Jews occupy a great place in general Iraqi literature to a degree that can't be found in any other eastern land. These writers are respected by the family of Iraqi writers. They fought to spread education among the people, to educate women. . . . They fought on behalf of the same principles among their own people as well. . . . In our opinion it is the Jewish writers in Iraq, and only they . . . who can fill an important role in creating a bridge between Hebrew and Arabic literature.[90]

These writers constitute part of the literary heritage of the Iraqi-born Jews who now write in Israel. If not for the social upheavals of the 1940s, they would most likely be contributing to the development of modern Iraqi fiction in ways similar to those of their literary predecessors. Instead, they have adapted their Iraqi literary background to an Israeli environment with varying success. The challenges are different; first and foremost among them is the question of language.

# PART TWO

## Narrative Writings of the Iraqi Jews in Israel

# 4

# The Choice of Language

> Everything can change but not the language that we carry inside us, like a world more exclusive and final than one's mother's womb.
>
> —Italo Calvino

> I envy those writers who experience their infancy, kindergarten years, first love and its disappointment, writing their first literary lines and the summing up magnum opus in the same country, in the same language, in the same culture.
>
> —Sāmī Michael

AT THE VERY BASIS OF THE CONDITION OF EXILE IS THE INABILITY TO communicate. The difference between the familiar language of home (the mother tongue) and the new language of exile is one of many the exiled person encounters and at the same time serves as a metaphor for them all. The difference is particularly significant for the writer.

Among the Iraqi Jews who came to Israel were writers who had begun their literary careers in Iraq and had written in Arabic. Now, in Israel, they had to choose whether to continue to write in Arabic or to brave the transition to Hebrew. There were those who left the field of literature altogether[1] and others who entered the academic sector.[2] Those who decided to continue writing had to adapt to the new language or remain in exile, using their native tongue in a "foreign" environment.

As we have seen, there were periods when the choice of Hebrew as an instrument for literary expression was by no means obvious, and many Jewish writers opted for competing languages—Arabic, Yiddish, or European vernaculars. In the Diaspora, the Jews lived among other peoples and developed a bilingual or multilingual culture. Hebrew was the language of scripture, ritual, and liturgy. Local languages were adopted for daily, bureaucratic, commercial, and other secular functions. In the medieval period, Jews living under Islamic rule were influenced by their hosts and adopted classical Arabic *(al-fuṣḥā)* for writing prose. It was in many ways a natural choice; the language was already established as a literary medium and was similar enough to spoken Arabic *(al-ʿāmmiyyah)* to be easily understood. Poetry, however, was written in Hebrew, following the tradition of Jewish liturgical poetry, albeit in metrical patterns and rhyme schemes derived from Arabic poetry. The poets were also inspired by and competed with their Arab counterparts, showcasing the glories of their respective scriptural languages. They made a conscious effort to revive and revitalize the holy tongue;[3] the results comprised the "golden age" of Hebrew poetry.

The writers of the modern Hebrew revival were also products of bilingual or multilingual backgrounds and traditions. Some of the most important Jewish writers of the nineteenth and early twentieth century wrote in both Hebrew and Yiddish. While Hebrew had a rich literary heritage and therefore prestige on its side, it lacked the audience to be found for Yiddish. Neither language was a natural choice; both needed to be recreated as literary media. One lacked the flexibility of a spoken language, the other the patterns and paradigms of a belletristric language. Each choice had powerful ideological undertones.[4] The writers' explanations of their choice of Yiddish *in Hebrew*[5] are also apologies to their medieval predecessors who earlier lamented the neglect of Hebrew.

By the time our group of Iraqi writers arrived in Israel, Hebrew had become well established as a literary (and national) language, and the issues in choosing a language had shifted once more.

Arabic was the principal language of the Jews in Iraq. Arabic is often described as existing in a state of *diglossia*, "where two varieties of a language exist side by side throughout the community, with each having a definite role to play."[6] Charles Ferguson stresses the importance of using the appropriate variety of language according to the situation[7] and differentiates the condition of diglossia from the more common situation:

> Diglossia differs from the more widespread standard-language-with-dialects in that no segment of the speech community in diglossia regularly uses H [the literary or written form] as a medium of ordinary conversation, and any attempt to do so is felt to be either pedantic or artificial. . . .[8]

In other words, Arabic has an ideal written or literary form *(fuṣḥā)* sufficiently distinct from the spoken or colloquial dialect *(al-ʿāmmiyyah)*. The literary form is more or less standard throughout the Arab world; dialects are many and varied. In actual usage many different registers form a multiglossic spectrum between the two poles.[9]

Dialects of Iraq are not only regional but also ethnic. The dialect of Iraqi Arabic spoken by the Jews differed from the dialects spoken by the Muslims and Christians respectively.[10] The Jewish dialect belongs to the "Qeltu" group as opposed to the Moslem "Geltu" dialect.[11] Its most distinguishing characteristic is the use of Hebrew vocabulary items. The Hebrew items are mostly names (personal names, family names, and nicknames), words for religious objects and observations, and titles of synagogues and other Jewish institutions.[12] The dialects also vary with respect to morphology, phonology, and syntax.[13]

Jews (and Christians) traditionally did not adopt the dialect of the Muslims. This was due perhaps to social isolation, as well as the lack of prestige historically accorded to the speakers of the majority dialect until modern times.[14] The ethnic division of dialects is especially true for the Christians, Jews, and Muslims of Baghdad. Sufficient numbers of the minority populations lived in the capital to keep the communities more segregated than in the smaller cities and towns. Thus, dialects remained distinct.[15]

However, members of the minority groups understood the Muslim dialect and used it when speaking with Muslims.[16] "In Baghdad the Christian Arabs speak a 'Christian Arabic' dialect when talking among themselves but speak the general Baghdad dialect, 'Muslim Arabic,' when talking in a mixed group."[17] And so it was for the Jews. The Jews spoke the majority dialect with varying degrees of proficiency.

> [In contrast to the situation in the smaller towns], in Baghdad, where there was a large Jewish community, of whom many, especially the women, did not often have any contact with an Arab school or grocery, the Jews did not speak the Muslim dialect with its correct accent, and sometimes addressed themselves to a Muslim in the Jewish dialect, which occasionally led to ridicule on the part of the Muslim listener.[18]

*Farewell Babylon*, a novel written in French by Naim Kattan,[19] opens with a passage that illustrates the use of different dialects. It begins in a Baghdad café where a group of high school-age boys—aspiring intellectuals—meet to discuss issues of culture, literature, and the future. The group is mixed; only Nessim and the first-person narrator are Jewish.

> The evening was marked by an unusual note. Nessim spoke in the Jewish dialect. We were the only Jews in the group. . . . In Iraq the presence of a single Muslim in a group was enough for his dialect to be imposed. . . . Every religious group had its manner of speaking. . . . We had only to open our mouths to reveal our identity. This emblem of origin was inscribed in our speech. . . . An inexhaustible source of confusion and ridicule. . . .
>
> Semi-literate Jews always studded their phrases with one or two Muslim terms when they spoke to other Jews. . . . The rich Jews were no less ashamed of their accent and they never missed the chance to slip a few words of English or French into their conversation. . . .
>
> The Muslims borrowed only from the literary language. They felt no need to cast an unfavorable judgment on their dialect. . . . A typically Jewish word in the mouth of a Muslim was synonymous with ridicule. . . .[20]

Nessim's words are a challenge to the entire group, but especially to the narrator. He tries to avoid the need to react, but he is forced to respond when Nessim asks him a question. He tries for neutrality: "I chose a middle course. My words were neither of the Jews nor the Muslims. I spoke in literary Arabic."[21] Nessim underlines the inadequacy of this dodge by translating his friend's words (which would surely have been understood by such well-educated youths) into Jewish dialect. The narrator himself regrets his choice.

> I was betraying him. I was ashamed to utter in the presence of others the words of intimacy, of home, of friendship. . . . I could not reject our common language without humiliating myself. . . .[22]

By the end of the evening, everyone has accepted the use of the Jewish dialect, and even the Muslims respectfully try to adopt it themselves.[23]

The dialect served as an ethnic marker. Speech was as much of a means of identification as dress had been earlier during the Ottoman period.[24]

Sāmī Michael refers to the identification factor of the languages in his novel *Ḥofen Shel Arafel,*[25] set in Baghdad on the eve of Israel's declaration of independence. Akram, the Zionist brother, is identified as a Jew when "in his excitement, the Jewish dialect slip[s] out."[26] George the Christian, in trying to explain to his wife the closeness of his friendship with Akram's Communist brother Ramzī, declares "I myself speak the Arabic of the Jews."[27]

The written, or literary, form of Arabic was acquired in school. Many of the Jewish children were sent to the free government-sponsored schools for their primary education as well as secondary education, and the language of instruction was Arabic.[28] Also, in the Jewish-community schools the children were taught in Arabic. Literary Arabic had been forbidden by the Ottoman Turks for any official functions,[29] but with their departure and the rise of Arab nationalism written or literary Arabic returned to the foreground. Written Arabic's return to importance necessitated educating the speakers of Iraqi dialects in the literary form of the language.

> The new administration demanded that all of its servants . . . know the official language of the country, Arabic. Jews and Muslims set out to relearn a language which they had spoken only in the degraded form of dialect. . . .[30]

Arabic had not been abandoned but, rather, eclipsed. The renaissance of the Arabic language had started even before the British replaced the Turkish government. The Young Turks revolution (1908) and the writing of a new constitution granted equal citizenship to all subjects and ushered in an era of greater freedom and near equality. This promise of freedom was reflected in the proliferation of the Arabic press beginning in 1909.[31] The Jews were enthusiastic participants in the revival of literary Arabic and acquired a reputation for excellence in the language, often scoring well on government examinations.[32] Their contribution to the development of modern Arabic literature is discussed in chapter 3.[33]

Knowledge of Hebrew was maintained throughout the ages, although largely restricted to the traditional domain of religion. For the most part, Jews were educated in the traditional *istadh.*[34] The schoolroom itself was sparsely furnished, but in the words of one scholar, "The teacher's punishment cane was most prominent."[35] Up to fifty or more children attended together without regard to age or level; the teacher would call each in turn and teach according to his or her knowledge, beginning with the alphabet and progressing to biblical verses. "Incredible though it may sound, many of the children who attended the *istadh* managed to learn Hebrew no matter how hard the way was."[36]

Hebrew was taught not as a spoken language in the *istadh* but as a language used to fulfill religious and business functions. Advanced students would learn to write business letters in what was called either *suki* or *sharh*:[37] the Iraqi Jewish dialect of spoken Arabic written in Hebrew characters.

The low standards of the traditional *istadh*, and to its conservative nature[38] contributed to the success of newer schools such as the modern "Talmud Torah," which followed the national curriculum in addition to teaching religious subjects. The more modern schools encouraged the learning of modern Hebrew alongside Western languages. The Alliance Israélite Universelle established the first modern school in Iraq at the invitation of the Jewish community of Baghdad in 1864.[39] Students studied Hebrew, Arabic, and a general modern Western curriculum including science and mathematics. The trends toward secularization and an openness toward the West were followed by many of the schools established by the local Jewish communities in the wake of the Alliance schools. These schools taught Hebrew, English, and Arabic beginning in the primary grades, following the state curriculum and using Arabic as the language of instruction—with the exception of the Shammāsh school, where the primary language was English. In 1920 the Jewish community in Baghdad supervised eight schools teaching 5,511 pupils; by 1949, on the eve of the mass emigration, the number had grown to twenty schools teaching 10,391 pupils.[40]

Many of the Jewish children attended these modern community-run schools, which spread in popularity, replacing the *istadhs* in the larger cities. Several of the schools imported instructors from Palestine to teach Hebrew.[41]

> Since the overwhelming majority of the Iraqi Jews, in contrast to the Egyptian, had attended at least elementary Jewish schools, up to the middle of the 20th century, only a few grew up in that country without learning at least a little Hebrew. Some young Jewish people could undoubtedly be found who could not recognize a letter of the Hebrew alphabet, but they were not many.[42]

However, the teaching of Hebrew was forbidden in 1935 by a government decree;[43] only reading the Bible in Hebrew was allowed, without any translation or commentary. In any event, the religious component of the Jewish schools had waned in importance, having been reduced to a minor subject taught once or twice a week.[44] The ban on teaching the Hebrew language was apparently lifted temporarily around 1947 when the government permitted[45] the publication of Ezra Haddad's textbook *Alpha Beta*.

In the meantime, the establishment of the Zionist underground (1942) contributed to the Jewish nationalist education of its members.[46] In 1946 teens between fourteen and seventeen were included in these educational efforts as well, and by the next year, most of the teachers of the Jewish elementary schools had joined the movement. Even those children too young to be a part of the underground were exposed to Jewish nationalism.[47] Modern Hebrew instruction was an important part of the teaching. However, the number of students who actually learned the language with any proficiency is questionable.[48]

Western languages were taught by the same modern schools that replaced the *istadh*. At the Alliance schools, Turkish,[49] French, and English were taught alongside Hebrew, Arabic, and general curriculum subjects. Fluency in these languages was not a guaranteed result. For the most part "those finishing elementary school had a good knowledge of French, knew some English and had acquired only the rudiments of the other three (after 1917, two) languages."[50]

Yet proficiency in French, and even more so in English, was richly rewarded with jobs both prestigious and well paying.[51] "[T]he knowledge they gained of European languages enabled the *Alliance* school graduates to be taken on as clerks by commercial companies and banks, and when the British occupied the country, many of them served in the administration."[52] The schools gave their students the edge over their non-Jewish counterparts in the job market. "As a result of the higher educational facilities provided by the activities of the *Alliance Israélite Universelle* and the Anglo-Jewish Association, knowledge of French or English is more common among the Jews than the Muslims."[53]

## TRANSITION TO ISRAEL

Upon coming to Israel, the Iraqi Jewish writers were faced with the problem of whether or not to adopt the language of their new home. To write in Arabic was to hold on to something familiar in a strange land and to use the medium in which one felt at home. It was the language that belonged to the past, to home, and arguably was the most appropriate in conveying that time and place.

The writers who turned to Hebrew had to confront several difficulties: it took time to achieve fluency, ingenuity to compensate for the comparatively limited vocabulary, and determination to prevent any intrusions on the part of the mother tongue. Additionally, it was a great challenge to translate into Hebrew an event experienced in an Arab context.

Writing in literary Arabic, in general, already creates a distance from the daily experience. The distance between the experience and its literary representation is arguably increased by the divergence between "written" and "spoken" Arabic, and continues to increase as time passes from when the writer lived within the Arab community. Writing in Arabic can no longer offer the same sense of immediacy. This distance is compounded by the gap between the writers and their audience. The potential readership for Arabic literature in Israel was small then and becoming smaller.

Most of the Iraqi-born Jews who continued to write in Arabic in Israel were those who made the move at a more advanced age (Murād Mīkhāīl, Ya'qūb [Lev] Bilbūl) or those who came many years after the mass immigration (Anwar Shā'ūl).

Of the writers discussed in this book, there are two—Samīr Naqqāsh and Yiẓḥak Bar-Moshe—who continue to write in Arabic to this day; three—Shalom Darwīsh,[54] Shimon Ballas, and Sāmī Michael—who have switched to Hebrew; and Eli Amir, who has written only in Hebrew.

Paradoxically, those writers who chose Arabic as their linguistic medium had some background in Hebrew from childhood, while those who chose to write in Hebrew had hardly any Hebrew background. Yiẓḥak Bar-Moshe and Samīr Naqqāsh learned a fair amount of Hebrew while still in Iraq. In his memoirs, Bar-Moshe recounts his days at the community-run Moriah school and the excellence of the Hebrew education he encountered there.[55] Samīr Naqqāsh knew the Hebrew alphabet by age four (as well as the Arabic and Roman alphabets) and began his studies in a Jewish school. When he transferred to a government school, his family hired a private tutor for him who, he said, "taught me much more than I would have learned even in school. He taught me to really read [Hebrew] and translate. . . ."[56]

Shalom Darwīsh, who had studied in the Jewish schools of Baghdad and had even served for many years as secretary of the Jewish community there,[57] deferred writing stories in Hebrew for many years after his arrival in Israel. He continued to publish in Arabic through the 1970s and only published his first work in Hebrew in 1981.[58]

Being neither Zionist nor religious, Sāmī Michael did not have access to a Hebrew education. His situation is clearly atypical of contemporary Baghdadi Jews. He claims not to have known more than a few Hebrew words upon his arrival to Israel.[59] Ballas studied in a school run by the Jewish community, but the study of Hebrew was not stressed.

> [There was] one hour a week to learn to read Tanakh, the book of Genesis, but we did not take it seriously, the grade was not included in the average. That was in elementary school. Then in the junior high and high school, we did not learn Hebrew at all. So I forgot. When I came to Israel, I could barely decipher the letters.[60]

## CHOICE OF ARABIC

Writing in Arabic in Israel presents several problems and further choices. An obvious drawback is the lack of audience. The Hebrew reading public is small: a book that sells twenty thousand copies is considered a best-seller.[61] Yet it still constitutes a larger potential audience than that for Israeli Jews who write in Arabic. Most Israeli Jews do not know Arabic, and in any case would prefer to read in Hebrew or a Western language. The opportunities for publication and distribution in the Arab world are further limited by a combination of political and economical factors. Few non-Arab Israelis are attracted to a language that represented "the other." Arabic is not only considered the language of an "inferior culture," as we will see below, but it is also the language of "the enemy." Arab readers are considered to be unlikely to be interested in a book by an Israeli author describing a Jewish childhood, even were it available.

Yiẓḥak Bar-Moshe acknowledges his ability to write in Hebrew (or English), but writes in Arabic because "it is easier," and he can write quickly. He has chosen Arabic also because it is the language that best matches his subject: the past. "It is the language in which we lived." Additionally, he admits to contrary motives, consciously choosing a language little read and even less well regarded. He hopes his writing will confront the negative perception of Arabic in Israel. He believes that it is a language everyone in Israel should know and that by writing in it he encourages more people to learn to read it.[62]

Naqqāsh, on the other hand, writes in Arabic because he "cannot write in Hebrew." He was twelve years old when he left Iraq for Israel in 1950–51. Despite the urgings of his colleagues and teachers[63] he has never seriously considered writing in Hebrew.

> Language is the writer's tool. A writer must choose the tool that is strongest for him . . . even if you speak another language well, you don't have words for smells, tastes, feelings. . . . Those who grew up on one language and later try to use another . . . as much as [they] try [they] cannot achieve 100 percent of what I want to achieve.[64]

In both cases, the writers stand firm against the pressures on them to switch to Hebrew. As a counterpoint, Eli Amir, who arrived in Israel at the age of twelve, never considered writing in any language other than Hebrew.[65] Another member of their peer group, David (Rabi) Rabeeya, continues to publish in Hebrew, despite leaving Israel for the United States in 1970 and maintaining strong academic and personal ties to Arabic. He asserts that he has forgotten how to write in Arabic, but hopes to return to it someday.[66]

Bar-Moshe, Naqqāsh, and the other Jews who continue to write in Arabic reach a very small and diminishing audience. For the most part they are limited to the private press—the equivalent of the vanity press in the United States—or depend on the largesse of organizations such as the Association for Jewish Academics from Iraq.[67]

Naqqāsh, a writer highly regarded by the small number of mostly academics who read him, publishes six hundred to a thousand copies of his work, many of which the author himself distributes.[68] He serves as an extreme example; his choosing to write in a specific dialect further limits his readership. Naqqāsh, in particular, seems very frustrated. A scholar's writer—he is proud of the level of linguistic complexity in his writing—he complains that no one knows how to read him.

Translation is virtually the only option available to increase readership among those who continue to write in Arabic. This is somewhat self-defeating, as much of the linguistic complexity inevitably gets lost in translation (although some of the stylistic intricacy and philosophical depth shine through). The fidelity to the past that Naqqāsh has preserved through his skillful Arabic is not transferable, almost by definition. One collection of his short stories has been translated into Hebrew thus far. His sister Ruth Naqqāsh was generally praised for her efforts in translating the work, but not for the results.[69] Bar-Moshe's memoirs have been published in Hebrew translations; not his short stories.

Another problem is the increasing distance between the writer and the source of his writing medium. "Writing in Arabic requires keeping up with the trends . . . in places to which one has no ties save memories of the past."[70]

The writings of Naqqāsh and Bar-Moshe are largely oriented toward the past, focusing on Iraqi Jews and the traditional neighborhoods in which they lived. They explore the connection with the past, documenting and preserving the very rich and ancient heritage of the Iraqi Jews. They do so by incorporating raw materials from the past into their stories—memories, dialect, and folklore. Bar-Moshe has written three long volumes of his projected four-part memoirs, almost exclusively based on his personal experiences in Iraq. (Only the very last chapter of *Khurūj Min al-ʿIrāq*[71] refers to the author's arrival and first few days in Israel.) In doing so he describes the lifestyle of the middle- and upper-class Jews in Baghdad before the exodus. Naqqāsh evokes the same period by his use of language and folklore materials. His story about an Iraqi immigrant who has brought his belief in the mischievous demon Tantal with him and "sees" him in Israel[72] in effect brings this demon to the pages of Israeli literature and preserves him.

Naqqāsh's use of the colloquial is not entirely unprecedented in the context of Arabic literature. At least since the middle of the last century there has been discussion as to the appropriate use of the colloquial in belletristic work.

The first "colloquialists" were tentative proponents, suggesting that dialect be restricted to contemporary novels and not be used in classic works or translations from foreign languages.[73] Those who championed the use of colloquial language in dialogue asserted that dialogue played an important dramatic role, whereas their opponents viewed literature as art and not mere documentation.[74] The arguments in favor of using colloquial language stressed its quality of authenticity and realism and the advantages of showing character through behavior (of which the speech act was an important component) rather than description. Opposing arguments ranged from dismissing its importance for character description[75] to a somewhat circular argument that it not be used because "in a translation it would be difficult to simulate the difference between *fuṣḥā* and *al-ʿāmmiyyah*."[76]

Iraqi writers began to write dialogue in colloquial language in the thirties. Shalom Darwīsh has been counted among the first to do so,[77] although the two stories in which he used *ʿāmmiyyah*—"Qāfilah min al-Rīf" and "ʿArūs"[78]—were published after his first collection (1941). However, as early as 1938, Ya'qūb (Lev) Bilbūl wrote the dialogue in a story in colloquial language, perhaps one of the only writers to do so before the Second World War.[79]

Bilbūl's dialogue is skillful enough to earn him the praise of several critics: his use of the colloquial succeeds,[80] "nears good artistic dialogue,"[81] conveys the personalities of the characters.[82] His use of *ʿāmmiyyah* demonstrates his clear commitment to realism, and not necessarily the espousal of any political or ideological beliefs. Both Bilbūl and Darwīsh used *ʿāmmiyyah* selectively. The colloquial is used only in selected stories, and then only in the dialogue, to reflect the socioeconomic and educational differences of the lower class *(al-shaʿb)* in relation to the middle and upper classes.

In each case the setting of the story, the character, or the plot determines the appropriateness of using colloquial language. "Qāfilah Min al-Rīf" is based on an event in the author's life when he was eight.[83] It takes place in a rural setting within a family context, making the use of colloquial language natural. "ʿArūs" tells the story of a young orphan girl from the underclass who becomes a prostitute in order to survive but doesn't give up her dream to be a bride. "Ṣūrah Ṭibq al-Aṣl" depicts two brothers who engage the services of a midwife to confirm their unmarried sister's pregnancy before they kill her.

In each story, the colloquial language used in the dialogues is always that of the majority Muslim population. The Jewish dialect was considered too parochial and, as mentioned, was often a source of derision among non-Jews. The Jewish writers were addressing the general public as their potential readers. None of the characters were identified as Jewish, with the possible exception of the midwife, Saīda-Habība, in Bilbūl's "Ṣūrah Ṭibq al-Aṣl."[84] In any event, she interacts with Muslim or neutral characters, in which case one would expect the Muslim dialect to be used. This holds true even in storytelling among the Jews. When a story is told in Jewish Arabic, the Muslim characters speak in their own dialect, as do the Jews when speaking to Muslims. The literary choice corresponds to reality: "A Jew knew the language of the Muslims; a Muslim would not know the language of the Jews. In an encounter between a Jew and a Muslim the language of the conversation would be Muslim."[85]

While not the first to use colloquial language, Samīr Naqqāsh was the first to use the Jewish dialect in his literary works. He did not use the *ʿāmmiyyah* until his third collection of stories.[86] Different dialects identify the ethnic-religious background of each character.

The writer's use of the dialect in these stories documents the quickly disappearing language, but his choice arises from the desire to express "what cannot be expressed in *fuṣḥā*." "In every word there is so much, [every word] needs a translation in full."[87]

The use of these dialects is, to some extent, a hindrance to reaching a wider audience but not to aesthetic achievement. The specific dialect of the Baghdadi Jews serves well to portray their recent past. It is truly the language in which they lived, a closer representation of reality than the more formal *fuṣḥā*. However, this choice also intensifies some of the difficulties for the Jewish writer of Arabic literature in Israel, especially as related to the issues of readership and change.

The potential audience for literature written in Jewish Baghdadi dialect is very limited. When Bar-Moshe, who claims to have decided to write in Arabic because he grew up with the language, was asked why then did he not write in the local vernacular, he replied: "Our spoken Arabic, of the Jews of Iraq, is understood by a very small group, a group that gets smaller and smaller."[88]

Naqqāsh attempts to overcome the disadvantage of the reader who is not conversant in the Iraqi Jewish dialect by providing glosses to his texts. His glosses are found at the foot of nearly every page, translating words, phrases, and entire speeches into *fuṣḥā*. He offers occasional phonetic or grammatical explanations in these notes. The format is daunting to the casual reader, and even difficult to those more committed.

The gloss does not necessarily make the text accessible to the Iraqi, much less the non-Iraqi. Naqqāsh's fellow Iraqi-born writers have expressed their own difficulties in reading his work. Darwīsh has admitted never having succeeded, despite his efforts.[89] Yiẓḥak Bar-Moshe declares his colleague's work to be "unreadable" and "not enjoyable," due to the effort it demands. In an interview he described reading Naqqāsh's writing as a Sisyphian task, every book a dictionary. "I know the words, but kill me if I know what is the context, how does he use it here, why?"[90]

In this function the dialect also loses the one characteristic that separates it from *fuṣḥā*: that it changes over time.[91] Naqqāsh's dialect is frozen, as if sealed in a time capsule; it is not open to the variation natural for a spoken dialect. He has chosen to hold on to this dialect even when the oral storytellers have begun a transition to Hebrew.[92]

In choosing Arabic, the writer remains linguistically at home, tied to the mother tongue. The advantage of not having to pour energy into mastering a second (or third) language is inestimable. Perhaps the greatest disadvantage with this option is that one is forced to remain on the margins. Without a reading public it is almost impossible to move into the literary mainstream; without readers one's works are not acts of communication. Those writing in Arabic are not exiled from their first language, but they are cut off from the source of the experiences and a potential audience.

## CHOOSING HEBREW

Already in the early fifties there was a growing awareness of the difficulties encountered by continuing to write in Arabic. Two young Iraqi immigrants, David Semach and Sasson Somekh, who had already joined literary circles in Baghdad, began a club for fellow lovers of modern Arabic literature.[93] The purpose of this club was to bring Arabic literature to Israel and to continue their own participation in its development. The club "Nadwa al-aṣdiqā' al-adab al-'arabī al-taqaddumī" (Friends of Progressive Arabic Literature) would meet for discussions, lectures, and other cultural events. Semach recalled the general tenor of these discussions:

> How to write, in which language to write? How could we continue to give expression to our love of literature—that is, to continue to write—and at the same time to have an audience we could influence? We began to understand that to write in Arabic, [who would be] the audience? On one hand we wanted to turn to the Arabs so that they would see that we were not strangers, that there are Jews similar to them, who think like them, write like them, love poetry and songs just like them, but we wanted more. We wanted to reach the Jewish audience and bring them closer to Arab culture.
>
> We thought it was only a matter of years. A matter of time . . . to fulfill this mission and also get self-fulfillment from writing. There was no escape from learning Hebrew. We could learn it and begin to write in it. Today I no longer remember who said what: who said no, we have to continue in Arabic; who said yes. Reality showed afterward that the debate was already decided for all practical purposes, decided before it heated up. As proof, the majority of people either crossed over to write in Hebrew or they stopped writing completely. . . . Those who continued to write in Arabic were older, and had already published in Iraq. They had written and published a great amount. For them it was much more difficult.[94]

The proceedings of an early meeting of the club in which the issue of language was debated were summarized in the Communist Al-Jadīd.[95] At the time, the club had come under the aegis of this journal, initially for practical reasons—to have a place to publish their writing. But the ideological aspect cannot be disregarded entirely; by this time the majority of club members were either party members or supporters.

Among those present were Shimon Ballas and Sāmī Michael. Ideological considerations guided the discussion. There were those who felt the choice of language to be less important "as long as literature executes its duty on behalf of the masses." The political rhetoric of the statement is clear. Others felt that the choice should be left to the discretion of the writer but that Hebrew was to be preferred because of audience. Stronger arguments were stated in favor of choosing Hebrew in accordance with the writers' obligations as progressives: to popularize and democratize the language; to unite the population and destroy the "Tower of Babel" in Israel; and to provide the progressive literary elements necessary in laying the foundations of a proletarian literature in Hebrew. No argument was stated in favor of choosing Arabic.[96]

It was ultimately a personal decision. Michael was one of the first to try to switch because of the need to match subject with language. Shortly after his arrival he realized that he could not write in Arabic about the Israeli reality, and he also took it upon himself to urge his peers to learn Hebrew.[97] Ballas was at first reluctant to follow.

> I was among those opposed. I said no, what, language, impossible. Language is a part of a person. Yes, it's the mother tongue, not just a mother's tongue, but the mother tongue. But in the end I came to the conclusion: I live in Tel Aviv, I speak Hebrew. [After all] who is my audience?![98]

Darwīsh reached a similar conclusion much later, waiting until he felt he had full command of Hebrew. In his opinion, it is a waste of time to write in Arabic.

> If I write in Arabic no one will read it. There is no market at all. The people who read me in Iraq have crossed over to Hebrew. Arabs are not interested in reading a Jew. . . .[99]

The transition to Hebrew, however, was not easy even for the younger writers. It was difficult to learn the language. Ballas and Michael both learned Hebrew in part by reading the newspaper and working for the Communist Party paper *Al-Ittiḥād*. Michael worked for the paper as well and learned Hebrew from his daily routine.

> My method of learning Hebrew was rather unsystematic. I picked up the language while taking walks in my neighborhood, riding the bus, or listening to conversations.[100]

Darwīsh waited thirty years before he felt he knew Hebrew well enough to attempt his first literary piece in Hebrew. Still he worried that his style would be "too lawyerly." Darwīsh, who is an attorney by profession,[101] enjoyed great popularity as a weekly columnist writing about legal matters, but was concerned that his fluency would not carry over to literary endeavors.

Despite the passage of time and the acceptance these writers have received from readers and critics, each considers himself to be different from the native Hebrew writer. At the beginning of his Hebrew career Ballas felt the need to prove to his readers that he knew the language. He studded his first work with anachronisms and neologisms to prove this knowledge. Michael has allowed himself less license with the language than he would as a native speaker.

> I still envy people who were born into the Hebrew language. They can castrate words on purpose or distort them. They are free to take the language, to make a dough from it, and play with it as they like. They have a legitimate right to do this. I feel as if I am not entitled to do this.[102]

The mother tongue is apt to intrude where the adopted language fails.

> Ballas: A child creates great metaphors in language without knowing the rules. At an older age he learns the rules of syntax, enters the system, and the imagination and instinctive energy in the language are stopped. Such is the writer who learns a second language at a late age. He feels that he writes in an artificial manner. From time to time words and expressions come to his mind naturally in his mother tongue and he has to push them aside, and put himself in the new framework.[103]

Knowing this, Ballas intentionally tried to forget Arabic. He forbade himself to read anything in Arabic—or even to listen to the radio—for three years while writing his first novel.[104] Yet proficiency in the language does not preclude the possibility of linguistic interference.

> Michael: Today I think in Hebrew and write only in Hebrew. However I still feel that I wasn't born into the Hebrew language. Sometimes the pen stops and my mind searches for the appropriate word, but the word appears only in Arabic or English garb.[105]

It is not just linguistic ability that is required in order to write in a new language, but also cultural background. Michael describes having been steeped in Arab and Islamic culture as a "feeble if not hopeless start for a Hebrew writer"[106] because of its irrelevance (and *not* because of any implied value judgement). Ballas's early style resounds with heavy echoes of Agnon, whom he read in a personal "crash course" to acquire the background in Hebrew literature. It was only when he matured as a writer that he freed himself from this influence and found his own voice.

The perceived simplicity of modern Hebrew style compared to the arabesques of more traditional Arabic rhetoric was seen as an advantage by those who switched. Even in Iraq Michael tried to rebel against the "fussy ornamentation" of literary Arabic.

> I love the simple word which expresses thought clearly and doesn't enslave reality in a magic formula. . . . I found refuge in modern Hebrew, for today it more closely resembles the languages of Europe than Arabic.[107]

Ballas concurs with Michael's preference for the simple over the ornamental. "I think if I had continued to write in Arabic . . . I would have westernized writing in Arabic as much as possible—Hebrew helped in this."[108]

The choice of Hebrew is not based on a pull from the adopted language, but is a recognition of the inadequate reach of the language left behind. The overriding factor in the decision is the question of audience. These writers began writing in Hebrew in order to reach a wider public.

## TRANSLATING CULTURE

After the acquisition of the language the next difficulty involves the process of conveying the flavor of the old culture in this new language. The challenge of cultural translation is to use the language of the target audience to present a rich description that draws a picture of the people and the culture of the source language. Strategies for doing so involve a combination of linguistic and nonlinguistic elements. Nonlinguistic elements included objects (food, clothing, etc.) and behavior (customs, traditions, habits). In Shimon Ballas's *HaMa'abarah*[109] one man wraps the *kaffiyah* around his head (p. 11), another fingers his string of amber worry beads (p. 10), a third reveals his gold tooth when he smiles (p. 24). They look forward to a dish of *pacha* (p. 28),[110] and *kofta*[111] and avoid the gefilte fish of the Ashkenazim. "For the Yiddish it's not Shabbat without the gefilte fish."[112]

Borrowing from the Arabic culture was not restricted to food and objects, but extended to the linguistic texture with some lexical items. Ballas begins his novel *HaMa'abarah*—the first Hebrew novel published in Israel by an Iraqi-born immigrant—with the words "Maqhā an-Na'ṣr li-ṣāḥbihī Shlomo Khamra."[113] These Arabic words, transcribed into the Hebrew alphabet, are asterisked and explained in Hebrew at the foot of the page as "Café A-Natsar [Victory]—Shlomo Khamra, proprietor." The original version of the novel also had entire poems in the Arabic (with Hebrew translation) but these were omitted by the editor as unacceptable to the Hebrew reader.[114] The unprecedented use of Arabic to open a Hebrew novel was a powerful statement in itself, carrying with it the risk of alienating the reader.

In general, however, Arabic is used in dialogue rather than in the narrative parts. The narrative voice remains neutral in order to gain the reader's confidence and to mediate the distance to an unfamiliar culture. The Arabic transcribed falls into four general categories: interjections, formulas, proverbs, and curses.

In his first novel[115] Sāmī Michael identifies dialect spoken in Arabic primarily by inserting the vocative *yā* before the name of the person addressed. The *yā* precedes the proper name *(Yā Reuven, Yā David*, p. 17, p. 18), title *(Yā Abū-Shā'ūl* [O father of Shaul], p. 21),[116] designation of relationship *(Yā Bnī* [my son], p. 25; *Yā Abba* [father], p. 13), or category *(Yā walad* [boy], p. 48; *Yā īsha* [woman or wife], p. 14). Arabic is also used for emphasis *(Yā-ḥaraām* [it's forbidden; for shame], p. 104). Interjections such as "*Yā'nī* (literally "it means," used as "that is" or "you know," p. 27), *tafaḍḍal, tafaḍḍalī* (please, come in, sit down, p. 40), and *dakhīlak* ("please, please!" p. 31) flavor the text. *Wallāh* (by Allah) is used as an intensifier: *Allāh lo yitayn, wallāh, allāh yishmor* (May Allah give to him, by Allah, may Allah keep him [the phrase itself is rendered in Hebrew], p. 23). Eli Amir similarly sprinkles the occasional Arabic expression in *Tarnegol Kaparot*: *Wallāh majnūn* (Boy, is he crazy!).[117] For the most part these words and phrases are familiar and not alienating. These expressions in Arabic serve as "markers" for Arabic, but at the same time they are familiar to the Hebrew reader, having already crept into Hebrew folklore, slang, and humor.

The characters' speech in Ballas's *HaMa'abarah* also contains formulaic expressions that are used as responses to other phrases or events. A person is greeted with *Khayr inshallāh*, glossed as *B'surah tova halvai* (Good news I hope) (p. 134); one who has returned after a long absence receives the greeting *ḥamdilla 'as-salāma* (glossed to *ha-sheveḥ la'El 'al ḥaziratkha bashalom* [praise be to God for your safe return], p. 125). This reflects the customs of Arab society, which depend on situation-appropriate formulaic phrases and expressions as an integral part of expected behavior.

In *HaMa'abarah,* Yosef is nicknamed Abū Ya'qūb (p. 84)—the Iraqi Jewish pronunciation[118] of what would be in Hebrew Abu Yaakov, referring both to the Arab custom of naming a baby after the grandfather, as well as the biblical (and Qur'ānic) genealogy of Jacob and his son Joseph. Shlomo Reshti is called Abū Ghā'ib—father of the absent one, because he has no male children—and is greeted with *Yom al-'indak* (May it be God's will and may you too have a son).

The characters curse in Arabic as well. *Tuz!,* Abu Helawa says to Ẓiporah in *Shavim VeShavim Yoter* (p. 29), *Yikhreb beetak* (may your home be destroyed) curses a character in another book.[119] In some cases these curses are rendered in a literal Hebrew translation rather than transcription: *ervat emam* (their mother's shame), *hashaḥor aleikhem* (black unto you).[120] These phrases, common in Arabic, do not otherwise exist in Hebrew. There are other phrases and concepts that are translated fully or partially into Hebrew words. The Hebrew translation substitutes for the original Arabic phrase in the text itself rather than supplementing the Arabic in a footnote. The response to Naima's news of her pregnancy is *Mabrūk ya Naima, mabrūk. Ben zakhar inshallah* (Congratulations, O Naima, congratulations. May it be a son, God willing).[121] Someone on the verge of vexation is urged to patience with the literal Hebrew translation of *ṭawwil baalak*: *Haarekh ruḥakha* (lengthen you breath).[122] The proverbs in *Paḥonim Veḥalomot* by Sāmī Michael are ostensibly translated from the Arabic: "Better a dog running around than a sleeping lion" (said by a mother to her son to encourage him to go out and do something); "When the monkey doesn't know how to dance he says that the ground is bumpy" (said by the grandmother to her partially lame granddaughter, who doesn't want to join her peers for a dance); "A man who asks you for an egg will die of hunger before you succeed in peeling it" (the character's friend expressing impatience with his slow pace).[123]

The use of Arabic words, phrases, expressions, and formulas in all of these novels is present mostly in the speech of the characters in the literature describing the period shortly after the Iraqis' arrival to Israel (*ma'abarah* literature),[124] and much less so in either the literature set in Iraq (pre-exile) or post-*ma'abarah*. The small phrases and single words of Arabic serve not only to convey an atmosphere, to hint at a cultural milieu, but also to highlight the gap between the characters and their surroundings. The linguistic dissonance brings the reader closer to the condition of exile. In the literature that takes place in Iraq, the characters are at home, in the only home they have ever known. The entire experience is translated into Hebrew words as if monolithic; there is no need to create a gap between the characters and their environment. The post-*ma'abarah* literature shows the characters in a later stage of adjustment in which the gap between them and their surroundings is less central; their conflicts come from within.

## EDITING

Editing is one phase of the publishing process that illustrates the difference in writing experience for the Arabists and Hebraists respectively. In joining the ranks of modern Hebrew litterateurs, the writers had to conform, at least in part, to their standards and traditions. One of the more difficult transitions was the acceptance of the institution of editing, something that was much less common in the Iraqi literary scene of the forties than in Israel twenty years later, when these writers began to publish book-length works. The majority of works published in Iraq were done at the author's (or perhaps benefactor's) expense.[125] The only incidence of prepublication editing by someone other than the writer in Iraq that I found occurred in the case of Ya'qūb (Lev) Bilbūl's short-story collection.[126] The editing concerned only one piece, the story referred to above[127] in which the two brothers kill their pregnant sister. Two (Muslim) brothers who worked at the press read the stories they were to print. They took offense that the characters portrayed as cruel and primitive had typically Muslim names, while the kind midwife had a common Jewish name. Bilbūl changed the names to more neutral names to please his friends.[128]

The writings of Samīr Naqqāsh and Yiẓḥak Bar-Moshe show the continuation of this noneditorial tradition. Neither Yiẓḥak Bar-Moshe nor Naqqāsh avail themselves of editors. Bar-Moshe edits his own work. On one occasion Maḥmūd Abbāsī—editor for numerous Arabic publications in Israel—suggested the omission of a particular story on the grounds it would not be well received by the Arab readership. Yiẓḥak Bar-Moshe filed the story away.[129] He disregarded other suggestions on the part of prepublication readers to shorten the manuscripts of the first and subsequent volumes of memoirs (596, 420, and 389 pages, respectively) towards a tighter narrative. As a result, critics have commented on the uneven quality of stories in his collections,[130] surprising errors,[131] and the length of his memoirs.[132] His memoirs are apt to try the patience of a Western reader with their repetitiveness and plethora of minor details.

Samīr Naqqāsh has been accused of being incommunicative, and not only because of his use of multiple dialects.[133] His style is complex, drawing on a broad frame of references, from local Iraqi folktales (*ʿIndama tasquṭ aḍlaʿ al-muthallāt* [When the sides of the triangle fall])[134] to the dadaist movement in art (*Nuzūlahu Wakhīt Al-Shayṭan* [Tenants and cobwebs]).[135] Careful editing could help him retain the complexity on which he prides himself without veering into obscurity.

Editing was yet another adjustment demanded of the writers who crossed over to Hebrew. Not only was it a difference between the literary traditions, but it had perhaps more urgency for those who were writing in an adopted language. According to the editor for Darwīsh's *Phraim! Phraim!*, extensive revisions were necessary to render the author's original manuscript into grammatical Hebrew.[136] The writer himself concurs in part: "A word here or there, yes he had many comments, especially about style."[137]

Ballas had difficulty in accepting the editing of his first novel[138] and never published its sequel because of editorial conflict.[139] Yet today he affirms the importance of editing for his own work and literature in general.[140]

At its best, editing can serve as a mechanism for quality control, eliminating errors, wordiness, repetition, and substandard pieces. It can also help the novice writer find his or her own style.

> When I wrote *HaMaʿabarah* I was influenced by Agnon. I tried the whole time, afterward when I went over it again and again, I tried somehow to free myself from him, but [his influence] remained. Some remained. Then it was edited.[141]

As both writer and professor of Arabic literature, Ballas has since come to appreciate the institution of editing and to feel its lack within the contemporary Arabic literary tradition.

> Editing involves another person coming from outside, someone who comes and looks, sometimes gives advice. [The editor] doesn't necessarily have to sit down and correct, but sometimes one piece of advice makes all the difference. It doesn't exist in Arabic [literature]. And that is a great failing.[142]

While the process of editing has gained greater acceptance in the world of Arabic literature, it is not as easily available for the writers under discussion. Those who write in Hebrew have to overcome the difficulties of adjusting to the process; those who write in Arabic are largely free from considerations of marketability and editorial interference. Yet they are cut off from the traditional sources of feedback: editing, criticism, and reader response. Judging by the lack of reviews, copies of books sold, and want of mention in contemporary literary studies, the voice they write in is their own, but it is rarely heard.

## THEMES

Editing is not the only difference between the Arabic and Hebrew works. The content, themes, and subjects differ in accordance with the linguistic media. The stories written in Arabic focus on more traditional (and insulated) Jewish neighborhoods in Iraq, while those in Hebrew generally explore the world outside these quarters. This difference reflects the difference in the authors' backgrounds and personalities, and suggests a solution to the paradox of their language choices.

Naqqāsh, Bar-Moshe, and Darwīsh lived within the Jewish community. Their writings set in Iraq (or looking back to that era) are peopled with members of the Jewish community and imbued with a strong sense of autobiography. The Iraq of Naqqāsh, Bar-Moshe, and Darwīsh's writing stays within a traditional Iraqi Jewish frame of reference. Most of the characters are Jews, of similar background; the lone Arab is "the other," the exception that emphasizes this homogeneity. Within this sector the world they create—particularly Naqqāsh's—is still very rich, full of life and texture.

In contrast, the stories of Michael and Ballas set in Iraq show a much more heterogeneous culture. Their Jewish characters move in a mixed society, and the themes explore close friendships among Jews and Arabs, Christian and Muslim, as well as Kurds and other minorities. Michael and Ballas themselves were members of the secular Jewish community who considered themselves first and foremost Iraqis. Their membership in the Communist movement attests to their desire to change the society from within, but also to their feelings of belonging to that society. The worlds they create in their Iraq-period literature are multicultural, inhabited by members of previously segregated societies.[143]

Michael and Ballas's stories set in Israel, along with Eli Amir's novel, *Tarnegol Kaparot,* present a similarly heterogeneous group. Whether in Iraq or Israel, the characters in the novels grapple with the same issues of identity and cross-cultural relationships. Ballas, Michael, and Amir have written novels describing the difficulties of acclimating to the new environment and present different strategies taken by the transplanted Jewish Iraqi. The problems specific to the transplant are generalized to include Israeli-Arab relations, questions of identity, betrayal, and refuge.

The writers who chose Arabic often came from more traditional insular families living in the Jewish quarters. Their marginal status as members of the Jewish minority in Iraq shifted with the immigration to the marginal status of being Iraqis in Israel. Their choice of language reflects this marginality, as well as an orientation toward the past.

> I live the past more [than I live] the present and the future. And without any doubt . . . all the baggage that I have I didn't get any of it in Israel. I got [all of it] in the twenty-three years that I lived in Iraq.[144]

On the other hand, those who have switched to Hebrew came from secular backgrounds and mixed neighborhoods. They brought with them from Iraq to Israel the desire to be part of the mainstream.

> When one lives in a certain reality, in a certain society, then, one must be a part of the society. To be part of the society is a matter of language, [it means] not to stay as a stranger forever, as an exile. Here [in Israel] it is impossible to be an exile. . . . You arrive, you become integrated in the society somehow, you take a new identity. If you take a new identity, you must take it fully, including the language.[145]

They were oriented toward the present and toward contemporary issues. As in the stories they wrote before immigrating, it was their challenge to generalize their experiences into a literature that embodied universal themes. For the most part the Hebrew writers concentrated on the period in Israel and on developing their personal relationship with the Hebrew language.

The case of the Iraqi-born Jewish writer in Israel is an example of the writer in exile who must choose the language in which to write. The choice is a determining factor in the writer's struggle both to communicate and to mediate between the past and the present. The choice influences the style and subject matter of the works, as well as readership. In the following chapters I discuss significant themes and formal aspects in the Hebrew and Arabic writings of these Iraqi-born Israelis.

# 5

# The Experience of Transition: First Novels in Hebrew

> Our expectations of the country were great, a mixture of messianic dreams and unrealistic aspirations, but the reality was different: crisis followed crisis—economic, social, religious and moral. The hardest of all was the search for identity, a search for the personal I and the collective; and on top of all of these came an additional blow—[the crisis] of culture.
>
> —Eli Amir

THE CRISES ELI AMIR DESCRIBES WERE SHARED BY MANY UPON THEIR arrival to Israel during the period of mass immigration (1948–51). Their experience has found expression in the Hebrew literary subgenre, *sifrut hama'abarah* (literature of the transit camp). This literature, written predominantly by Israelis of Iraqi origin, is frequently characterized by the sharp contrast between the newcomers' expectations and the lack of welcome they received, the bleak physical conditions of the transit camps in contrast to life in the country of origin, and the clash between the cultures of the newcomers and the veteran settlers. The plot describes the difficulties encountered by the characters, including fragmentation of the family unit and the crisis of identity. These novels, written in the realistic mode, create adolescent protagonists and large casts of secondary characters that often remain underdeveloped. The authors make use of institutions central to Israeli society as background, examining them as mechanisms for promoting integration of these characters. Foremost among these institutions is the *ma'abarah.*

The root of the word *ma'abarah* implies transition or passage. One of the writers puts the following explanation in the mouth of one of his characters (Eliahu Eini):

> I asked why they called these camps *ma'abarot;* they told me that they are a passage *(ma'avar)* to full absorption into the way of life. I looked for the word in the Bible and found it in the Book of Samuel . . . a verse about Jonathan who passed between the *ma'abarot,* where [there was] "a crag from this passage and a crag from that one." Here you have the *ma'abarah!* A rock on both sides![1]

## SOCIOHISTORICAL BACKGROUND

With the influx of the mass immigration to Israel in the early days of the state, the factors affecting the integration of the newcomers changed because of the rapidly increasing rate of immigration, the shaky postwar economy, and the creation of a complex bureacracy.[2] Shlomo Hillel, an Iraqi-born Jew already living in Palestine at the time of the mass immigration, was recruited to help organize the illegal immigration of those Jews wishing to leave Iraq; he describes this last development as an overnight change. Returning from a successful mission, he finds his own entry to Israel challenged. He had never been issued an official passport.

> The Israel I had left nine months earlier was like one big family; it was enough for you to speak fluent Hebrew to prove that you "belonged." But the intervening months had turned us from a family into a state, with the standard bureacratic rules and formalities that could not be winked at.[3]

The conditions encountered by the newcomers were caused in large part by the very success of the programs organizing the immigration movements. The scale and suddenness of the mass immigration severely strained an already overburdened postwar economy. The bureaucratic structures developed to ease the "absorption" of the newcomers compounded the difficulties. Immigrants first met the more veteran Israeli citizens within an impersonal bureaucratic setting. This initial encounter not only emphasized the difference in status between the immigrants and the veterans (a status based on date of entry) but also established a hierarchical-relationship pattern of supplicant and provider.[4] The veteran Israeli citizen was in the position of knowledge and power; the *oleh* (immigrant) was reduced to an ignorant and therefore passive client.

Economic and employment opportunities were very limited. The *ma'abarot* (plural of *ma'abarah*, i.e., transit camps) were set up as a temporary measure. The intention was to furnish the immigrants with their basic needs (food, shelter, clothing, sanitary facilities) until they could learn the skills (including Hebrew and often job retraining) necessary to function independently.[5]

Upon their arrival in Israel, the Iraqi immigrants faced a set of conditions for which they were ill prepared and for which the Israelis were ill equipped. They were settled in these overcrowded *ma'abarot*, often sharing with another family a tin cabin *(paḥon)* or a canvas shack *(badon)* that could not withstand the winter rains. The shacks had neither electricity nor toilet facilities; the communal lavatories were located as much as a kilometer or more away.[6] The material deprivation and difficult physical conditions were intensified by the contrast they posed to the comfortable way of life that many left behind in Iraq.

> The same papers that trumpeted the arrival of the first plane-loads of immigrants from Iraq were filled with items about the shortage of food, the black market in sugar and oil, and the prospect of "new cuts in imports." Unemployment, still rampant, was now leading to violent clashes between veteran, unionized workers and new immigrants who were willing to work outside the union framework for lower pay.
>
> But most difficult of all were the conditions in the transit camps. Fresh off the boat or plane, the immigrants were taken by truck (buses being considered a luxury) to one of the camps dotting the countryside, where whole families, from infants to the elderly, were crowded into asbestos huts or tattered tents from British Army surplus. The furnishings they received for their temporary home consisted of narrow iron cots and straw mattresses. The water faucets and sanitary facilities . . . were located at the far edges of these sprawling camps, and reaching them required waiting on long lines in all kinds of weather. . . . In a way, the immigrants from Iraq were even worse hit than the others, because their short and relatively comfortable journey made the shock of these conditions all the more stunning. Some of them had left large and well-appointed homes in Baghdad in the morning and within hours found them-

> selves installed in a tent or hut somewhere in a remote and seemingly forsaken transit camp.[7]

For those who had been committed Zionists the shock was perhaps greater. The difficulties were not unknown to the Jews in Iraq; reports from relatives who preceded them to Palestine often discouraged further *aliyah* (immigration).[8] The Iraqi government spread reports as well, as part of a propaganda effort; but the knowledge did not necessarily cushion the shock of actual experience.

In addition to being uprooted from home and living in unfamiliar, harsh conditions, the Iraqi Jew suffered an immediate fall in status partially arising from the difference in cultures (different values and priorities) and partially from a prejudice on the part of the new society, which assumed that Jews from Arab and Islamic countries were less modern and less educated. A professional or businessman who had been highly respected in Baghdad would be asked if he was familiar with electricity and plumbing, and, if lucky, would get a job as a day laborer.[9] Physical work, disdained by the elite in Iraq, was glorified in the pioneering culture of the newly established State of Israel. Work was scarce, and anyone over forty-five or fifty was in danger of being dismissed as too old.[10]

Iraqis, together with other immigrants from non-Western countries, were labeled as "Sephardim"[11] and often judged as inferior and primitive. There was little distinction made between the Jews from Arab and Islamic countries despite their highly varied backgrounds.

> The more modernized Jews from Iraq, Syria, Lebanon, [and] Egypt fared as badly as did the less modernized Jews from Kurdistan, Yemen, [and] North Africa. The Oriental Jews from an urban background were not distinguished from those from rural communities.[12]

In his book *1949: The First Israelis* Tom Segev discusses the complicated attitude the Israelis, and especially their leaders, had toward the newcomers.[13] The institutions and people charged with facilitating the integration of the newcomers were frequently insensitive to their needs. While it can be argued that many of these bureaucrats were well intentioned, they were often more concerned about strategy than about individuals. The common use of the term "absorption" in the contemporary writing concerned with the mass immigration reveals the attitude prevailing in the societies at large. Not everyone believed that the melting-pot model afforded the same opportunities to all.

> The term *misug galuyot* [sic] . . . literally means the merging or mixing of the exiles. . . . In Israel, however, the mixing—*misug galuyot*—apparently means simply the Ashkenization of the Sephardim.[14]

The dominant culture of the day, based on Ashkenazi traditions, was accepted as superior. Well-meaning programs to aid the "culturally deprived" or those from "culturally impoverished environments," i.e., children not from Ashkenazi backgrounds,[15] were simply less insidious manifestations of the same ethnocentrism espoused in Kalman Katzenelson's *HaMahapekhah HaAshkenazit* (The Ashkenazi revolution, 1964).[16] While among the most extreme, Katzenelson was not alone in asserting the superiority of the dominant Ashkenazi culture and the fear of the "Levantinization" of the country.[17] Sammy Smooha cites Abba Eban, then Israel's foreign minister:

> So far from regarding our immigrants from Oriental countries as a bridge toward our integration with the Arab-speaking world, our object should be to infuse them with an Occidental spirit, rather than to allow them to drag us into an unnatural Orientalism.[18]

The sociologist Samuel Klausner predicted in 1955 that the Oriental immigrants' cultural contribution would be "largely limited to some gustatory and esthetic symbols and preservation of a primitive folk religion in the lowest classes."[19] Until recently the general consensus held this prophecy to have been accurate, but the works under discussion in this book are evidence of important cultural contribution by Mizraḥi (eastern), and in particular Iraqi, immigrants to Israeli culture.

## THE TRANSIT CAMP NOVEL

For each of the writers to be discussed in this chapter—Shimon Ballas, Sāmī Michael, and Eli Amir—the *roman ma'abarah* (transit camp novel) was the first book written and published in Hebrew. Those who made the commitment to Hebrew were impelled to write about the experience of being an immigrant in Israel. By writing in Hebrew they addressed the general Israeli reading public. Ballas began his novel in Arabic but made the conscious choice to rewrite the story in Hebrew. Amir intended to write a completely different novel, which would focus on the period in Iraq on the eve of leaving, but felt compelled first to write *Tarnegol Kaparot* (Fowl of atonement).[20]

From their own experiences, and those of their friends, relatives, and neighbors, comes the subgenre of immigrant literature—*sifrut hamaʿabarah* (transit camp literature)—which is concerned with this period in both the immigrant's personal history and the collective history of Israel. While these stories create worlds familiar to their authors, they are written as novels and not as autobiographies or memoirs. As such they require participation in the fictional contract on the part of the reader. At the same time that they reflect a specific reality, they are presented as fiction, with the customary ingredients of plot, theme, setting, and characters.

The figure of the adolescent plays a prominent part in the literature of the *maʿabarah*. The protagonists in Shimon Ballas's *HaMaʿabarah* (The transit camp),[21] Sāmī Michael's *Shavim VeShavim Yoter* (Equal and more equal),[22] and Eli Amir's *Tarnegol Kaparot* (Fowl of atonement)[23] are sixteen or seventeen years old.[24] The authors use the age of adolescence to serve as a central metaphor for the condition of the exile.[25]

## THE METAPHOR OF ADOLESCENCE

These stories of the adolescent exile describe crises of identity initiated and intensified by abrupt change. The identity crisis is caused by several factors: the disparity between expectations and reality; between previous status and standard of life and that in Israel; the fragmentation of the family (a strong element of Iraqi society); and the clash of "western" and "eastern" cultures.[26] The move to Israel requires the renegotiation of the position of the individual within the family, the family within society, and the individual within society.

In an early study titled *The Absorption of Immigrants*, a leading Israeli sociologist, S. N. Eisenstadt, describes migration as a process that

> entails not only a shrinkage in the number of roles and groups in which the immigrant is active, but also, and perhaps principally, some degree of "desocialization," of shrinkage and transformation of his own status image and set of values.[27]

Rivka Weiss Bar-Yosef develops these ideas further in her essay "Desocialization and Resocialization: The Adjustment Process of Immigrants."[28] She draws on theories of adolescence to explore the condition of the immigrant. She ascribes the "complete disorganization of the individual's role system"[29] to migration. The desocializing effect of the situation "is undoing those social adjustment patterns the achievement of which is the aim of socialization, and the sign of normal maturity."[30] In other words, the process of migration strips even the adult immigrants of the maturity they attained previously, sending them back to the age of adolescence.

Adolescence is a crucial stage in the formation of identity. It is the beginning of a person's functioning as an individual within society. This identity is based on self-image and acceptance and rejection of familial and societal values. Identity, according to Erik Erikson, is "a subjective sense of an *invigorating sameness* and *continuity*."[31] It is formed by "a process 'located' *in the core of the individual* and yet also *in the core of his communal culture*."[32] Elsewhere, Erikson defines the identity crisis as a loss of the sense of "personal sameness" and "historical continuity."[33]

Adolescents attain an awareness of themselves as individuals distinct from their families; exiles are forced into an awareness of themselves as individuals distinct from their society. In effect, adolescents are exiled from their childhoods by chronological distance; exiles are banished from their childhoods by geographical distance as well.

Adolescents must leave home to find and take their rightful places in the society of adults; exiles must leave their homelands and find or make their places in a new society. Both face the challenge of conforming with their new peers without losing their uniqueness as individuals.

The exile's identity crisis arises from being uprooted from home and transplanted to an unfamiliar society. Historical continuity has been broken; the exile is separated (in space as well as in time) from the past. In addition, the exiled person is alienated from the present, living apart from the people and the environment in the place of exile.

The bureaucratic system reinforces this isolation and the resulting regression. Government officials treat all clients in a similar fashion, without deference to age. Furthermore, the newcomers are forced into childlike dependency on the officials; their decisions are made by the officials according to the system, and their privacy (an adult privilege) is not inviolable.[34]

Rivka Weiss Bar-Yosef even borrows from theories of adolescence to describe the stages of desocialization and resocialization. In his theory of adolescence, Erikson states:

> By psychosocial moratorium, then, we mean a delay of adult commitments, and yet it is not a delay. It is a period that is characterized by a selective permissiveness on the part of society . . . and ends in a more or less ceremonial configuration of commitment.[35]

During the moratorium period immigrants, like adolescents, are confronted not only with re-forming their own (social) identities but also with revising their "cognitive map." Eva Hoffman, a Polish-born Jewish immigrant to Canada, offers this description:

> The reference points inside my head are beginning to do a flickering dance. I suppose this is the most palpable meaning of displacement. I have been dislocated from my own center of the world, and that world has been shifted away from my center. . . .[36]

Without a well-defined cognitive map, the adolescent and immigrant are adrift. Kurt Lewin's categorization of the adolescent as a "marginal man"[37] applies as well to the immigrant. Just as the adolescent is caught between childhood and adulthood, so too the exile is caught in between two cultures. The immigrant and adolescent are caught in the liminal phase of becoming.[38]

Several factors have been recognized as affecting the success of the immigrant, that is, the ability to "resocialize" or become integrated into the adopted society. Bar-Yosef concentrates on external factors: the cultural distance between the original and adopted societies, the information gathered before migration, and the extent of communication with an interpreter.[39] Eisenstadt relates adaptive ability to the immigrant's "ego strength."[40] He roots this ego strength in the family unit (the more stable the family, the greater the individual's ego strength). Ego strength enables the individuals to survive and adapt by raising their tolerance of the ambiguities inherent in the process. The immigrant's situation is seen as ambiguous due to the newness encountered and the contrast between hopes or expectations and reality. A strong ego also helps the individual immigrant weather the frustrations of immigration and integration, to overcome the loss of status symbols, and to develop a sense of belonging to the new home.[41] Those with the least to lose from the transition are generally the most successful.

> [T]hose who have least "vested interest" in high social positions and roles . . . show the greatest "openness" and flexibility in their levels of aspiration, as change cannot affect their privileged position.[42]

In addition to the psychology of the individual and the difference between the two societies, the attitude of the "absorbing"[43] society must also be considered in predicting and evaluating the immigrant's successful integration. Clearly an open pluralistic society that celebrates diversity will be more welcoming than a homogeneous one.

An additional factor affecting the resocialization of the immigrants from Iraq was the changing status and structure of the family, the primary unit of Iraqi society. Family life was turned upside down by the move. Parents, and especially fathers, no longer ruled over the home. The disintegration of the family structure was noted in the sociological writing of the day:

> Immigration into Israel [by the Iraqi Jews] accelerated the process of disorganization in all classes. Eventually there was some work for the son who had learned Hebrew, whose back was strong, or who had a trade or profession. If the father is in his late forties he is too old to meet the new conditions and sits in his hut day after day or walks down to sign the register at the Labor Exchange. The son has become both provider and interpreter of Israel to his family. Now he challenges his father's authority openly, while the father, confused by the new conditions and without the institutional supports of an integrated community and tradition, can only passively accede. This premature supersession of family authority is not easy for the son, who feels blame for having led his family into a difficult situation. . . . Whatever gap had grown between the generations has been widened and the tensions that had existed have been sharpened. [44]

The father, the traditional head of the household in Iraq, could no longer fulfill the role. He lost the status that he held in Iraqi society and his ability to provide for the family; therefore he also lost his standing within the family. Economics played a large part in the disintegration of the family. In many cases the adolescent replaced the father, assuming the role of the head of the household (in whole or in part) in an uncomfortable realization of a common fantasy.

While the Iraqi Jewish family as a unit was losing its prestige in this new culture that favored the individual and the nation, it was also relinquishing its cohesion. Just as the individual's reputation would take precedence over the family's in Israel, so too the good of the individual was privileged over the family good, and the collective good was privileged above all. Most important was the individual's contribution to the collective. This was a difficult concept for the family-oriented Iraqis to understand, much less accept.

## THE EXILE AS A MALE ADOLESCENT

The literature of the *ma'abarah* exploits the similarity between the condition of exile and the age of adolescence to explore the transitional process. Ballas's *HaMa'abarah*, the first novel under discussion, emphasizes the collective nature of the experience. The story of the main adolescent character mirrors that of the figurative protagonist. The second novel stresses the alienation felt by the central character. Adolescent anger propels the plot toward full integration. The third novel covers a shorter span of time and of transition in the life of the protagonist. The open ending suggests the inability to resolve completely the conflicts of adolescence and exile.

In Ballas's novel *HaMa'abarah* a broad panorama of Iraqi immigrant characters encounter different problems of life in the camp (poverty, unemployment, water and food shortages, poor sanitary conditions) and conflicts with their new home. The main plot, which details the organizing of the camp, is embedded within, and almost submerged by, many side plots. The point of view shifts with the various characters and their roles. The narrative often "tells" rather than "shows"[45] and frequently employs indirect speech[46] to present the thoughts of the different characters.

The story of Yusuf Shaby, perhaps the central character in the work,[47] brings out issues and themes similar to those in the previously discussed works. Here is another example of the breakdown of the family structure. Yusuf takes the place of the absent father and becomes the man of the house. He disciplines his younger brother Sa'id. His change of status within the family makes him "almost like a husband to his mother" (p. 77).

Yusuf's struggle to maintain a sense of his identity is given expression when a disturbance in the camp results in the arrests of several of the residents. Yusuf refuses to be fingerprinted in jail. He says he is not a criminal and he will not let the prison define him. It reminds him of the day he voluntarily gave up his Iraqi nationality in order to be allowed to leave for Israel. He will not relinquish his personal identity (chap. 18).

While Yusuf Shaby comes the closest to being the protagonist, no one character emerges as central from the large cast of undeveloped characters. In fact, *HaMaʿabarah* is an ensemble novel. The role of protagonist is filled by the transit camp itself. The *maʿabarah* sits at the center of the novel just as it sat at the center of the immigrant experience.

Most of the story takes place in the transit camp, which is divided between public spaces (coffeehouse, synagogue, work council) and private spaces (the canvas shacks that serve as homes). The only setting outside of the camp is the prison where several of the camp residents are sent after an organizational meeting erupts in violence. A subtle connection is drawn between the camp and the prison; both are closed areas that offer minimal physical comfort. Furthermore, both institutions limit personal freedoms and de-emphasize the individual.

Even though most of the story takes place indoors, there is great emphasis on the weather. This is not only because the shelter the indoors offers is inadequate (canvas shacks in winter rains) but also because of the multiple functions the weather serves. It is generally stormy, with cold blustery winds and rain falling or overcast skies threatening. *Ruḥōt hasagrir* (winds of the [cold and] heavy rain) and similar combinations are used to describe the weather (pp. 14, 29). These descriptions engage the reader in the physical discomfort and suffering of the characters, signal the development of the plot (the proverbial storm brewing). They also serve the plot directly as a catalyst for the main story line.

At the beginning of the novel, the camp is clearly in disarray. In addition to the poor conditions—shortages of food, water, jobs—the camp is rife with infighting and threats of violence. After the expository introduction in the beginning chapters, the first real event of the plot occurs. A doctor refuses to come to the camp (storms have made the dirt roads impassable) to attend to a woman in labor.[48] As a result, she loses the baby and is rushed to the hospital in critical condition. This personal trauma is seen as a collective tragedy, symbolic of the many hardships and indignities immigrants suffer in their new home.

In response to the incident, a meeting is called to organize a protest. Nearly everyone in the camp turns out, despite the threats of the camp thugs who have been hired by the camp director. These thugs create a disturbance, thereby permitting the police to break up the meeting and make arrests (*HaMaʿabarah*, chap. 15).

The second meeting is arranged by Ḥaim Vaʿad (Council) who has been called home by the camp director. Members of the same group hired to disrupt the earlier meeting help publicize this one by posting notices. However, it too ends abruptly (although without violence) when Ḥaim's right to leadership is challenged by members of the audience.

The third gathering is more spontaneous. On hearing of a disturbance at the tents,[49] the residents rush over. In a show of unity, they halt the government workers who are dismantling the illegal tents. The women, no longer passive nor divisive,[50] help by hurling fistfuls of mud at the officials trying to cart off the tents. The director, who is behind the efforts, is pushed into a pit from behind and breaks his leg. He is literally and figuratively toppled in his last attempt to undermine this struggle for self-determination. He is replaced by Ḥaim Vaʿad; the tent people are allowed to stay; and more jobs are made available for tent and shack people alike.

The community of the *maʿabarah*, as the eponymous protagonist of Ballas's novel, is itself similar to both adolescent and exile. As an exile, it is alienated from the society surrounding it, cut off from mainstream Israeli society. In the role of teenager, it first rebels in its struggle for autonomy. The first meeting is held contrary to the wishes of the authority (the director, the police, the establishment). The second meeting—implicitly condoned by the director if not organized by him—is disrupted from within. Only when the transit camp learns to adapt to the trappings of democracy favored by the "host" society does it succeed in gaining independence. A resident of the camp itself (Ḥaim) becomes the new director. He signifies the adjustment to the new ways; he has been educated outside of the camp in a special leadership training program. While sharing the same Iraqi background with the others, he is also fluent in Hebrew and proficient in Israeli bureaucratic methods.

*Shavim VeShavim Yoter* is the story of one character's initiation into a new world, his transition from youth to adulthood, and from exile to absorption. It is set against the backdrop of the Ashkenazi-Mizraḥi conflict.[51] The narrative is told from the point of view of David Asher, an Iraqi immigrant, in his own voice. It alternates between David's fighting in the Six Day War and his earlier experiences as a youth in the *maʿabarah* with his family, where he falls in love with an Ashkenazi girl (to the consternation of her mother). The two parts of the narrative merge at the end, corresponding to David's integration as a whole person. The integration process is shown to be prolonged and painful. For David, leaving the transit camp does not mean leaving it behind. He achieves both psychological and social integration when he finally accepts Israeli standards, allowing them to complement his original values. By the strength of his inner character, he saves his Ashkenazi army comrade and becomes a wartime hero. While he has not yet won back his Ashkenazi bride, she gives him reason to hope. Yet his son is the greatest source of optimism. David can now bequeath to him—the result of a mixed marriage—not only his dark skin (Iraqi heritage), but also heroic status (full Israeli citizenship).

The areas in which David's transition is expressed include work, sex, and the family. Two months after his arrival in Israel, David gets his first job assignment working in the Tenuvah dairy. This is recognized by both himself and his older brother as a rite of passage into adulthood.[52] It is also, however, one of the first steps toward integration into Israeli society, an entry into the social and economic systems outside the *maʿabarah*.

His companion from the plane, Madeleine, introduces him to the world of sexuality. Their first night in Israel, Madeleine takes advantage of their shared quarters to begin his initiation. "I discovered *my body*," he realizes afterward, "this combination of parts which until now I had hardly considered suddenly became a rare and precious treasure full of possible sensations which I could only now imagine."[53] His subsequent loss of virginity (to Madeleine) is at best anticlimactic ("Is that all?" he asks) (p. 46) and less than romantic. It is significant that David first has sexual intercourse in Israel with a fellow Iraqi. Suspended between the two communities, he has transgressed the norms of the Iraqi community yet falls short of full integration into the Israeli community. Also, the anticlimactic aspect of this experience echoes the disappointment of the newcomers upon their arrival in Israel.

At the same time David is discovering aspects of the adult world and Israeli society, he begins losing the pillar of his childhood in Iraq. His family is crumbling. The father, the traditional head of the family, is in ill health, going blind, and losing control of his own body. The oldest son, Shā'ūl, takes charge even before his father's death. He marries off his sister: he needs to be consulted before a suitor can see the sister Ḥanīna; he buys the furniture the suitor demands as part of the dowry; he also deals with the extortion bid of this suitor-turned-bridegroom, who falsely claims his bride Ḥanīna was not a virgin. Moreover, he takes care of the other children, guiding David in his studies and making arrangements for his younger brother Ze'ev to go to a kibbutz. The counselor sent from the kibbutz is kept waiting for Shā'ūl because, as his brother David explains, "[H]ere we don't do anything without Shā'ūl" (*Shavim VeShavim Yoter*, p. 84). This premature replacement of the father by his son is a reversal of the roles they had in Iraq.

The slow disintegration of the family—the father's debilitation, the scattering of the children—is finished by quick destruction. A fire races through the transit camp, destroying the Ashers' home and killing the father, the mother, and the little sister. This serves as both a dramatic depiction of the hostile environment for the Iraqi family and a projection of David's own anger at their circumstances.[54]

David attempts to build a new family unit. He marries Margalit, the only Ashkenazi girl in the *maʿabarah* (and the only resident to go to high school in the city). Together they have a son. The marriage ends in divorce, and the young family is torn apart. The difficulties caused by their lack of realism are exacerbated by the mother-in-law's attempts to keep Margalit dependent on her. The girl is too young to break away from her mother; the boy is too insecure to oppose this dependency. The failure of their marriage contrasts sharply with the conventions of contemporary movies dealing with the Mizraḥim. Ella Shohat summarizes these films succinctly: "In most 'bourekas' films, the ethnic/class tensions and conflicts are solved by a happy ending in which equality and unity are achieved by means of unification of the mixed couple."[55] Here the marriage of the mixed couple is presented not as a solution to the ethnic gap but as a source of more ethnic conflict.[56]

David's anger fuels the narrative and gives his life direction. At times, it is a constructive anger, such as when it spurs him on to set and attain his goals: a university degree, an accounting job, and the girl of his dreams. Its destructive nature takes over once he has achieved his initial goals. It prevents him from coming to terms with his past and his present. It leads him to the very depths of despair, causing him to lose his job, his family, and his self-respect. The anger is always directed against the Ashkenazim, whom he blames for his difficulties and failures.

The army, which first is seen as demoralizing, eventually serves to integrate David fully into Israeli society. He enters the war under protest:

> They won't do a job on me . . . I go out to war not as a Jew, nor as an Israeli; I go out as a black Sephardi. If I return from this business alive—I'll return to my previous status . . . my skin color and ethnicity marked on my forehead like the sign of Cain. *(Shavim VeShavim Yoter,* p. 54)

Previously, he refers to various acts of discrimination against Sephardim in the army and the high incidence of suicides. "Guys like me had no place in the army" (p. 142). He emphasizes the ethnic gap when he describes his unit, which includes "Yoram, the commanding officer—Ashkenazi, of course"; Rafael the Yemenite; and "that Efraim." Efraim, a Sephardi soldier with special training, is the exception that proves the rule of Ashkenazi officers and Sephardi privates (p. 9).

David's heroic act during the 1967 war is an act of redemption. This heroism makes him belong: ". . . I am an Israeli citizen. For the first time in my life I acted as a citizen whose skin color was not an obstacle, not a physical defect" (p. 254). The maturity he gains through his experiences in the army allows him to go beyond the categories of Ashkenazi-Sephardi, oldtimer and newcomer, and to become an Israeli.

The kibbutz, like the army, is another fundamental Israeli institution which offers a useful context in which to explore the socialization process of the new immigrant. In *Tarnegol Kaparot*, the kibbutz setting highlights many of the crises of the immigrant; it functions as a microcosm for the Zionist nation. The kibbutz is one of the most ideologically charged institutions; it is founded on the principles of socialist Zionism: the privileging of the communal good, agricultural work, and secularism. Members, potential members, and guest workers are expected to conform to the kibbutz ideals, which stand in opposition to those of their parental society. In the days of the *maʿabarot* children were frequently placed in a kibbutz away from their families on a temporary basis. The novel tells the story of a youth caught in the conflict between the Iraqi and the Israeli ways of life. Nūrī is forced to decide between joining the kibbutz and staying there permanently or returning to the *maʿabarah* to help support his family. His dilemma is played out in the cultural context: challenging his musical appreciation (Beethoven versus the *layālī*),[57] his accent, habits, and religious customs. The cultural clash leads to questions about his identity.

Many of the same issues present in the other works under discussion in this chapter are explored in this novel: the changes in status, conditions, and social expectations, and the difficulties of adjustment. In *Tarnegol Kaparot* the cultural differences enrich the novel and illustrate these difficulties.

Nūrī's crisis of identity results from feeling torn between his family and his new home. He states: "I was neither one nor the other . . . we were torn between two worlds. . . . Like the ball in a game of tennis, I bounced from court to court . . ." (p. 123). His desire to adapt to Israel[58] is constrained by his loyalty to the family.

Even without family considerations, Nūrī is hesitant to accept the immediate transformation the new place seems to expect. He explains:

> They tried to provide us with ready-made identities, which we were supposed to put on like a new suit of clothes in order to be like them. We had, indeed, shed our old clothes, but the new ones were too new, as uncomfortable as brand new shoes. (P. 68)

The renaming of the immigrants symbolizes this process, this imposition of instant Israelihood. Nūrī balks at becoming Nimrod, the biblical hunter (Gen. 10:8–10), and retains his Iraqi name.[59] He carefully walks the thin line between adaptation and absorption.

His reluctance to adopt a "ready-made identity" does not preclude him from entertaining curiosity about the new ways and educating himself. This is illustrated in the musical scenes. Nūrī's first introduction to (Western) classical music mystifies him.

> Who was Beethoven? What strange music it was. Everything in it was the same. . . . And the way they [the Ashkenazim] listened to the music—without interjections, without exclamations of admiration! What point was there to music if it didn't do something to your heart—something that softened your face and your eyes? *(Tarnegol Kaparot,* p. 118)

Nūrī learns about classical music and participates enthusiastically in the next Western classical music quiz.

His introduction to "Israeli" culture (that is, Western culture) is less traumatic than his introduction to Israeli secularism. Along with cultural identity, Nūrī is confronted with questions about his religious beliefs and practices. The paradoxical nature of the situation—traditional Judaism as less of a presence in the Jewish state of Israel—is the source of the conflict. The secular nature of the new Jewish nation is difficult for Nūrī and his friends to understand. Many of its founders were ardent socialists intent on creating a society that stood in opposition to the traditional religious enclaves of European Jewry. Nowhere is this secularism more apparent than on the kibbutz, the epitome of Zionist ideology. In order to leave the youth transit camp and get placed on a kibbutz, Nūrī lies and says that he is not religious.

The issue of religious custom and belief is largely seen in terms of the confrontation of members of a traditional, religious society (the Iraqis) with a modern secular society (Israel). This is an oversimplification and ignores the fact that the Jewish community in Iraq was already open to less rigidly proscribed religious observance and had incorporated secular subjects in the curriculum. The Alliance Israélite Universelle established the first modern school in Iraq (Baghdad, 1864).[60]

> Western education had already led the children into a new world. . . . They developed a feeling of superiority to their past and an abyss opened between the generations.[61]

Nevertheless, this simplification is based in part on reality. The immigrants were faced with more sudden change in the direction of secularization. The natural stage of questioning religious and ideological beliefs at adolescence was compounded by the abrupt transition to the secular culture of Israel.

The adult characters complain about the difference between their life in the *ma'abarah* and how they lived in Baghdad, or elsewhere in Iraq; they bemoan the lack of spiritual leadership and ritual observance. One of Nūrī's neighbors from the camp tells him:

> Back in the diaspora we were better Jews than we are here in our own country. Over here everything is falling apart. There's nothing sacred, there's no respect for the rabbi. Not only among those atheists on the kibbutz but even here, in the *ma'abarah.* (P. 165)

In the *ma'abarah,* the move away from religion seems to be an expression of lack of faith and a further unraveling of society as known in Iraq. On the kibbutz, the move toward the secular expresses a specific ideology. Secularization is part of the indoctrination of the prevailing Zionism of the day. The rabbi of the *ma'abarah* warns the youth about the evils of the kibbutz. "On your kibbutz people desecrate the Sabbath, they eat nonkosher food, and the girls are wanton. Leave the kibbutz. They are making infidels of you there" (p. 164).

Nūrī and his peers who arrive at the kibbutz from their *ma'abarot* are dismayed at the absence of space and time for Jewish observances. Noticing the lack of synagogue,[62] they wonder where they pray and what to tell their parents. The Sabbath is not sanctified as the day of rest, nor is there time set aside for religious rituals. Nūrī describes his resentment at this state of affairs in recounting his daily routine: "occasionally skipping the laying of *tefillin* and feeling a frightening void opening up inside me, simply in order to arrive in time for my stinking, dirty job [in the cowshed]" (p. 65).

The great conflict arises when Nūrī brings home a chicken for his family in the *ma'abarah*. His parents do not believe Nūrī when he lies and says that it was slaughtered according to Jewish ritual. They accuse him of being spoiled by the kibbutz. He is torn by self-recrimination, realizing the enormity of the gap between his life on kibbutz and his life with his family.

> How could I have brought a headless chicken home to the ma'abarah? Who ever gave a thought about ritual slaughtering on the kibbutz? . . . Ever since the big fight about God in the youth group everyone had stopped thinking about Him. . . . Night after night I was afraid to fall asleep: they had killed God. (P. 200)

The incident gives the novel its title and serves as a powerful image. The phrase *tarnegol kaparot* literally refers to the rooster used as a substitution for a sacrifice on the eve of the Day of Atonement. The bird is whirled in a circle overhead while the following is recited:

> This is my exchange, this is my substitute, this is my atonement. This rooster will go to its death while I will enter and go to a good, long life, and to peace.[63]

The youth, caught in the middle of two incompatible cultures, must choose what he is to sacrifice from either in order not to become a sacrifice himself.

While rebellion is considered a typical stage of adolescence, the Iraqi teenagers have no clear authority figures to rebel against. Those against whom they may have rebelled in Iraq have lost their authority, and those in Israel encourage rebellion! The Israelis par excellence of *Tarnegol Kaparot*, the kibbutznikim Sonia and Dolek, try to explain to Nūrī that "here, rebellion is a principle of society." Sonia continues,

> There's simply no room in our lives here for Baghdad or for the way of life in the Jewish shtetl of Eastern Europe either. We came to this country because we rebelled against that way of life . . . we don't have to deny our cultural origins. Don't you think we didn't suffer from the infantile disease of cultural adjustment ourselves? . . . we didn't bring Poland here with us, and you're not going to bring Iraq

> with you either. We cast the yoke of the past off our necks for the sake of the future, and that is your mission too. (Tarnegol Kaparot, p. 114)

Dolek advises the same: "You must rebel against your parents" (p. 63).

The Iraqi youth from the *maʿabarah* have difficulty understanding the call to rebellion. "Why don't they ever talk about loyalty to your family instead of rebellion against your parents? Why revolution, not tradition?" (p. 136). The narrator of *Tarnegol Kaparot* is particularly eloquent in pointing out the source of the dissonance between the kibbutznikim and those from the *maʿabarot*.

> The difference is that I didn't come here on my own, like you, like Dolek and Faivush. I came here with my family and relations and friends, all of Jewish Baghdad moved out here, and now it's in the maʿabarot. Which makes it much harder to burn our bridges. You've built a society founded on individuals, because you came here alone. I belong to a clan. (P. 186)

In Israel, rebellion against "that way of life," against diaspora conventions, takes on different meanings. The rebellion urged is, in effect, based on conformity to a Eurocentric ideal and life experience. It is also a limited rebellion. The counselors are quite upset when their authority is challenged (such as when the Iraqis ask for a holiday to visit their families, contrary to the counselors' wishes). For the Iraqi youths, therefore, it is a rebellion from the outside, rather than motivated from within.

The family is devalued in Israeli society compared to society in Iraq. The Iraqi teenagers find it a dilemma to reconcile the expectations of their families with those of their new home. The conflict between their responsibilities to their families and those to their new home is explored in *Tarnegol Kaparot*. Most of the children of the *maʿabarot* who are lucky enough to be placed on kibbutzim do not stay to join those kibbutzim as members. This is a failure from the perspective of the kibbutznikim who host the children as part of their recruitment effort. The immigrant children leave the kibbutz in order to return to the *maʿabarot* because they know they are needed to help their families. They are potential wage-earners. Nūrī finds himself torn in this conflict.

> At this moment, I, Nūrī, the son of Fahīma from Iraq, knew that my parents, who were waiting for me to come home to help support the

> family, would never in a million years understand the ideal of "self-realization" and that they would never forgive me if I abandoned them to their fate. (P. 192)

Nūrī's family feels dependent on his support: "When are you coming home? . . . we won't be able to manage without you" (p. 199). Nūrī's own confusion makes him a wholly sympathetic character and gives the book its strength. His conflict arises from being torn between opposite poles: the past and the present, the *maʿabarah* and the kibbutz, responsibility and self-realization.

Despite Nūrī's pride at wearing the kibbutz clothes and representing the kibbutz to the people of the *maʿabarah,* he does not choose to join. He rejects the ready-made identity and the call to rebellion. However, when he returns to the transit camp he does so fluent in Hebrew, Beethoven, and the ideals of the kibbutz.

## IMAGES OF FEMALE ADOLESCENCE

While the above discussion focuses exclusively on the teenage male character, not all of the adolescent characters are male. The female characters have a different status in the narrative. They are not the protagonists, but in general serve to illuminate issues relating to the conflicts of a more traditional society encountering one less traditional, the changing place of women, and sexuality.

Issues concerning sex and sexuality are central to the age of adolescence. Yet here the exiles deal with their burgeoning sexuality in a society much different than the one in which they were socialized, and thus the issues become even more complex. Adolescence, a time that is confusing in the best of circumstances, becomes more so for these Iraqi-born immigrants in Israel. Women are not required to dress "modestly," girls are not sequestered, and previous sexual taboos are not necessarily avoided. The code of honor is completely turned around. The novelist Eli Amir clearly remembers his first encounter with some of these differences in Israeli society:

> On the sandy soil in front of me, there were many people, fair haired, with shining countenances—and among them an embracing couple! I had never witnessed a scene like this. Instinctively I covered my eyes.
>
> I had already beheld strange sights, smelled different odors, walked on unstable sandy soil—and here was a boy publicly embrac-

ing a girl clad in short pants. For me this was a moral-religious shock.[64]

This is not to say that the process of modernization had not already begun to take place in Iraq before the emigration, especially among the more educated. Girls were admitted to institutions of higher education. The Alliance Israélite Universelle established a high school for girls in 1892. Some girls began to work outside the home in the 1930s.[65] Some were active in the Zionist underground, participating in coeducational activities that were permitted because of their nature (and because they were always concluded before dark).[66]

Yet the Iraqi immigrants' reaction to modern Israeli society was still one of shock. The disorienting effect of sudden freedom from traditional expectations of behavior was not counterbalanced by the family. The family no longer functioned as a strong unit. Home could not serve as a stable base from which to confront new ideas and new freedoms; those representing the "old ways" had lost their authority.

In *HaMa'abarah*, the women play roles that illustrate the changes in the Iraqi family and social mores upon arrival in Israel. Esther, the female counterpart to Yusuf, keeps her family together by postponing her army service and working as a domestic. Her mother has died and her father has gone mad. She performs as the head of the household until her uncle comes to take charge of her younger siblings. The novel leaves her poised to begin her army service and her real initiation into Israeli life.

Changes in family structure are not far behind when long-standing female roles are challenged. Rumors fly when Shaul Reshti's wife Salima comes home late from her job outside the *ma'abarah*. Shlomo Ḥamra, the café proprietor, remarks, "[Our fathers] didn't send their women to work and didn't allow them to do as they wished. A woman has to sit at home. Outside her head gets dizzy" (p. 136). After getting Esther to admit to her special feelings for Yusuf, Miriam Shabat reminisces, "Thirteen years ago in Iraq courting was through messengers and parents. Now a girl can go out with any boy she wants, no one cares, as long as they are happy" (p. 72). And indeed, Me'ir the barber courts the woman of his desires, planning to marry her against her parents' intentions.

Although some changes are tolerated within the closed society of the transit camp, they are limited in scope. While affected by the move to Israel, the *ma'abarah* allows little change, instead trying to recover as close as possible what was left behind. The family structure is not abandoned, and the father is replaced (as necessary) by a father figure. Esther remains head of the family until the father is hospitalized and her uncle comes to take the children. Yusuf "adopts" his friend Na'aman's father. Moreover, even when women have greater opportunity (and need) to work outside the home, and rules of courtship are freer, tradition ultimately reigns. Salima Reshti quits her outside job. When given the option to decide for herself, Me'ir's sweetheart abandons him for the family's choice. She has been engaged to her cousin since childhood, which was also when her brother became engaged to the cousin's sister. In this way, both branches of the family saved on dowry payments, and the family inheritance stayed within the family.

The other two works offer less conservative pictures. In *Shavim VeShavim Yoter* the changes resulting from the move to Israel cannot be ignored or reversed, but must be confronted. Neither can they be embraced without a challenge or modification. Those who accept the new way of life without question are in danger of losing their past. Madeleine, who is so enthusiastic about the freedom that awaits her "there," in Israel ("Tell me, David, is it true that *there* a girl can do whatever she wants?" p. 16) is defeated by it. She turns to prostitution, falling into the hands of an unscrupulous pimp who does not allow her to recuperate after she has had an abortion. He then kills her and her mother with his own hands. Her family had offered her little in the way of support and guidance.[67] David, who was at first attracted to her coarse language and open ways, is then appalled and finally saddened by her. While Madeleine is presented as a participant in her own destruction, it is clear that the circumstances of her life are assigned the greatest portion of blame. Even with the help of his older brother Sha'ul, David cannot save her from her tragic end.

David's narrative does not present sex as a moral issue. Madeleine's death is not a moral judgment against her. David's neighbor Na'īma is married to Reuven, but both of her children are fathered by Sha'ul. Rather than judging her, David sees her as a model of femininity. He rushes to assure her that his mother never knew about the affair, and he does what he can to contribute to the adulterous couple's happiness. Reuven, on the other hand, is not seen as the wronged party but as the cuckolded husband. He loses his standing among his own community. Having compromised himself in public life (thereby winning the shallow approval of the Ashkenazim in power but losing any respect he had among his former neighbors and fellow countrymen) he is compromised in his private life. For David, good sex involves a loving relationship regardless of marital status, ethnic background, or any other factor. He comes to this conclusion as part of his growing-up process. Through the different women characters and their stories, David explores the nature of male-female relationships and his own sexuality.

In *Tarnegol Kaparot* the women and issues relating to sexuality are again seen through the eyes of the main character. Here the question of sexuality is presented as a clash between two cultures. In Iraq, boys and girls were separated after elementary school and girls were expected to dress and behave modestly. Nūrī gives convincing expression to the social order "back there" in Iraq:

> Back there I had seen women only with their faces veiled. Once when an Englishwoman in long trousers walked past the shop windows in the main street, she was pursued by the whole of Baghdad. Whereas here there was a riot of bare thighs, provocative breasts and cascading hair. . . . (P. 179)

Such segregation is so well ingrained that its absence on the Israeli kibbutz (featured in *Tarnegol Kaparot*) demands greater adjustment than the Iraqi youths can afford. The girls insist on eating at tables separate from the boys in the communal dining room. The boys predictably react to the unfamiliar forced integration with false bravado, spying on the girls in their huts, taunting them.

> The classrooms filled with noise, curses and shouts, the boys undid the girls' kerchiefs and shamed them as protest against the counselors who had forced us to live, work and study with them. . . . (P. 57)

Their greatest fear in coming to the unknown entity "kibbutz" was the fear of mixed living quarters. They are somewhat relieved to find their fears allayed, but wish for even greater separation of the sexes than the kibbutz grants. After a long stay at the kibbutz, the girls agree to the necessity of sex education, but still demand that the discussions among the boys and girls be held separately (p. 179).

The differences they find in Israeli society are not immediately accepted by the Iraqi immigrants, particularly by those who remain within their own communities in the *ma'abarot*. Florentine is taken from the kibbutz in *Tarnegol Kaparot* by her parents and later is seen, "a kerchief on her head, wearing a long dress with long sleeves and supporting an old man walking heavily at her side. He was her husband . . . rabbi of the *ma'abarah*" (p. 141).

The young Iraqis on the kibbutz begin to rebel. Florentine's peer Farīda runs away from her family when they come to the kibbutz with her "grey-bearded fiancé" (p. 59). Refusing to return to the transit camp, she instead offers her family the hospitality of the kibbutz. Nilly takes to wearing "the merest strip of cloth barely covering her groin" (pp. 129–30) like the kibbutz girls, instead of a long skirt.

Of all the Iraqi teens on the kibbutz, Nilly most wants to be like the Israelis. She tells Nūrī, "You're like me. You know Iraq is dead" (p. 139). But in abandoning the past she misreads the moral code ("I thought all the locals 'did it,'" p. 140) and courts disaster with her out-of-wedlock pregnancy. The abandonment of old values, without their replacement by the new, results in near tragedy. She is rescued from a life of shame by the efforts of the counselor Sonia and Nūrī; as a doubly marginal person (a woman in a male-oriented society and an Iraqi among Israelis) she requires the efforts of both an Israeli and a male. She ends up living "happily ever after." Sonia (representing the kibbutz) joins forces with Nūrī (the "new" generation) to talk with the girl's parents. They first reject these efforts and declare her dead. Only when she names the child after the grandfather in accordance with her father's wishes do they reconcile with her (p. 145). Amid all the changes (and revolutions!) there is still the need to pay homage to tradition.

Each novel presents remnants of the old ways and beginnings of the new. Ballas's novel shows the most modest changes of the three. While Esther is not chastised for failing to conceal her affection for Yūsuf, neither does she act on these feelings. It is merely another signpost of the changes in the lives of these uprooted Iraqis. *Shavim VeShavim Yoter* presents a more extreme situation. The penalty imposed on Madeleine for her misjudgment of the freedom offered by her new home is harsh and uncompromising. Amir strikes a more moderate tone in his book. Nilly's case does not conclude with the censure of her peers, but, through the combined efforts of Nūrī and the kibbutznik counselors, it is resolved; she marries the "local" youth and finds reconciliation with her family. The child brings together the two cultures, serving both as remembrance of the Iraqi past (through his name) and hope for the Israeli present and future.

Despite the strength of some of the characterizations of these female adolescents, they still remain on the margin of the narrative. When compared to their male counterparts (Esther to Yusuf, Madeleine to David, and Nilly to Nūrī) they appear to be inferior. Of the three, we know the least about Esther—due to the ensemble style of *HaMaʿabarah*—but we do know that her Hebrew is nowhere nearly as fluent as Yusuf's, nor are her abilities to take a leadership role at all on par with his. Madeleine ends up dead, defeated by the move to Israel despite her embracing the possibilities she thought it presented. David is not only saved from life-threatening danger, but the danger is ennobling and he is glorified by it. Nilly is publicly shamed in her efforts to be like the locals and needs to be rescued by Nūrī. The move to Israel does not truly afford great opportunities for women within the reality of these novels. For the most part they serve as "functions"[68] rather than as developed characters. They illustrate the differences between Iraqi and Israeli society, and serve as a focus for sex and sexuality. Even when similar to their male counterparts, they are the "other." It is difficult to find a male character who would not concur with David's exasperation in trying to figure out "What is the *true* nature of a woman?" (*Shavim VeShavim Yoter*, p. 33). As the "other" in a place of exile, women remain on the margin of the margin.

## THE CONCEPT OF THE OTHER

The notion of the "other" is central to the understanding of the development of adolescents and as such has great potency in the literature of exiled adolescence. In the normal course of development, young children become aware of the other as they develop their understanding of self. However, it is during the teen years that one starts to move away from one's family and grant the "other" outside greater significance. Teens begin to look to their peers rather than their families as their central reference group.

The young Iraqi characters in the novels under discussion experience a sudden and radical change in their reference groups as a result of their move to Israel. The familiarity and continuity they could expect to find in Iraq is nowhere to be found among their new reference groups. These shift in definition, significance, and characterization from novel to novel. In each case, however, they are Ashkenazim who seem to the youth to be drastically different from them. At first glance, Ballas's novel seems to all but ignore the notion of the other. Almost all of the characters of *HaMa'abarah* are Iraqi. Ashkenazim do not play a large role, because it is the transit camp, not the ethnic question, that is under discussion. However, the Ashkenazim serve as the reference group for the protagonists, setting the normative standard. They are called "the Yiddish"[69] by the Iraqis, highlighting the centrality of language. Their presence is evoked by the *ma'abarah* residents to check unruly behavior: "The Yiddish are laughing at us. They say the Iraqis are savages—each at his brother's throat. . . . They say we are uncivilized, lazy. . . ." (pp. 128, 148).

The only exceptions to the absence of Ashkenazi characters are the government official in charge of the *ma'abarah* and the blond sabra (native Israeli) named Zvi, who shares a cell with some of the transit camp residents in prison. The blond sabra stands in ironic opposition to the heroes of novels popular in the previous generation. Those blond sabras represented the ideal "new Israelis" and often died fighting for their country.[70] In explaining why he is in jail, Zvi states, "I was simply sick and tired of staying in the army. There are all sorts of characters and each one gives an order. I can't stand orders" (p. 164).

Zvi's character contrasts with the accepted ideal and can be seen as criticism of the earlier literature. Zvi represents the new individualism that was replacing the commitment to group cohesion. By placing Zvi in prison, the novel also equalizes the sabra and the newcomer and thereby calls the established hierarchy into question.

Outside the home, most of the Iraqis find that they no longer command the same respect that they did "back home." They bemoan their diminished status, which is due in part to the different criteria prevailing in Israel and in part to conditions drastically different from those previously enjoyed by many of the immigrants. Selim sadly reminisces about his work in Iraq: "I used to sit next to the desk and ring, and servants would come and serve tea and do as I ordered" (p. 92). He is now employed as a porter by the Tenuvah company. Eliahu Eini likewise recalls: "In Iraq we sat among ministers, senators and sheikhs. When I would enter the sheikh's drawing room, everyone present would stand. Here—who knows me? I have become one of the ignorant rabble." Even Ḥaim Va'ad has lost his title (Al-Kātib), which signified his higher status as a government clerk.

The camp society itself exhibits its own social stratification. The people living in the tents clearly have higher status than those who squat in tents. And while the thugs gain power through brute force, they do not gain the respect of the *ma'abarah* residents. Within the camp characters retain—or regain—their former status. Eliahu Eini is one of the VIPs of the community; Shaul Reshti, who earlier bemoaned his reduced circumstance, gets himself promoted to a desk job; and Ḥaim al-Kātib Vaʿad becomes director of the camp.

*HaMaʿabarah*'s lack of emphasis on the Ashkenazim is in stark contrast to *Shavim VeShavim Yoter,* where the conflict is all-encompassing. The title itself is derived from the cynical formulation of George Orwell's *Animal Farm.*[71] It expresses the basic conflict in the book: the tension between the expectation of equality and the blatant inequality between the Mizraḥim[72] and the Ashkenazim, the other.

While the perspective presented in the book is that of David, the protagonist and narrator, certain generalizing tendencies are implied. Each group depicts the other group in unflattering terms. The Ashkenazim call the Mizraḥim blacks and *frankim;*[73] the Mizraḥim return the favor with *vuz-vuzim* and *itz.*[74]

The arrival scene helps set the stage for the ethnic gap and carries with it a powerful symbolic resonance. The first and perhaps most potent blow to the newcomers' expectations was delivered upon arrival in Israel. Not only was there no welcoming committee, "no flowers, no band, not even bread and salt" (*Shavim VeShavim Yoter*, p. 25), but the expectant Iraqis, dressed in their finest clothing, were sprayed with DDT. The spraying is a rite of passage, a toxic baptism.

The narrator of *Shavim VeShavim Yoter* blames the reception for destroying his father: "[W]ithin five short minutes the new homeland succeeded in turning my father from an energetic man standing at the height of his powers into an old humiliated broken human being" (p. 18). It is the scene of his father's last victory: he manages to hold in his sneeze. After that, he loses control of all his bodily functions, one after the other.[75] The DDT scene illustrates the various feelings of exile: feeling unwelcome, feeling impotent, and feeling alien. It is a sign of what is to come.

The division between Ashkenazim and Mizraḥim is not equivalent to the categories of veterans and newcomers. One of the most hateful of all of the Ashkenazi characters in the book is Ẓiporah, a newcomer who lives in the same *maʿabarah* as David and his family. David instinctively senses the disdain Ẓiporah feels toward him[76] despite her daughter Margalit's denial ("My mother [doesn't hate you]; she respects your family very much," p. 89). Love is not lost on either side, but Ẓiporah's attitude toward Mizraḥim becomes clear first. One evening David startles Margalit in the dark. Ẓiporah's hysterical reaction ("Thief, murderer, *gevalt* . . . they're attacking my daughter!") does not abate upon either seeing David, the alleged attacker ("What did he do to you," she asks her daughter, ". . . that black?" p. 43), or hearing Margalit insist that nothing had happened.

The situation hardly improves as the romance develops between David and Margalit. Ẓiporah does everything she can to prevent and destroy the marriage. The prejudice is expressed in many ways. A dish as simple as gefilte fish is made to function on a symbolic level as well.[77] The appearance of a jar of the fish signals the insidious intrusion by the hateful Ashkenazi mother-in-law into David and Margalit's life. The daughter's query, "What do Sephardim know about fine food?" (p. 168) is not merely a question of taste but alludes to the basis of the conflicts in the story: the Ashkenazi image of the Sephardi as ignorant and unappreciative, and therefore undeserving of the finer things in life.

Ẓiporah is not unique in her attitude. David's boss Mr. Goldberg chastises him for his tardiness the day the bus drives by the *maʿabarah* stop. "Laziness . . . is a contemptible Arab trait. . . . You've left the Arab world behind. Here you can't live on lies and excuses" (pp. 52–53) He reinterprets David's desire to study as a wish to "live the life of an effendi" (p. 53) and avoid real work.

Margalit's classmates—all of whom are Ashkenazim—see David as a novelty when his bride takes him to a party. The hostess's father is shocked by David's erudition and his brother's ambition. "A lawyer . . . an accountant," the father says, "and who will do all the work?" (p. 178). His brother Shāʾūl encounters similar ignorance on a kibbutz. "They trilled shrieks of excitement when they found a book of Baudelaire's poetry in my hands," he tells the kibbutznik, surprised at seeing a work by Spinoza on his bookshelf, "or when it became clear to them that I didn't chew grass" (p. 82).

Further expressions of such attitudes are evident in the different uses of languages. In *Shavim VeShavim Yoter* Yiddish is a language of curses and quarrels. When Ẓiporah, the Ashkenazi shrew of the *maʿabarah*, catches David kissing her daughter, her Hebrew swiftly breaks down into Yiddish. "But here the artificial Hebrew that was in her mouth betrayed her—she shifted to Yiddish—[the tongue] of the masses, common, vulgar" (p. 94). Later arguments between David and Ẓiporah begin in Hebrew and degenerate into Yiddish and Arabic (p. 214). The driver of a full bus, trying to pass the people of the *maʿabarah* who are already late for work, mutters something in Yiddish (p. 151).

The Israeli soldiers sighting the protagonist of *Shavim VeShavim Yoter* on the road call out "taʿāl lahūn" (come here) to tell him to get off the road, having mistaken him for an enemy soldier. David literally saves his own life (and those of his army comrades) by his knowledge of Hebrew. The soldiers are content to let him die, until he speaks to them in Hebrew. "He's Jewish!" they exclaim in surprise, and rescue him (p. 231). His use of Hebrew proves his identity as an Israeli soldier and his worthiness as person to be saved. He then insists on returning to his comrades and saving them too (p. 242). By doing this, he becomes a war hero, recovers his self-respect, and finally acquires a sense of belonging.

Before this drama David finds sympathy with others who do not fit into the mainstream. Holocaust survivors are depicted as exempt from the Ashkenazi label: "This was a non-ethnic type; not Sephardi and not Ashkenazi. In the classification system I grew used to in the *maʿabarah* there was no place for them. The unfathomable suffering they had known purified their souls" (pp.145–46).[78]

Depressed that Margalit is marrying her Ashkenazi suitor, David drives to the seashore. There he meets another man and offers him a drive home. On the long ride, they talk and share similar stories of failed marriages. It is not until the passenger takes out his cigarettes that David realizes that his new friend is an Arab. "Until now I had never imagined that an *Arab* could be miserable because of a woman. . . ."[79] (The reader can only imagine whether or not the passenger categorized David as an Arab.) Whereas earlier comparisons to Arabs were meant derogatorily (see for example his employer's comments),[80] here the likeness in their stories serves as an antidote to alienation. David goes to the beach alone, but he returns with a companion. Likewise, David's otherness in Israeli society is diminished in the presence of someone further and more permanently outside the society. While until this point in the narrative David has been an outsider among Ashkenazim, he is an insider compared to Arabs.

*Tarnegol Kaparot* presents a further elaboration of the us-them categorization scheme in *Shavim VeShavim Yoter*. In this novel, "they" are divided into the redheaded Ashkenazim and the blond sabras. The sabras, or locals, are models for integration and greatly admired by the Iraqi youth, while the Ashkenazim are generally negative characters.[81] "Why did every place have to have its own redhead?" the narrator asks in dismay.[82] Yet the Ashkenazim cannot be easily dismissed because of their dominance over early Israeli society.

When Nūrī falls for Vera, the new Polish arrival, he thinks to himself: "My father had been right when he said to me, 'Learn Yiddish, my boy, and you'll get whatever you want in this country'" (p. 171). Here the humor does not hide criticism of the dominance of the European Jews and their culture, nor the resentment.

Among the Mizraḥim there are differences and assorted stereotypes. For example, the Moroccans are the fighters and the Iraqis are seen as "Charcoal-faced, idiots, [who] don't sing, don't dance, and don't fight back" (p. 20). Neither are all Iraqis the same; the different class backgrounds that are referred to in the earlier works are further explored here, as are regional variations.

Not surprisingly, the Iraqis who came from more marginal or lower class backgrounds are more embracing of the new society. Abdallah, orphaned at a young age in Iraq and left to roam the streets, instantly renames himself Herzl and refers to the kibbutz as "ours" before he ever sees it. Nilly is from a remote village in northern Iraq. She takes advantage of the possibility offered by switching to Hebrew to cover up her much-mocked peasant accent. Nilly represents the case of the successful integration of a once-marginalized person into the mainstream. She makes one of the most abrupt transitions to Hebrew complete with native Israeli pronunciation. Nilly, who wants so much to be one of the local sabras, is rewarded for her efforts by the next best thing: she marries one.

Those from more prestigious backgrounds adapt much less easily, clinging to their previous status. Faced with a new situation, new acquaintances, and new standards, the characters in *Tarnegol Kaparot* fall back on this family status to risible effect. As the basis of their campaigns for peer elections, "everybody boasted about his family and its prestige in Iraq" (p. 76). A bitter worker on the kibbutz complains, "They sent me to clean human shit, you hear? Me! Do you know what my father was?" (p. 55).

The new arrivals discover that their previous standing in Iraq is ignored as irrelevant. Not only do they lose the status they held in Iraq, but they must contend with prejudice and discrimination. Several of the veteran kibbutzniks—redheaded Ashkenazim—make no distinctions between the newcomers. When the Iraqi youth begin to play their own music, the singularly unsympathetic Gutman remarks: "We wanted to turn them into human beings and just listen to them: howling like a pack of jackals" (p. 111). His friend Ze'ev calls the Iraqis animals and asks, "Where did you grow up? In a jungle?," alternatively suggesting that they used to live in caves (p. 45).

The local sabras have no higher opinion of the Iraqis. They freeze the newcomers out of their own youth group activities, leaving them to organize their own. When Ẓvika faces marriage to Nilly, his friends torment him with endless stories of Iraqi primitiveness and remark, "for what sane person would marry an Iraqi?" (p. 142).

The adults do not fare any better. The leaders and professionals of the Jewish community in Iraq are reduced to unemployable figures without even the financial means to be able to while away their free time in the local café. Nūrī cannot dispel the image of his unemployed father.

> I saw my father. However hard I tried to get rid of him and think about the color of the flowers, I went on seeing him, bowed and shamefaced at the entrance of the Pole's cafe, like most of the men in the *ma'abarah* who besieged the door of that dirty, miserable hut every afternoon.
>
> *Mafish fluss! Rukh min hon!* (There is no money! Beat it!) (P. 49)

This image of the father stays in the reader's mind as well. It serves as a powerful representation of the attitude that the novel ascribes to the behavior of the Ashkenazim vis-à-vis the Iraqis.

The flip side of the use of Arabic by Ashkenazim is introduced by the character of Kuba in *Tarnegol Kaparot.* The husband of Sonia, he is the kibbutz counselor in charge of the Iraqis' adjustment and friend of local Arabs, "known throughout the country for his excellent Arabic" He gets great joy from greeting the protagonist with the words "Kīf ḥā-lek, ya Khwājah Nūrī?" (How are you, Mr. Nūrī?) (p. 147). Yet, for all of Kuba's good intentions and his enthusiasm for Arab culture, he makes his young friend uncomfortable. Nūrī is too embarrassed to refuse the Turkish coffee he dislikes or to admit his ignorance in the matter of swords and daggers. "I was ibn Arab, wasn't I?" (p. 148). The well-meaning Kuba sees the Iraqi youth as exotic, and Nūrī has no more an idea of how to react to the enthusiastic Orientalist than he does to the bigots. It is as if, in his confusion about his own identity as an Iraqi-Jewish-immigrant-to-Israel-on-the-kibbutz, Nūrī begins to accept Kuba's stereotyped image of the exotic Arab Jew.

The author illustrates the gap between the newcomers and the others through the example of music. The Iraqis on the kibbutz are invited to a musical quiz that is based on knowledge of Western classical music. One of them complains, "[T]hey're imposing their music on us . . ." (p. 115).

Music becomes an arena of social conflict. Their teacher convinces them to perform a Hasidic story in front of the kibbutz audience. The contrast between the Iraqi performers and the Hasidic characters they attempt to portray strikes the audience as ludicrous. At the uproarious laughter, the Iraqis stop the play and leave the auditorium in protest. They hold a *ḥaflah* (an Arab-style music party), bringing their musical instruments out of hiding to play *taqāsīm* (improvisations based on scales) and sing *layālī* (songs in a vocal style specific to the Arab world). They use their music as a collective assertion of self-worth and identity.

> The party was a great success and redeemed us from our disgrace, if not in the eyes of others, then at least in our own eyes. And that meant a lot. (P. 108)

The Iraqis do not remain culturally isolated. Nilly brings newly learned Hebrew songs to the *ḥaflas*, and the rest of the girls chime in. When Masul rejects the suggestion of ending their play with Israeli dances ("a dance for donkeys") (p. 106), Rina asks, "Don't you want to be like them?" referring to the "locals" (p. 108).

The *ḥaflah* gives cultural expression to their communal self-assertion in reestablishing their connection to their past. This frees them to become more receptive to new influences without requiring them to abandon their own identities. The novel calls for mutual recognition of the other's value, and cultural coexistence.

## CONCLUSION

Having explored these three novels as examples of *sifrut hama'abarah* it may be constructive to examine their sociopolitical context and their relationship to contemporary Hebrew literature. The realities of Israeli society at the time of their publication contributed to their critical reception and current status.

The same year (1964) as Katzenelson's polemical *HaMahapekhah HaAshkenazit* (The Ashkenazi revolution), Shimon Ballas's *HaMa'abarah* (The transit camp) was published. This book is recognized as the first literary work about life in the transit camp by a former resident, but it is not without precedent. *Shesh Kenafaim LeEḥad* (Each one has six wings), by Hanoch Bartov,[83] winner of the 1955 Keren Kayemet Ussishkin Prize, was the first work to be recognized as a transit camp novel *(roman hamaʿabarah)*.[84] It takes place in a poor neighborhood outside of Jerusalem rather than in an actual transit camp and tells of various immigrants from different countries of origin. Included is the story of young Menashe, who leaves his family to join a kibbutz. In doing so, he realizes the Zionist dream as held by the early settlers. The novel ends happily with the birth of a child to a pair of Holocaust survivors—their own sabra, to be named after the native-born teacher who first helped them adjust to their new life.

Iraqi readers complained that their past was not well represented by Ballas's novel,[85] but such representation is clearly not the aim of the work. Life in Iraq remains outside of the narrative, serving as a distant context for life in the camp. Instead, the book emphasizes the present of the *maʿabarah* with only scant references to the glory of the past. Ballas has said, "I wanted to represent a certain reality . . . the reality of life in the transit camp."[86]

The contemporary critics, all Ashkenazim, varied in their judgments of the novel's literary merit. Some even ignored the standard questions of literary criticism, much to the author's dismay.[87] One reviewer dismissed the book as "literary reportage" and commented that it was "not the story of the Second Israel [i.e., Jews of Middle Eastern background] which we have long been awaiting."[88] A more favorable review characterized the style as "quasi-documentary" and opined that Hebrew literature was not yet mature enough to have the Tolstoy such a story required. However, she judged the novel as "readable," "interesting," and "relevant,"[89] and in a different review she remarked on the success of the book in being "[a window to a world] we couldn't find our way to by ourselves."[90]

Another reviewer praised the author's ability to write and to engage the reader from the beginning, as well as his mature perspective. She concluded that "it was good that *[HaMaʿabarah]* was written, and seventy times more so that it was written without bitterness."[91] The writer of the review titled "The genre of 'I accuse' in the transit camp" clearly disagreed.[92] This is undoubtedly a very personal reading, as the tone of the novel itself is not bitter.[93] A few of the characters express their dissatisfaction with regret or clever irony. One immigrant in *HaMaʿabarah* coins the phrase "the Second Babylonian Exile," inverting the idea of the original exile of the Jews from the Land of Israel to Babylon to signify the return of the Babylonian Jews to the Land of Israel.[94] His neighbor composes a poem in the form of longing for Zion to lament their fate: "Hoy yonah homeiha bekirvati / hoy

Shekhinah, lu yada'at tsorati."[95] Yet the bitterness is not directed against anyone, and comes only from the characters and not the narrator.

More than twenty years after the publication of *HaMa'abarah*, Yaḥil-Wax described it as "a novel about Israel in which Zionism is not mentioned."[96] The book clearly did not belong to the canon that focused on the collective experience and the promotion of positive values. However, it is not because it has nothing to do with the discussion on Zionism that it could not fit into the canon, but rather because it asks a different question than the canon. Contemporary stories began the quest to define a new Israeli identity for the majority (Ashkenazi) with recognition of a minority (usually Arab) presence.[97] According to one critic, the novel causes the Ashkenazi reader to ask, "Did we build a new Diaspora?"[98] The canon has had difficulty finding a place for the novel[99] because of its difference. It offers a new perspective on the experience of the ingathered exiles in the promised land of Zion.

The decade following the publication of Ballas's book bore witness to the rise of the Black Panthers *(Panterim Sheḥorim)*, a mostly Moroccan ethnic group that came to the attention of the public in 1971 and expressed the frustrations and anger of the "Second Israel" and challenged the Ashkenazi hold on political power.[100] The ethnic question, declared politically dead in 1969,[101] was revived as a social issue by the Black Panthers. The protest took most of Israel by surprise. The Panthers achieved modest success before fading into the background.[102] The Labor Party, which had been in power since the founding of the state (and before) until 1977, has frequently been blamed for the *ma'abarot* and the institutionalized discrimination against Middle Eastern Jews.[103] In 1974 Sāmī Michael published his novel *Shavim VeShavim Yoter.*

The critics generally decried the novel's bitter tone and its artlessness. One critic described it as "sewn with a black thread on white fabric."[104] She complained that the writer did not take the situation of the newly established state into account in his protest.[105] While admittedly the book shows the common flaws of a first novel, the oversimplification of issues into binary categories (black and white, good and bad, Sephardi and Ashkenazi) serves to reflect and underline the protagonist's perspective. In questioning the validity of the protagonist's generalizations, the opposing generalizations are called into question as well.

The novel, like the Panthers, was seen as more radical than it actually was. While it exposed an issue problematic to Israeli society, it did not seek to undermine the structure of society. Nor did the Panthers. They did not call for a revolution; rather, they asked to be allowed to participate in the social institutions of Israel, and in particular the army.[106] In the novel, the army serves an integrating and democratizing function. *Shavim VeShavim Yoter* validates a primary Israeli social institution and embraces the mainstream myth of heroism. Of the three novels under discussion, it is arguably the most affirming of Zionism and Israel.

The ten years following the publication of Michael's novel (1974–84) brought many changes to Israel, including a rise in immigration from East Europe and the West. No longer were immigrants automatically associated with Arab and Islamic lands. The ethnic question shifted to being constructed as a cultural issue. *Tarnegol Kaparot* (Fowl of atonement) by Eli Amir reflects this change in emphasis. His novel takes place mostly on the kibbutz and emphasizes the psychological and cultural crises of its main character.[107] Of all the characters in these novels, young Nūrī is by far the most likeable and believable.

Although still critical of the establishment and the Ashkenazi domination over Israeli culture, the book is much less overt in its criticism than Michael's book. Even the humiliating DDT scene is presented with humor by the narrator-protagonist.

> We already had the spraying with DDT behind us. Whenever I looked at a new victim I couldn't help remembering that humiliating and funny experience. Yes, funny too, after the first shock was over. As soon as we landed at Lydda airport, the disinfectors rushed towards us, waving their sprays in their hands. The white dust burned my eyes, I wanted to cry, to shout: "I'm not infested fruit! What are you doing to me?" And suddenly I saw my father, in his best Sabbath suit, coming to greet the yearned-for Bride, the Land to which he had turned his face three times a day—and his pinstriped suit was spattered with white blotches, the black stubble on his face was spotted with white. He looked so dismayed I wanted to weep. What were they doing to my father?! My father! Then he turned to look at his youngest son, dripping with trickles of white powder. Just as my brother's face crumpled into tears, my father burst into peals of laughter at the sight of him. The whole sprayed, groaning hall followed suit.[108]

The novel has enjoyed a warm reception by critics and the Israeli establishment alike.[109] It received the Youth Aliyah Prize for Literature and was adopted by the Department of Education for inclusion in the high school curriculum. One journalist proclaimed it "a revelation for understanding the social and political upheavals of the seventies."[110] These include the aforementioned rise of the Black Panther movement and the 1977 defeat of the Labor Party.

Yet in actuality it is more revolutionary than the books preceding it. *Tarnegol Kaparot* is critical of the kibbutz, "the experiment that did not fail," that bastion of Zionist principles, equality, and communism. In this story, the kibbutz does fail: it fails to offer true hospitality to the Iraqis; it fails to integrate them into the values of Israeli society; and most importantly it fails to convince them to join the kibbutz. This book also presents a surprising transformation in which the value of self-realization becomes a reason for joining the kibbutz[111] rather than for leaving it. [112]

The books and the reactions to them are reflective of their times. In *Hamaʿabarah*, the emphasis is more on the contrast between present and former status than settler versus immigrant, Ashkenazi versus Mizraḥi, native versus foreign-born. The presence of the "other" (the settler, the European, and the native born) is scarcely felt and hardly as central as in the later books. *Shavim VeShavim Yoter* highlights and polarizes these oppositions. The act by which the character of David achieves his position is necessarily one of epic proportions. It takes a dramatic event to actuate a change so extreme according to the book's ruling paradigms. Although the oppositions at the core of Michael's novel are present in *Tarnegol Kaparot*, they play a less central role; Nūrī's heroic actions are less dramatic and display a grasp of the more subtle criteria of status and prestige.

The arrival scene is absent in Ballas's work because the scope of the novel is almost entirely confined to the characters and events within the transit camp. The story begins and ends in the coffeehouse that serves as the focal center for the *maʿabarah* and the novel. In *Shavim VeShavim Yoter*, the humiliation of the experience is presented as justification for the narrator's anger and antiestablishment stance. It belongs to the era of the Black Panther protests. This contrasts with the humorous portrayal in Amir's novel, which has been made possible, perhaps, by the further passage of time and the changes taking place in Israeli society.

Until recently the *maʿabarah* literature had assumed a marginal position, despite the centrality of the concerns it addressed in a country of immigrants. As Ammiel Alcalay suggests in his postscript to *After Jew and Arabs,* "anyone who strays from the dominant ideological or 'thematic' consensus" is kept out of the mainstream.[113] The departure from the Zionist master narrative is not the only reason for this literature's neglect. These novels began to appear while Israeli literature was undergoing a transition from social realism to existentialism and postmodernism. Written in the style that mainstream Israeli writers considered passé, the *ma'abarah* literature did not appeal to the literary taste of the period and as a result was either judged unfavorably or was ignored.

The *ma'abarah* novels continued the social realism trend of the literature of the forties and fifties. An assumption of shared values common to the author, narrator, characters, and audience underlies the literature of the War of Independence.[114] These values were based on the principles of building and defending the land and the community. Identification with these values has created the "novel of the collective."[115]

> Literature of the War of Independence was born, due to the circumstances which shaped it, with the sign "we" . . . and asked . . . what right of existence does the "I" have without any connection to social realism.[116]

Little distinction, if any, was made between the points of view represented by the various narrative levels in these works. Characters tended toward types; protagonists were heroic men of action—builders and pioneers. They were the new sabras, as different from the image of the *galut* (exile) Jew as possible. Plot schemes favored the death of the hero as a martyr,[117] rewarding characters who behaved according to the accepted values and punishing those who did not. Irony was absent. The language used was generally highly stylized and formal, whether, as Shaked suggests, to express the noble greatness of the values expressed[118] or due to the lack of a modern literary idiom.[119] Nurit Gertz emphasizes the core of shared values in creating the genre.

> The possibility of using different aspects of the work (especially plot and external characterization) in order to shape and direct the moralistic norms comes from complete confidence in these norms.[120]

This confidence waned in the "New Wave" literature of the next generation.[121] This literature asks:

> What happens to the hero, brought up on the voluntaristic, romantic notions of the pre-state when confronted with an established state with its routines and duties?[122]

The belief in shared values central to the realization of Zionist collectivism and pioneerism is questioned when it falls short of the high moral ideal.[123] The disillusioned and alienated individual wanders through these works as an antihero. The confusion in values and goals is expressed through irony, unreliable narration, and the absence of any clear authority. The narrator or protagonist's point of view is differentiated from—and undermined by—that of the implied author.[124] The almost classical style of the earlier works gives way to a more colloquial, non-normative language. The Palmaḥ generation's literature is discounted as simplistic and naïve; aesthetic sensibilities are given precedence over social realism.

The New Wave writers transformed Israeli literature from a literature of belonging to a literature of alienation. The notion of exile was transformed from a national concern to be "resolved" by the establishment of the State of Israel to a metaphor for modern life.

Written during the period of New Wave literature but in a style closer to that of the Palmaḥ novels, *sifrut hama'abarah* belongs to neither of the two literary generations. These are novels of *collective* alienation, exploring the shared, rather than the individual, experience of not belonging. They question the values lauded in the writing of the 1940s, and challenged in the 1960s, from the position of the outsider wanting to come inside. Instead of the sabra protagonists of both the Palmaḥ and the New Wave novels, the characters central to the stories of the *ma'abarah* are marginal to Israeli society. In this respect, the literature of the *ma'abarah* preceded the mainstream Israeli literature that incorporated marginal characters in the 1970s and 1980s.[125]

The *ma'abarah* literature works within the conventional schema of the canon in form if not in content. The language and rhetorical style follow the development of the literary idiom in "mainstream" Israeli literature. The Hebrew of *HaMa'abarah* echoes the earlier classical style; Arabic is used to demonstrate the characters' distance from their surroundings. In *Shavim VeShavim Yoter* the language is more informal and less stylized; Arabic words and phrases signal dialogue between fellow outsiders. *Tarnegol Kaparot* is written in a language close to the daily idiom. The use of Arabic and nonstandard items seems the least self-conscious and nearest to the spirit of contemporary works.

With the publication of the first *ma'abarah* novel[126] the critic Azriel Okhmani recalled a remark made by Moshe Shamir:

> A year ago or so someone declared that the child who grows up in a transit camp will write the first *ma'abarah* novel. Apparently it was not Menashe[127] who wrote the first story about the neighborhood of immigrants.[128]

These then are the stories by the Menashes of the transit camps. "The one who has lived the reality of the *ma'abarah* is obligated to write about it."[129]

# 6

# Childhood and Home in Iraq: Narratives in Arabic

> The past is not just people and events, it is childhood too.
>
> —Samīr Naqqāsh

> Not only the past and the world of childhood are in a timeless world—but also the path to them, the path of writing and the story belong to the same current that continues within a timeless frozen structure of the creative act.
>
> —Ehud Ben Ezer

WHAT IS HOME? FOR THE EXILE, IN PARTICULAR, HOME IS LOCATED IN a specific time and place: childhood in one's motherland. Home is the house in which one grew up, the members of the household, and the different routines, customs, and traditions of the household. Home serves to give one a sense of identity, of history, and of belonging. The state of exile causes a loss of these senses and leads to efforts to recover all of them. Writers often attempt to do so through their writing.

"How do you find your way back to the past," it has been asked, "when the past is discontinuous?"[1]

By the very nature of exile, the actual physical place is lost to the individual forever. Those in exile cannot return home except through memory. Memory mediates between past and present, recalling and often distorting. It brings the past to the present, viewing this past through the perspective of the present.

> When we look back, we always discover that things we didn't understand then, we can understand now—possibly another trick of memory.[2]

Nostalgia lurks around the corner of every memoir, ready to reclaim positive events and to ignore or recast in rosy hues those that are negative. One Iraqi Jewish immigrant recalls:

> I was seven when we came to Israel. Life in Baghdad is preserved in my memory like reality from another world. If not all of it is happy, a magic aura of childhood is still poured over it, something that makes it unique, that, arrow-like, separates the event from reality like the mythical river of Sambatyon.[3]

Eva Hoffman begins her memoirs in a similar vein: "[T]he wonder is what you can make your paradise out of . . . happy, safe enclosures of Eden."[4]

Nostalgia is recognized as the most subjective of all forms of memory;[5] in it even sadness is bittersweet, and time bears no relation to the clock.[6] It evokes a past based on personal experiences that is remembered as superior to the present. The sharp contrast between the past and the present suggests a condition of discontinuity such as that caused by leaving one's home. While nostalgia uses the past as its source material, it is a construction of the present. Conditions of the present determine the materials and moods of this construction. In his sociological study of the nostalgic mood, Fred Davis describes it as "a *distinctive aesthetic modality* in its own right, a kind of code or patterning of symbolic elements, which by some obscure mimetic isomorphism comes much as language itself, to serve as a substitute for the feeling or mood it aims to arouse."[7] He concludes:

> As one of art's more enduring resources nostalgia need not merely feed upon or revel in the past; it can become the means for creatively using the past as well.[8]

Memory can thus be manipulated by selection and coloration: what is remembered and how it is remembered. Yet, just as importantly, the ordering of the fragments of memory is also subject to interpretation. Narration, in particular, orders events, and, in so doing, asserts control over them.

> Looking back sometimes I can gather all the details, sometimes I can't. Sometimes I don't get a logical chain [of events]. Doubt tortures me whether the chain of events is right. Aren't the events more important and not their order? (*Bayt Fī Baghdād,* p. 23)

The two Iraqi authors under discussion who continue to write in Arabic have both revisited the places of their memories in narrative. Through narrative, Yiẓḥak Bar-Moshe and Samīr Naqqāsh present an ordering of place in a linear representation of three-dimensional space through the fourth dimension, time.

*Bayt Fī Baghdād* [A house in Baghdad] is the second volume of Yiẓḥak Bar-Moshe's memoirs to be published, yet it predates the others (including one not yet published) in autobiographical content. It covers Bar-Moshe's memories of the first ten years of his life, as well as stories handed down from his parents, grandparents. and great-grandparents.

*Laylat 'Urābā,* (The night of Hoshana Raba)[9] by Samīr Naqqāsh is a novella included in a collection with three other medium-length works. It tells the story of one family's celebration of the harvest festival Sukkot on the eve of their exile from Iraq. The narrator of the frame story describes the evening twenty-nine years ago in the fictional past to an implied audience in a small coffeehouse in Israel.

Both of these works are written in Arabic,[10] from a first-person perspective, and are among the best and most accessible works of each author. Due in large part to the specificity of setting, these works are vividly realized. Unlike some of the writers' other pieces, these works are not obscured by treatment of the abstract. In addition to his memoirs, Bar-Moshe has published short-story collections. The settings and characters of most of his stories are unidentified—the few names used are neutral, lacking in connotation—with the exception of his one book of Jerusalem stories.[11] He attempts to deal with the universal questions of existence and reality. His memoirs are more widely read, and the first two volumes have so far been translated into Hebrew.

Naqqāsh has also written stories set in undefined places and time (his second book is titled *Ḥikāya Kull Zamān Wa-Makān* [Stories of any time and place]),[12] but he anchors most of his stories, plays, and novels in Iraq, writing from a familiar background. He views man as wretched and miserable because of his limitations and inabilities. In his works Naqqāsh argues against the possibility of knowing reality because of its fluid and ever-changing nature.

Both of the works under discussion treat the same time and place

(Iraq in the thirties and forties) from a similar vantage point. The narrators of both deal with childhood in Baghdad. While the narrators accurately record their experiences and feelings as children, they narrate from a more adult perspective. Childhood is presented as a time of innocence, in which home is safe, permanent, and all-encompassing.[13] The narrative of childhood is an established literary tradition.[14] A structure common to these narratives results from the shared theme of growing up.[15] Growing up means losing one's innocence and leaving home. The story of the Garden of Eden serves as the basic paradigm.[16]

Despite the shared themes and structures in the narratives of childhood, there are significant differences between the authors' works. The most obvious difference is that of genre. Bar-Moshe's book is autobiography, while Naqqāsh's is fiction.

The genre of autobiography as a narrative form has been the subject of much recent analysis.[17] It seems to deny or at least downplay some aspects of fictionality. It collapses the distance between the author (implied and biographical) and the first-person narrator, leaving only the distance of time between narrator and protagonist. The genre leads to expectations of historical accuracy and the assumption of chronology as the organizing principle, rather than completeness and an imposed structural order.

In reality, autobiography is subject to many of the same rules as fictional narrative. In their studies on autobiography, Pascal refers to the "elusiveness of truth"[18] whereas Egan discusses the "inevitability of fiction."[19] Events are selected, ordered, and presented from a particular viewpoint. Even in autobiography that "moves in a dutiful line from birth to fame, omitting nothing significant,"[20] a strict chronology is impossible to follow. The very linearity of narrative distorts a true time sequence;[21] overlapping or simultaneous events must wait their turn in the narrative.

> By the time experience is distilled enough through our minds to set some particular thing down on paper, so much unconscious rendering has gone on that even the naïve wish to be wholly "truthful" fades before the intoxication of line, pattern, form.[22]

In autobiography memory acts as an additional filter. Both memory and narration select, order, and present events according to the principles that shape the autobiography. These principles, in turn, color the events. "[T]he narrative *confers a meaning* on the event which, when it actually occurred, no doubt had several meanings or none. This postulating of meaning dictates the choice . . . according to the demands of the preconceived intelligibility."[23] Thus, at least in terms of narrative control, the generic expectations of autobiography do not differ greatly from those of fiction.

In his first volume, Yiẓḥak Bar-Moshe leaves the question of genre to his readers:

> The book *al-Khurūj min al-ʿIrāq* is therefore a novel if you wish, and a collection of [short] stories if you wish, and a personal history [or autobiography] if you like as well, but in the end it may be a mixture of all of these things together.[24]

The second volume, *Bayt Fī Baghdād*, is labeled by Shmuel Moreh as an autobiographical novel because its point of departure is artistic *(fannīyah)*.[25]

Pascal points out the contradictions inherent in the genre of the autobiographical novel:

> What happens in the novel should be self-sufficient and completed, while the autobiographer must refer us continually outwards and onwards, to the author himself, and to the outcome of all these experiences. [26]

This contradiction is even more apparent in the work of Bar-Moshe itself. On one hand it is a self-contained work, but it also stands as part of Bar-Moshe's other autobiographical works. *Bayt Fī Baghdād* is itself composed of seventy self-contained story units; it is one of four volumes. At the same time that it claims wholeness as a novel (or short-story collection) and a book, it admits incompleteness, since as an autobiography it is one in a series.

The paradox of complete and incomplete is thematized in the story by Samīr Naqqāsh. *Laylat ʿUrābā* is not offered as an autobiography but as a novella in a collection of fiction. However, the first-person narration in which the narrator's younger self is the subject suggests that it is an autobiography, as does the real-life basis of the story.[27] Its self-conscious emphasis on storytelling is apparent in the setting (a coffeehouse) and its use of typical rhetorical devices (addressing an unseen audience); this keeps the work within the realm of fiction.

Andrew Gurr has written, "For the exile home is a static concept rooted in the unalterable circumstances of childhood."[28] In both works under discussion here the concept of home goes beyond fulfilling the primary need for shelter. It grants security, tradition, and identity. Reclaiming the childhood home leads to reclamation of one's past and oneself. As Gurr also says, "For . . . exiles the search for identity and the construction of a vision of home amount to the same thing. Typically the home is set in the past, in memories of childhood . . . the home of memory, which is the only basis for a sense of identity which the exiled writer can maintain."[29]

## BAYT FĪ BAGHDĀD

### *The Man and His Home*

> "A Man without his house is only an illusion."
> —Bar-Moshe, *Bayt Fī Baghdād*

In the first chapter of *Bayt Fī Baghdād,* the reader is introduced to the narrator's grandfather and his house. The narrative thus links together man and house from the beginning, and then further develops this parallel of identification by describing the qualities they share. Both the house and the grandfather are presented through the filter of imperfect memory and time. While the narrator knows both the man and his house, his own personal recollection is fragmented and needs supplementing from other sources. "Most of what we [the cousins] knew about grandfather was what our mother, father, uncle, grandmother, and aunt told us" (*Bayt Fī Baghdād,* p. 9). Yiẓḥak Bar-Moshe fills in the gaps with his own personal memories of the family patriarch and of the photographic portrait on the wall.

While the house has left a strong imprint, Bar-Moshe's memories are incomplete: "The house was unlike any other. I would pay a very great sum if only someone could sketch a picture of the house as it was. I only remember parts of it. . . . I don't remember the rooftop, or actually, how we'd get up there . . ." (p. 10).

Despite the incompleteness of the narrator's personal memory, both the house and his grandfather leave behind a strong impression. They serve as the center holding together and unifying the family. The house is an expression of the grandfather's love and his hopes for his family.

> My grandfather loved his house deeply, for it was the house of his youth. . . . My grandmother ʿAzīza told us that our grandfather worked industriously to buy this house, and that he put everything he saved and earned into it. My grandfather was a very hard worker. His three sons and daughter meant everything in the world to him. He wanted to be at peace with himself and to feel content that he had fulfilled all his worldly and religious obligations to them. (P. 10–11)

The house that makes such an impression on the narrator has three main divisions: the basement, the main floors, and the rooftop. These can be seen as loosely corresponding to the underworld with its resident spirits, the earthly world of daily activities, and the heavens above, home of the celestial bodies.

> I know the entrance was a spacious, high-ceilinged area, and that this foyer led into the courtyard of the small house. Indeed, the house was two houses, one inside the other, and from the small house you would pass through from one side of the courtyard to the big house. I would feel a type of awe when I would look at the wide courtyard, the rooms around the courtyard, and the second story. [The second floor was composed of] a number of rooms set on top of the first floor, encircling the courtyard from above. . . . I remember the spacious rooftop above the rooms that was almost divided into rooms for sleeping in the summertime. (P. 11)

The basement is home to the jinn (demons).[30] Even though the children are aware of the scientific worldview that would deny the existence of these underground spirits outside of the imagination (the unconscious), the children remain scared of the cellar. The women of the house laugh at the ignorant folk belief of the servants who fear the jinn, but they themselves avoid the cellar.

The jinn seem innocuous enough. They use the dialect of the people who live in the house—a dialect that shifts, if necessary, when the house's ownership changes—and observe the accepted norms of hospitality. A visiting child claims he is wary of the resident jinn only because they are unfamiliar to him. "It's okay," say the children of the house, encouraging him to descend the stairs they themselves will not, "[the jinn] know you're our guest" (p. 48).

Similar jinn occupy the basement of other houses they move to. They occupy all the homes in Bar-Moshe's short stories. Shmuel Moreh describes one of Yiẓḥak Bar-Moshe's fictional worlds as "the naïve childhood world of spirits, demons, and supernatural powers".[31] "Al-Sirdāb" (The cellar),[32] for example, tells the story of a ten-year-old boy who cannot enter the cellar because of his fear of the jinn. As a law student he decides to conquer this fear. When he goes to the basement, he sees the jinn and flees in fear.

The narrator of *Bayt Fī Baghdād* and his playmates tell similar stories of feet grabbed on the cellar stairs and even of befriending one of these underground spirits. While it is not clear from these stories why the jinn are to be feared, the underground remains the domain of the underworld for the characters in Bar-Moshe's narratives.

Bar-Moshe describes the rest of the house with more nostalgia than detail. Upstairs and downstairs rooms encircle the courtyard. Bedrooms are on the second floor; on the first floor are rooms for cooking, eating, playing, and entertaining. The house is divided into four wings, one for each branch of the family. The four servants (one for each branch) sleep in the attic, a spacious but poorly insulated room.

It is the rooftop, where the family sleeps on hot summer nights, that extends the view of the household members.[33] The rooftop is connected to those of the neighbors and the heavens seem within reach of the roof.

> There was no window in our house that looked out onto the street. But the house overlooked the whole world. In it were the sky and air, the earth and clouds, the sun, the moon, and the stars. The house was on the doorstep of the entire universe. I used to sit on the rooftop during the summer when we would sleep up there and stay up to watch the stars. I learned a great deal about the stars—fixed and moving—before I ever read about them in books. (P. 306)

Life in the house was oriented around the inner courtyard. The world contained within the house was a secure and insulated world.

> But the Jews usually leaned and continue to lean towards preserving their former lifestyle. They realized the risk which faced them from great societal change. Their houses were safe, well-fortified [impenetrable] and closed on themselves and their rich Jewish lives. (P. 370)

This static insular life contrasts with the life of the streets, where different peoples mix and lifestyles are in the process of changing. The threat this presents to the Jews' feelings of security and well-being is similar to that posed by the reign of King Ghāzī. The monarch is introduced in the narrative immediately after the description cited above. For most of the time frame covered by the events depicted in the book the inward orientation of the "Jewish home" provides security enough.

*Home as The Universe*

In *Bayt Fī Baghdād* the members of the extended family live together in one large house.[34] Each of the four wings houses one branch: the grandparents and their daughter, Lulu, until she marries; Uncle Abū Albert; Uncle Sāmī (and later, his wife); and the narrator's immediate family. This physical closeness mirrors the intimacy of the family dynamics. Aunt Lulu (the grandfather's youngest daughter and the narrator's aunt) continues to visit daily after she marries and moves out of her house. Even after the different branches of the extended family move to different homes, the closeness continues. The uncles continue to consult with each other about everything and to make weekly visits to the grandmother's home Saturday nights. "It seemed to me that the ties between the uncles became stronger rather than weaker [after the move to separate households]" (p. 359).

The grandfather and his house leave behind a legacy of family unity. They presumably leave such a lasting effect because of their centrality in the family members' lives. The grandfather serves as the unifying link among the family members who live together (even after his death) and out-of-town relatives: Great-uncle Asher, Great-aunt Tuffāḥah, and her husband Uncle Ibrāhīm. The house is central. "I don't think that the elderly couple [Tuffāḥah and Ibrāhīm] visited anywhere else in Baghdad. Baghdad, according to them, was my grandfather's house in Qambar ʻAlī" (p. 121).

Both the house and the grandfather are self-sufficient. "[Grandfather] was not ambitious, he was satisfied with himself and his family" (p. 52). So too the house: "Everything was in the house. Sky, sun, moon, stars, a spacious courtyard, wings, and huge rooms" (p. 210). Indeed, for the protagonist as a small child, the house is almost the entire universe. As he grows older, this universe extends to include the school and synagogue, but these are extensions of the house. To the narrator-child the house is central to his life and lifestyle. When he hears that a family friend is moving to Palestine, beyond his realm, he asks, "What would a house be like there?" (p. 26) and later wonders, "Why go if the houses there aren't as nice as here?" (p. 263).

The school is compared to the house by the narrator: "I felt as secure [at school] as in our own home" (p. 392). His sense of security comes from a feeling of familiarity. In comparing the school with home he assigns the role of grandfather to the principal, "the father of us all" (p. 138).

The other institution located in the child-narrator's world, the synagogue, is also compared to the house. Both are all-encompassing. "The synagogue had the same warm relationship with God, the sky, the stars, the sun and the moon as did our house" (p. 311).

*Rootedness*

In addition to being the universe, home in these works is created by the authors from the concepts of continuity, tradition and permanence (or at least the perception of such). The home is a stable, unchanging anchor. In his memoirs, Yiẓḥak Bar-Moshe constructs his "house in Baghdad" on a foundation of tradition and continuity. This foundation is composed, in part, of the stories about his parents, grandparents, and great-grandparents. The stories have been handed down over the generations. These stories establish lineage and validate the boy's membership in the household. They include the grandfather's building of the house, the father's escape from the Ottoman army and his survival, and the parents' "courtship" (the child-bride's fear of the groom's beard and her wedding-day flight). All are events that lead to the child growing up in the house.

There are also stories from before the narrator's time about the other household members. For example, a story is told about the time Uncle Abū Albert was threatened with being thrown out of the house unless he reformed his ways; he complied with his grandfather's wishes and became a tailor's apprentice. This one story validates the uncle's presence in the house and contributes to his characterization (fleshed out in later stories), but it also defines household membership as a privilege that carries with it benefits conditional on complying with family expectations of behavior. The ultimate punishment is banishment from the family home.

The permanent nature of the home is maintained despite the series of moves. "That year we knew that Grandfather's house remained in each house we lived in, whether all of the families lived in our house or whether each family chose its own house" (p. 26).

Despite their "Jewish tendency to conservatism,"[35] the Bar-Moshe family finds that nothing stays the same forever. The extended family moves from "Grandfather's house," a move that actually takes place in two stages.

The grandfather chose the location of the first house across from the mosque. Security considerations were then, as later, foremost in mind. While perhaps an all-Jewish neighborhood would be considered most safe, being a minority was not necessarily cause for concern. The important factor was a healthy respect for others' beliefs and practices, no matter how different. People who pray do not cause trouble.

Changes in the neighborhood motivated the family to leave this once desirable location. While the changes are not clearly specified, the story of their neighbor Awāsha serves as an illustration. Awāsha's story alternates with that of the move. Here we have an example of narrative order, not strictly chronological, implying a causal relationship. The grandfather has warned his family not to get involved in the dispute between Awāsha and her son-in-law, but they can hardly ignore it, as they share a rooftop with only a wall dividing the two households. Awāsha intimidates everyone in the neighborhood except for her son-in-law, who stays out late and drinks. In response to her complaints about his behavior, he tries to set her on fire but fails. The situation ends in tragedy: both are found shot to death. (The court decides that he shot her.) The Jewish family, well aware of the traditions of blood revenge, fear further violence (which could easily spill over the one wall). But as the narrator writes, "[T]here were many reasons for the decision my grandfather made to sell the house facing the mosque of Qambar 'Alī" (p. 33).

The advent of electricity is an additional reason. Not only are they moving away from the neighbors, but they are moving to an electrified quarter.

Their second home in al-Diḥānah is similar to the original home. A small house is connected to the larger house and used for storage. This house is rented on a temporary basis because of its proximity to the market. The location is evidently unsuitable for a Jewish family, because the market attracts large numbers of people from outside the neighborhood. These "outsiders" would presumably feel less obliged to offer protection if it were to become necessary. The house was also on the route of the Sbāyā (a procession marking the Shiite Day of Remembrance of the martyrs Hassan and Hussein). Naim Kattan, the Iraqi-born Jewish writer (now living in Canada), recalls the occasion in his memoirs:

> Some distant cousins of my father lived in the Shiite section, a rare thing for Jews. The Sbaya, the Muslim "passion," took place

> before their windows. Each year they shared their privileged vantage point with about thirty friends and cousins. . . .
>
> All the shutters were closed except for a small crack that did not let in any light. No one would suspect the presence of the curious. We pressed our heads against the edge of the shutters so that we could view the spectacle. We did not say a word, afraid of our own whispers. The excited crowd could attack any sacrilegious spectators. I was afraid of the demoniacal perturbation of this human wave and I dreaded my own shadow. . . . I can still see the bare-chested men, panting in the chains that bound their arms and legs, waiting open-mouthed for a drop of water to quench their thirst, unbearable but sought and accepted. They flagellated themselves and inflicted as many blows on themselves as on their companions. They were reliving the slow death of Hassan and Hussein, martyrs for the faith. There were even more men armed with swords and daggers. The unfurling of the apparatus of war and of a panoply of green-and-black banners attested to the passage of death—so that the faith might triumph and live. I crouched down in bewilderment. I was convinced that the slightest gesture would signal my presence to that multitude of demons.[36]

In Yiẓḥak Bar-Moshe's account, the Jewish family and curious visitors hide inside as well, concealing their presence from the parade of those consumed by passion and fervor. A knock at the door sends tremors through the household. The young narrator innocently opens the door, against his parents' direct orders ("We must not open the door. . . . Do not go downstairs . . . I will break your leg if you do that") (pp. 157–58) to find a sheikh on their doorstep. The sheikh requests water and asks if the boy is Jewish. He then cleanses the glass, drinks the water, and blesses the boy: "May Allāh preserve you, my son. The heat is fierce" (p. 158).

Despite the innocuous outcome of the encounter, the family cautions the child never to take such a risk again. "This time nothing happened, Allāh be praised. But next time you must be careful and obey your mother" (p. 159).

Yet according to the evidence within the narrative itself, the principal impetus for the second move comes from within the household rather than from any concern abut security or location. Within six months of the grandfather's death in the rented house, Sāmī's wife dies in childbirth. The recently widowed mother and son (Grandmother and Uncle Sāmī) decide to move away from the sad memories contained within the walls of the family home. Uncle Sāmī and the grandmother move to Bataween, a relatively new neighborhood that had just begun to attract Jewish families. (Aunt Lulu and her husband ʿAzīz had already moved to Bataween when interethnic relations had deteriorated in al-Mamlaḥah, the old neighborhood.) The narrator and his family moved with Uncle Abū Albert to another house in a different area. This house was, first and foremost, secure. It shared an alley with only one other house, and the alley was locked at night.

The moves are away from changing neighborhoods and threats of danger, and toward the fruits of progress of the twentieth century, such as electricity. The change reflects the march of time, increased mobility, urbanization, and improved material culture. The incipient dissolution of the extended family into subnuclear units is another indication of modernization. Yet the families maintain warm, close relations with each other.

Despite the move(s) away from the grandfather's house, the house itself is presented as a permanent fixture. This comes from a conflation of all the different residences into the eponymous house of the title; the preservation of warm ties among former and present household members; and the balance between inside and outside. The house itself is secure; it is closed to the dangers of the street, and yet it is open to the infinity of the heavens from the rooftop. The narrative fixes "home" by the preservation of the remembered home(s) in the written text.

### *Safe as Houses*

Security is the single most important thing a house can offer, even above comfort and privacy. Not everything in childhood is gloriously stable and unchangingly secure, nor are those recollections untainted. In both Naqqāsh's and Bar-Moshe's narratives there are foreshadowings of ominous times.

Bar-Moshe's book places a strong emphasis on security. Each home is judged according to the safety of its location; nonrental homes are purchased for the security they offer. The first home is chosen because it is opposite the mosque and then abandoned once that location does not provide sufficient protection; the second home is temporary because it is unsuitably located next to the market; the third is in a semiprivate alley locked at night.

The very act of moving reflects the beginning of the changes. The decision to move is influenced by the forces of modernization (increased urbanization attracts a less desirable element to the mosque area; a neighborhood with electricity is preferred to one without). Modernization contributes to the breakup of the extended family into subnuclear units.

The narrative repetition of the occasions of moving underlines their significance in the life of the young narrator. It is potentially a premonition of future events, of the great move to come.

Despite the inward-looking orientation of the house, the street can no longer be ignored. "Everyone felt safe at home; the adults felt safe in the street" (p. 336). The narrator becomes aware of the outside world as it becomes more threatening. The outside world somehow intrudes; German propaganda, Pan-Arabism, and Iraqi nationalism join forces in a new and virulent form of anti-Semitism. Adults no longer feel safe on the streets. Fear increases.[37] One night the father and narrator come home late to find the door unlocked. The father's reaction is one of controlled panic until he discovers that someone simply neglected to lock it. Not long after, Jews are murdered in the streets. The first two become victims upon leaving a social club on the eve of the Jewish New Year; a third dies on Simḥat Torah (two days after Hoshana Raba); and shortly thereafter a pharmacist and a train station manager are murdered.

Next, children are sent home from school when there is shooting in the streets. Home is still safe, but school, the extension of home, no longer is. How much longer will home be safe?

Bar-Moshe ends his narrative with a description of the atmosphere of fear that begins to pervade their daily lives:

> I knew deep down that the fear would never leave me. It would settle inside me forever whether I forgot the house that shook or whether I just pretended to forget it, whether the house stopped shaking or not. (P. 420)

## LAYLAT 'URĀBĀ

Central to the story of *Laylat 'Urābā* by Samīr Naqqāsh is the *sukkah*. The *sukkah*, a temporary home, is a boothlike structure erected as part of the celebration of the Jewish holiday of Sukkot. According to Jewish tradition, not more than one of its four walls may be permanent; the roof must be partially open to the sky. The *sukkah* represents the tents and shacks used as shelter by the Israelites during their forty years of wandering in the desert after their exodus from Egypt. The *sukkah* substitutes for the home during the eight-day holiday. According to Jewish law one is required to dwell in the *sukkah*.

On the narrative level, the *sukkah* functions to introduce the reader to a rich cast of characters and to explore the close ties among them. As a symbol of enclosure, it parallels the narrative situation—the narrator is telling the story of the last Hoshana Raba in Baghdad to an implied audience in a coffeehouse in Israel, twenty-nine years later.[38] Inside the *sukkah*, inside the narrative, all is secure and happy, while outside the storm begins to brew, and the narrative frame offers dismal updates on each of the characters present in the *sukkah*.

The relationship between the narrator's grandfather and his house in Bar-Moshe's *Bayt Fī Baghdād* finds its parallel in the relationship between the builder and his *sukkah*. The narrator's uncle is in charge of putting up the booth every year. "My uncle was the expert in building the *sukkah*. . . . [He] never liked to pass up the mitzvah of erecting the *sukkah*. This pious deed was to give my uncle a ticket for a rocket trip—fast and direct—to heaven on the Day of Judgement" (*Laylat 'Urābā*, p. 165). As soon as the fast of Yom Kippur is broken, the necessary materials and tools are gathered. The building of the *sukkah* proceeds according to the uncle's prescribed ritual. A four-sided frame of willow poles tied with hemp rope is set up and an extension cord is brought from the house to give light. Not until the day of the holiday is the frame filled in with palm fronds, decorated with gilded fruit, and furnished with wicker chairs and embroidered cushions. The procedure itself becomes ritualized, fraught with tensions between the young narrator and his uncle during the period of waiting between the beginning and the completion of the project.

The *sukkah* itself is part of a very old tradition. It is always erected at the same time, after the end of Yom Kippur and before the start of Sukkot, and in the same place, the northeastern corner of the garden. The ritual is presented as an annual event; its description shifts in tone to a specific performance of the ritual. It is made permanent through the narrative discourse, the narrator's memory shared with his "fictional" audience in the frame story, and with his "real audience," readers outside of the narrative itself.

Once completed the *sukkah* functions as home. The family eats there, celebrates the holiday there, and greets friends and relatives there. The narrator's pious aunt even braves the chilly autumn nights and sleeps in the *sukkah* all eight nights of the holiday.

During the evening, prayers are recited in the names of the forefathers. Candles are lit in honor of the dead. Simultaneous remembrance of the personal and biblical forefathers establishes a symbolic genealogy and validates tradition. The temporary structure of the *sukkah* is also imbued with the qualities of tradition and continuity. Not only does the *sukkah* function as a gathering place for friends and family, but it also recalls the personal and shared ancestors.

The *sukkah* seems to encompass everything: it holds friends and family, the known and the unknown, the holy and the mundane, the living and the dead. The night of Hoshana Raba is dedicated to the memory of the dead; the living feel the presence of their souls.

> My being that night was overflowing, mixed with the facts of existence. All that exists was enclosed in a circle of welcome, at the limit of the senses, the seen, the heard, the smelled, the felt. (P. 175)

The visitors represent an entire range of personalities, occupations, and philosophies, from Selīm the lute player, who entertains at happy occasions (such as weddings and celebrations), to Ezra Kamāl, a reader at funerals and houses of mourning. Some represent the extremes of solemnity (Uncle Heskel Ezra) and gravity (the *sukkah*-building uncle); others represent levity (Baba Sida and his storehouse of ribald jokes).

> The loved ones were many and each had one thousand tales. They all differ in their ways, styles, personalities, and thoughts, but all of them were in our sukkah, beads on the necklace. (P. 183)

The buildings, whether temporary or permanent or somewhere in between, house the characters just as the narratives house their stories.

*The Stories and Their Significance*

There are multiple narrative and story levels in Naqqāsh's *Laylat 'Urābā*. The frame presents the storytelling situation, the setting, the narrator, and the narrator's implied audience. The characters introduced by the storyteller each have their own stories; occasionally these lead into other stories. These stories are loosely linked by a theme of belief; its presence implies naïveté or even gullibility, and its absence indicates spiritual death.

Each visitor to the *sukkah* is an entire world or at least the window to many other stories. The appearance of Uncle Heskel Ezra leads to stories about his absent son Sāliḥ, the narrator's exploration of the world of hypnosis, his classmate Edmund, and his jacket.

The digression to the story of Edmund, the good-hearted classmate, introduces the notion of gullibility. Edmund is so good-hearted and so gullible that he doesn't think to question a stranger who accosts him on his way to school, takes his jacket, and claims, "Your father is sitting at the tailor's. He wants you to give me the jacket because he wants to get you a new one. You wait here. As soon as he takes the measurements, I'll bring it back to you. It won't take ten minutes . . ." (p. 179). As a result he loses his jacket and the school-day and still remains innocent. He tells the story to his classmates without the least thought of feeling foolish.

The narrator concludes the story about his classmate with a contrast between "then" and "now": "Edmund's goodness in those days wasn't stupidity. But doubtless today it would be considered pure folly" (p. 172).

While not as extreme an example, Da'ūd al-'Ajamī's son, Ṣāliḥ, is labeled "naïve"—that is, naïve according to "today's" terms. "Today we call goodness naïveté. We call goodness foolishness. In those days we called it all goodness" (p. 186).

Ṣāliḥ's father has his own story, a story "straight from the pages of *1001 Nights*" (p. 195). Da'ūd al-'Ajamī was an entertainer in Iran, a type of court jester. According to the story told, a beautiful princess fell in love with him (despite his comical appearance) and more or less seduced him, thereby forcing him to flee. At the same time, the narrator assures us that he is not as gullible as Edmund and doesn't for a moment believe the story. The disclaimer appears only after Da'ud's story is first retold.

The sequence parallels the story of Uncle Heskel Ezra in Israel. As a younger man, he served in the Jewish battalion during the war, and from then on longed for "Ẓion Rishon" (his name for Rishon Leẓion, an early village in prestate Palestine). The narrator tells his audience that he sought out his uncle in Rishon (in Israel) after both had left Iraq in the mass exodus. He describes his encounter with an aged man, oblivious to his surroundings and the fulfillment of his lifetime fantasy. The narrator then ends the recital of this incident with a disclaimer, "But this never happened" (p. 214). The narrator is testing the gullibility of his audience, both the implied coffeehouse patrons and the readers.

At the same time the narrator offers a disclaimer about his own reliability.

> I might get confused or make mistakes. My memory might not be as reliable as the electronic variety, nor as precise. I am a human being

> discussing the bygone days. And when people talk about the past, they skip things. They don't necessarily put things in the best order. (P . 163)[39]

This warning is offered with a good deal of irony, steering his audience in the wrong direction. After relating the story of Uncle Heskel Ezra in Israel, he admits to the sin of addition rather than of omission, and it is the order in the narration that gives meaning. He presents the incident as if it has happened and then denies its truth, trying to erase the unerasable and casting doubt on the occurrence of the events that follow. Truth slips through the reader's hands.

The story of Heskel Ezra, the dyer, is the first of the postscripts offered by the narrator. This updating highlights the contrast between the living conditions in Iraq and those found in Israel. The other postscripts are left to stand unnegated by any such disclaimers.

The narrator runs into an impoverished, shabbily attired Ezra and hears through the grapevine that Selīm al-ʿAwwād has broken his lute and has become a lowly garbage collector. Selīm the Inspector has left work at a mental hospital after being attacked by the patients, and later he meets an untimely death caused by high blood pressure. Daʾūd suffers the loss of his wife in a car accident, is crippled, and finally, almost mercifully, dies.

Baba Sida's family at first finds good fortune. Each of the sons finds work in his field. Baba Sida's death is met with the characteristic laughter of the family (he was, after all, one hundred years old). Yet eventually even the seemingly infinite reservoir of laughter dries up. Little Heskel, married to the daughter of his older brother, Big Yūsuf, mourns the loss of several children in infancy. He rejoices when one child manages to live to maturity, but that son is killed on an Israeli battlefield at the age of twenty. With this tragedy the laughter dies.

The narrator differentiates between spiritual death and physical death. Hoshana Raba commemorates the physically dead. The spiritually dead are those who have suffered the death of illusions and the naïve faith that fostered these illusions. Since naïveté is equated with goodness by the narrator and those of whom he speaks ("In those days we called naïveté goodness," p. 198), the narration may be seen as a eulogy to the memory of goodness.

The world has changed. According to the narrator, not only is goodness more scarce and more suspect but materialism has eclipsed spirituality ("[In those days] we did not mean things in purely material terms," p. 186), and selfishness has dislodged generosity.

> We used to get together for no apparent reason. Today people don't get together without seeking some potential gain . . . such ulterior motives were not to be expected from the pure-spirited. (P. 176)

Light, which is very important to the story and to the celebration of the holiday, is absent in the postscript. The updates of each character's story, like the coffeehouse in which they are told, are dark and dreary. The light of innocence and naïveté has gone out, relit only in memory and narrative. The narrator recalls the holiday for his audience: "This is Hoshana Raba. Each piece of it emits rays of pure light" (p. 163). It remains in his mind as a shining memory.

The holiday itself is defined by natural light and celebrated with electric and other light. The celebration begins at sundown and continues "until the full moon *[sic]* fades into the light of the sun" (p. 167). The *sukkah*, the site of the gathering, is decorated with light. "Candles burning and lamps lit. . . . Lights stretched to the *sukkah* turning night into day" (p. 170). Four or five lanterns ("one lantern is not enough," p. 169) are hung in the booth, creating "our gloriously furnished *sukkah* of shining lights" (pp. 178–79).

The light symbolizes the happy memories of the bygone holiday: "These dreams shine with the light of many sparks. In a sea of light, our hidden happiness flows, like a boat made of blazing fire" (p. 167). Positive traits, goodness and intelligence, are imbued with the quality of light. Selīm al-Muraqqab lights up the entrance with his goodness; Big Yūsuf's "great and keen mind" emits "rays of light that stun you . . . [they are] impossible to escape" (p. 178). What is connected with childhood remains radiant and flourishing. The world lost is a world of lights. Without these lights night stays night, unrelieved by goodness and virtue, only perhaps by their memory.

The narrative ends when our storyteller is "interrupted." His uncle is missing, and he must go and look for him. This is the uncle who once took charge of building the *sukkah* (in order to earn his rocket trip to heaven). He has stopped participating in the ritual, no longer believing in the rocket trip to heaven. His loss of faith translates itself into his loss of direction, perhaps his identity, and certainly his home. The faith that once gave direction to his life has been lost, as has his ability to construct his own home.

Similar in tone to the end of *Bayt Fī Baghdād,* Naqqāsh's novella hints at a negative future, foreshadowing the events leading up to exodus. While on the narrative level the story is told through hindsight that has already witnessed the change, within the narrative itself (that is, on the story level of "then"), the changes are merely foreshadowed.

The setting of the story—the time of Sukkot and the place of the *sukkah*—recalls the wanderings of the Children of Israel and their return from the (Egyptian) exile to the Land of Israel. The pillar of cloud that accompanied the children of Israel by day summons its counterpart: the pillar of fire, the companion by night. Fire hovers on the edge of the narrative, in the flickering candles and gas lanterns. Its presence is presaged by Selīm's smelling smoke, the harbinger of fire. The smoke itself does not exist outside of Selīm's insistence that it does. His sensation of smelling the smoke has possibly been dreamed. The whole incident—of Selīm smelling the smoke, alerting the others who find nothing, the rebuke by Baba Sida, and Selīm's refusal to retreat from his position—is invested with meaning. Baba Sida represents the majority view of the Jewish community who believed that the ancient roots would withstand the temporary unpleasantness. Selīm and those similar to him saw the impermanence of the *sukkah* structure, of the home the Jews made for themselves in Babylonia. Only in hindsight can one understand Selīm's insistence: "Warning is a duty" (p. 211).

The other ominous note of this otherwise pleasant family gathering at a holiday celebration is the absence of Cousin Ṣāliḥ, Heskel Ezra's son. The narrator is unsettled by his absence: "[T]he necklace isn't complete." Therefore the circle of family and friends is not closed and cannot offer a guarantee of safety.

The quality of wholeness or completeness is extremely important to the narrator of *Laylat 'Urābā*. His desire to finish the *sukkah* and see it complete gives way to great impatience.

> Nothing seems further away than tomorrow, my friends, when we wait for something complete like the sukkah . . . when we wait for tomorrow when our wish would come true . . . when we await the coming of a close friend, what comes between today and tomorrow is an eternity. (P. 170)

Once the *sukkah* is completed, the boy's impatience in waiting for the guests to arrive is tinged with anxiety. The absence of one family friend disappoints and vexes him.

These omens are given credence by the frame of the narrative where the reader learns that the evening described was the last Hoshana Raba to be celebrated in Iraq. The narrator emphasizes the difference between "then" and "now." According to him, the world has changed and grown ugly; as mentioned, people who were then considered naïve and trusting are now considered foolish.

The narrative structure of *Laylat ʿUrābā* is composed, in good novella fashion, of a frame story and an inner narrative.[40] The story frame parallels the actual structure it describes—that of the *sukkah*. Both frame "home": the *sukkah* frames family and friends, their stories and customs; the narrative frames the story of the *sukkah*. The frame narrative is also "framed" with references to a *qaṣīda*[41] context ("like the traces of an abandoned campsite," p. 166). Here the narrator mourns what has been lost in the past, yet stops short of the description of the journey, merely hinting at it by reference to the wanderings of the Children of Israel.

Naqqāsh's masterful use of the Arabic language reinforces the difference between the frame and the framed. It also contributes to thematization, tone, and characterization. The characters presented in the framed story speak in *al-ʿāmmiyyah*, the informal Jewish Baghdadi dialect.[42] How they use words differs according to their personalities and backgrounds. Young Sāmī speaks prematurely in old-fashioned cadences ("You shouldn't know from it. . . . Even the strength to pant I didn't have," p. 190); Baba Sida speaks in the lusty tones of one who sees the world as full of laughter; Da'ūd al-ʿAjamī,[43] encountered in the marketplace of Maḥaneh Yehudah (in Israel), speaks in a garbled, confused jargon.

The language in the framed story differs from that of the frame; description is more lyrical, dialogue more lively. The narrator speaks modern Standard Arabic to his implied audience, who do not share a common background with him (nor perhaps with each other). This presents a contrast between the homey and the formal, reinforcing the contrast between the lyrical past and the nightmarish present. The sense of community is gone.

Bar-Moshe's memoirs are also framed. Conscious references to the past, to memory, and to narrative serve to place the text. An introduction by the Iraqi-born Israeli scholar Shmuel Moreh and the author's foreword also contribute to the context, as does the author's categorization of his work as "short stories . . . or novel."[44] By defining the genre the author frames the work within certain sets of expectations.

A large portion of his memoirs is recorded dialogue. The rest of the text is written in modern Standard Arabic in a style that betrays the author's training and interest in journalism. The dialogues are written simply, minimally colloquial. The dialect is modified so as to be intelligible to a wide audience (without glosses). The dependence on dialogue creates a sense of immediacy that narrative description cannot; the style "shows" rather than "tells"; and ironically it contributes to the inferred reliability of the text—"ironically" because many of the discussions recorded are such that the author could not have been present.

Fred Davis points out three qualities characteristic of nostalgic fiction: first-person voice, past continuous tense, and intransitive verbs.[45] The first decreases the distance between the narrator and the narrated; true nostalgia can only be for that which has been personally experienced.[46] The inflection of the verbs distances the events temporally (past), and yet emphasizes their enduring nature (continuous). This latter quality is reinforced by the intransitivity of the verbs chosen.

The works under discussion build on these three qualities through the subjective treatment of time. Bar-Moshe creates the illusion of chronology ordering the events, and yet the moving-house sequence is only one example of the elusiveness of an objective time frame. It is the very conflation of the different episodes that helps cultivate the permanent character of the house(s).

Naqqāsh plays with time in a different way, but to similar effect. The iterative sense of the *sukkah*-building ritual shifts almost imperceptibly to a specific occurrence.[47] The *sukkah*, and that night of Hoshana Raba, achieve a permanent existence in the narrator-character's memory and the written text. Ironically, Naqqāsh's *sukkah*, a supposedly temporary building, is no less permanent than Bar-Moshe's *bayt*.

The images of both homes—the temporary-made-permanent and the permanent-turned-temporary—are fixed by nostalgia. The nostalgia filters out, or at the very least softens, anything unpleasant. What remains is a wonderful vision of home and childhood, emitting "rays of pure light" (*Laylat 'Urābā*, p. 163).

For the works under discussion the question of genre is less illuminating. Both works are carefully constructed narratives based on real-life experiences, people, places and emotions. "Fiction is true because it truly expresses aspects of human nature and experience. Autobiography is fictive in its turning to these forms in order to say whatever is more than commonplace."[48]

# 7

# Different Perspectives on Life in Iraq: Narratives in Hebrew

> The world of childhood is a timeless world which belongs more to the imagination than to reality, it is an experiential completeness that you cannot break into pieces or find in words. . . . I don't give much credence to stories from childhood, just as I don't give much credence to stories from dreams. I especially don't believe childhood stories of writers; those whose powers lie in fiction are less credible in conveying things as they actually were, and this is even more likely to be true about things from childhood.
>
> —Shimon Ballas

THE HOMES IN THE NARRATIVES DISCUSSED IN CHAPTER 6 SERVE TO separate inside from outside and childhood from adulthood. Inside all is warm and secure. Childhood is safe. It is only when threats from the outside can no longer be ignored that the glow of childhood begins to pale and the necessity of leaving home presents itself.

In the four works discussed in this chapter, most of the action takes place on the outside, away from home. The characters are older than those in the Arabic narratives, and the center of their life shifts away from the home. The threat to these characters and their community comes from the outside. The forces of modernization create an atmosphere inhospitable to the Jews. The rise of modern nationalism in its various guises—Nazi anti-Semitism, Iraqi nationalism and anti-

British sentiment, pan-Arabism, Zionism and the question of Palestine—changes the very nature of what once was home. Home itself ultimately proves to be the flimsily structured booth built for a temporary two thousand year-long harvest celebration, a booth that offers little protection from the outside world.

The works offer little nostalgia. The homes described in them are already on the verge of becoming not-home, and as such, provide less opportunity for idealization.

These "older" characters are approximately the same age as the adolescent protagonists of the *ma'abarah* novels. For all of them, the confusion created by puberty is intensified by their changing environs. Their lack of orientation arises from the once-familiar becoming unfamiliar. Home as presented here no longer provides enough protection against the outside and can no longer provide a sense of orientation.

These works present a different notion of "home" in Iraq than the narratives analyzed in chapter 6. All of them have been written in Hebrew. Except for Darwīsh, these writers turn to their childhood in Iraq only after dealing with their transition to Israel.

### *PHRAIM! PHRAIM!*

*Phraim! Phraim!*[1] was the first book-length work written by Shalom Darwīsh in Hebrew.[2] Twenty-seven years after his second collection appeared in Iraq, he published *Bayḍat al-Dīk* in Israel,[3] a collection of short stories written in Arabic. Several of the stories are set in Iraq, and were in fact written there.[4] The most obvious difference between these stories and their earlier counterparts published in Iraq is the use of Jewish markers in these later works. "Abū Liḥyah"[5] is the story of a religious man hired to teach the Jewish children in the *istadh* (the traditional religious school referred to in chapter 2). The later stories place their characters in Israel, where either romance (as symbolized by the Parker pen in "Romeo and Julia")[6] or calamity ("Tale of Misfortune")[7] has followed them. These stories continue the simple style and realistic vein of Darwīsh's earlier works.

*Phraim! Phraim!*, Darwīsh's first longer work, tells of a young girl in Iraq being married off at a very young age. In Iraq, as elsewhere in the Middle East, the principle of "the family good" is especially evident in family matters, and, above all, in arranging marriages. Unlike the custom among their Muslim neighbors, the Jews of Iraq required the bride's family to pay the entire dowry.[8] The demands from the groom's side could be quite costly, thereby placing a sizable burden on the shoulders of a family with several daughters. Marriage was more of a transaction than a matter of the heart. The son of a well-to-do family who would bring wealth to the bride's family through the marriage—or rarely, one who would waive the dowry—was a financial blessing to the whole family. In choosing the match, the collective good of the family took precedence over that of the individual.

The first page of the text remains "outside" the story narration and merely establishes the "truth-value" of what follows, recounting the incident that inspired the fictional account. The situation described in *Phraim! Phraim!* in which the girl Doris is engaged at nine and married off at twelve, is based on a real-life incident that occurred approximately sixty years ago. The bride was a young girl of eleven.

> Girls of nine, ten, were married, without a second thought . . . and they chased after them, and caught them. Seven, eight years old, they fled. . . . The gatekeeper at the kindergarten knew how to catch a little girl, and he would bring her back to the room.[9]

Shortly after the author's own wedding, he and his wife were guests at another wedding. His wife, aged seventeen, was summoned to the bride who had run away from the groom. She spoke to the bride for more than an hour (*Phraim! Phraim!*, p. 5). Curiously Darwīsh's wife's intervention is left out of the fictional account.

Doris narrates her story in her own voice. The structural units, whether phrases, sentences, or chapters, are short and relatively free of complex constructions. Descriptions of people focus on physical attributes, accentuating the unusual. The point of view is limited to hers. Her emotions are presented as pure: love for her Aunt Dinah, revulsion towards her fiancé Yehudah. Ambivalent feelings and subtle shadings are left for the reader to construe. The simplicity of the language, style, and structure add to her characterization. The language also creates irony in allowing the reader to understand more about what happens to her than she does.

Doris is, in effect, exiled from her childhood by the premature betrothal. Until that occasion, she enjoyed her childhood of going to school, playing with the other children, and, above all, spending time with her beloved David. All of these activities are abruptly put to an end when she is engaged to the suitor her sister has rejected. Yehudah is an albino who is much older than Doris. His close presence, his breath reeking of araq and tobacco, brings his reluctant fiancée to the point of nausea. However unappealing he is to the young girls, his wealth is attractive to their parents.

As mentioned, Doris's rebellious sister Rivka has refused to accept the husband her family has chosen for her. The parents of five daughters cannot afford to lose this wealthy suitor, and they overcome their misgivings through consultations with the rabbi, encouragement from the good Aunt Dinah, and an agreement to delay Doris's marriage to him until Doris reaches puberty. Doris herself is too young to lodge any serious protest. For her, the evening of the matchmaker's visit is merely another game of "dressing up," and all the attention that she receives is pleasing.

Although the actual marriage is to be postponed until Doris reaches puberty, she is treated like a bride from the start. The girl does not at first understand the implications of the betrothal. She sees it as a onetime event rather than a drastic change in her lifestyle. The day after she is presented to the matchmaker, she is forbidden to resume her usual activities (by the very aunt who initiated the situation): "Doris! From today onward you do not play in the street. You are a young lady now" (p. 34). The prohibition against joining her peers is not rescinded as the official betrothal nears. In response to Doris's reply that she is going out to play with the other children, her aunt cries: "What children? Tomorrow is the engagement. You must not be seen playing outside, do you hear? Go back to your room" (p. 38). The prohibitions are stricter after the ceremony. "After my betrothal I stopped going to school. I no longer went out to the street and played with the children. I no longer knew the pleasures of childhood" (p. 50). The ludicrous attempts to make Doris appear older meet with tenuous success. Aunt Dina stuffs a brassiere for the little girl and powders her face. She resembles, in her own words, "a dolled-up dwarf" (p. 45). Her tender age is neither disguised nor forgotten. Some spectators of the wedding procession throw rocks in protest and cry, "[S]he's a baby" (p. 93). They echo Aunt Dina's own words of "she's just a baby" to prevent the *haffāfah* (female equivalent of a barber) from removing Doris's nonexistent pubic hair.

Her youth and relative innocence make her a target for her envious older sisters. The sisters, perversely named Tovah (Good) and Mazal (Luck),[10] scare Doris with misinformation about menstruation and sexual intercourse. Whenever reminded of their comments, she reacts by vomiting, fainting, losing her appetite, and becoming weak.

When the marriage does finally take place, it does not transform Doris into a mature woman overnight. She continues to long for her childhood companion David and tries to recapture her childhood with varying degrees of success. She is very happy with the life-sized doll her husband Yehudah brings her (at the suggestion of his mother), yet she still wishes to play with children. Her own playroom is a lifeless substitute for the playground; expensive toys offer meager compensation for lonely days. At one point, she invites children much younger than she to come and play; she realizes that her peers have outgrown such activities by now. The six- and seven-year-olds are awkward playing in front of the sixteen-year-old matron, and the artificiality of the situation never fades. The maturity forced upon her remains superficial and only serves to retard her actual progress toward adulthood. Yet she clearly cannot recapture her lost childhood.

Only her mother-in-law seems to understand the situation from the beginning. She is more of a mother figure than Doris's own mother. She protects Doris from her son's advances during a prenuptial visit and keeps his ardor in check after the wedding. "What is your crime, what is your sin that adults have so betrayed you?" (p. 102). A pious woman, she tells her daughter-in-law stories from the Bible for entertainment. Doris herself identifies with the biblical ram sacrificed as a substitute for the patriarch Abraham's son Isaac.

Doris's first pregnancy causes great excitement: "A young girl doesn't bring a baby to the world every day" (p. 106). It ends in a miscarriage; she is not ready for motherhood. The mother-in-law hopes for a grandson to name after her deceased father, Phraim. However she does not want the baby to be an albino like her husband and her son. (Her disaffection for her late husband seems to be the reason for her alliance with Doris against her son.) She seems to condone Doris's rendezvous with David, promising her daughter-in-law: "I will stand by your side like a rock. I'll stop the tongues from wagging" (p. 114) if Doris gives birth to a non-albino child. Doris's first son, an albino, is named after Yehudah's father Menashe; her second is the eponymous dark-complexioned Phraim.

The story is framed by a prologue ("Reshit Ḥokhmah") and an epilogue ("Sof Davar"). In both, Doris professes, "Of all my children I love Phraim the most" (pp. 19, 159). The frame encloses the story in a circular narrative structure that begins and ends with the narrator's declaration of love for the title character.

Binarism is one of the major structural principles organizing the narrative. Doris and Rivka (the "good" sisters) are pitted against the nasty Tova and Mazal. The latter pair equate wealth with marital happiness; the former are passionate romantics. Rivka's love for Yūsuf parallels Doris's love for David; both are forbidden. The two sisters act as mediators for each other in their love affairs: Doris acts as lookout for Rivka and Yūsuf; Rivka arranges her sister's rendezvous with David. In the end, Doris convinces her parents to allow Rivka and Yūsuf to marry.

This play between similarity and difference resounds in other pairings. Both Aunt Dina and Yehudah's mother are much loved by Doris and play more significant roles in her life than her own mother. Why Aunt Dina is so adored by Doris remains a mystery. While Dina is a source of comfort to her niece, she is also the one who instigates and implements the plan to marry her off. This is part of the irony in the novel. Doris is too young to understand her aunt's betrayal. On the other hand, the mother-in-law has Doris's best interests at heart and even helps reunite Doris with her beloved David, betraying her own son. Doris is a simple woman, yet by reacting to her own lesson in "obedience" she is able to advise her older sister Rivka and help her achieve a happy ending. The binary structures are used to reflect a child's simplistic polar perceptions.

Along with the characters and their interactions, the attitudes toward sex also fit into the list of opposites and doubles. Sex is both pleasure and duty; child's play and adult obligation; desired and feared.

The children's game *bulbul khakh* and the stick used to play it serve intermittently as a multivalent leitmotif throughout the story.[11] It symbolizes Doris's days of carefree childhood, David's superiority over the other children (he is the neighborhood champion at the sport), and Phraim's resemblance to his father.

> The day Phraim lifted a big stick and tried unsuccessfully to bat a small stick into the distance was a day of celebration for me. I picked him up, hugged and kissed him, and promised him that he would succeed the next time. (P. 19)
>
> When Phraim was bigger I used to take him to play with the children in the field next to my father's house, and I wasn't satisfied until he began to grasp the big stick, and with it, bat the small stick into the distance. Ha, ho, hee! *Bulbul khakh.* (P. 159)

The sticks used in the game also symbolize the misinformation about sex with which Tova and Mazal would frighten their baby sister.

In addition to athletic prowess, the stick represents the fear of sex rooted in ignorance and nourished by spite. The stick, clearly a phallic symbol, is directly linked to Doris's view of David as well as her fear of Yehudah. The symbol of the stick ties together the prologue and epilogue, the son and his father, and the opposite faces of sex.

The tone of the novella is a clear departure from the tone of nostalgia in the works discussed in the previous chapter. It is very critical of the society and its traditions. The antinostalgic mood is given succinct expression in one particular incident. Doris remembers and longs for the sweets David used to bring her. She buys them and finds them a tasteless disappointment: "I must weep over my lost childhood" (p. 123). Sweeter in memory than in reality, the candy serves as a metonymical reference to childhood. The treat fails to evoke the happiness of earlier days and instead brings Doris to the realization that her childhood is gone forever.

Darwīsh reworked the memory of a personal experience into this novella by shifting from memoir to fiction, extending the incident, and developing the characters. He filled out the story with the background leading up to the wedding to explain the cause and effects of the situation. While finances in the form of the dowry are an important motivating factor, they are not the focus. The true story is one of growing up.

After mentioning his role (as observer) and his wife's (as observer-participant) in the introduction as an authenticating device, he does not include either in his account of the incident. Instead, he casts the bride as protagonist and presents the events from her point of view. The story is told in Doris's own voice. This is perhaps the most interesting choice by the author in transforming the core incident into a novella. This voice grants greater authenticity to the narrative and makes Darwīsh's achievement more impressive. It allows the author to get closer to the events described, while the use of Hebrew potentially creates distance. Both authorial choices—of narrative voice and language of narrative—accord more freedom to present the intimacies revealed. Darwīsh would have been more constrained by using a male voice as a third-person narrator, as he would have by writing in Arabic. He could no more have written such a frank account of a girl's sexuality in his mother tongue than he could have penned as severe a critique of the community in his motherland.

The story remains within the confines of the Jewish community. All of the characters in the story are Jewish, but this is an identification which, although central, is not an issue. Nor is the religious aspect discussed at any length. Opportunities for religious expression are not exploited; the description of the wedding focuses on the celebratory rather than the ceremonial; the occasion of Doris bearing sons passes without mention of a *brit milah* (circumcision). While the groom's mother is described as pious (and she is the only character whose religious life is mentioned), her piety takes the form of delight in biblical narratives. She offers these stories to Doris more for their entertainment value than for spiritual guidance.

Darwīsh returns to childhood, describing the Jewish community in Iraq as if it were frozen in time. While the presence of Yehudah's motorcar indicates that the story is set around the same time of political changes and fomentation, none of these sociopolitical events infiltrates the narrative. There is no indication that anything other than an early match (except, perhaps, the two oldest sisters) would disrupt Doris's happy childhood. Neither is there any hint that the Jewish community will not continue to exist as it did in the past.

Darwīsh, like the Arabic-writing authors we discussed, presents a picture of a stable, unchanging community. Like Naqqāsh's *Laylat 'Urābā,* his novella is not concerned with Jewish-Arab relations in Iraq nor the effects of modernization and secularization. He differs from Naqqāsh and Bar-Moshe in his unflattering perspective of the Iraqi Jewish community. Writing in Hebrew in Israel after living there thirty-five years, and in Doris's voice, permits him to assume this very critical and not at all nostalgic view.

## *BA'IR HATAḤTIT*

The stories published in Shimon Ballas' *Ba'Ir HaTaḥtit* (Downtown)[12] first appeared in *Mul HaḤomah* (In front of the wall)[13] with three stories added to the original collection.[14] They make use of a first-person participant narrator and are loosely connected by both setting and mood. The stories are arranged "chronologically" according to the approximate age of the narrator-protagonist, who may or may not be the same character in the different pieces. The last story in *Ba'Ir HaTaḥtit* features a middle-aged narrator who encounters many of the characters previously introduced. The collection is characterized by the blurring of the boundaries between the real and the surreal, its fracturing of time, and the ambiguity of memory in regard to fact and fiction.

The first story, "The Race" opens with the nightmarish scene of an old man, eyes dripping blood, who appears at the young narrator's window, demanding something to eat. The narrator recognizes the man from the beggars' lane on the way to school. In exchange for loose change, the beggars bestow blessings for good health and success in school.

One day the boy is late for school ("I don't now recall the reason why"). As he passes by the beggars, they are already counting the morning's receipts. They all start running after him. The blind old man grabs the boy, tells him to continue running to the synagogue (Sheikh Yiẓḥak), and bites him. As in the dreamlike episode that opened the story, the old man seems to be able to read the boy's thoughts. The old man accuses him of threatening to trip him (the boy's active thought). The boy feels powerless, as if he were tied to his bed. This description powerfully conveys the sense of dreaming and refers the reader back to the first scene. Suddenly the bells are pealing and he finds himself at the school gate.

The narration shifts between the worlds of dreaming and waking. "Even when I was awake," the narrator says, "it wasn't clear to me that the vision I imagined was not reality" (*Ba'Ir HaTaḥtit*, p. 7). The narrator shares this confusion with the reader. He works at establishing the realism of the central scene, yet does not leave the potential for rational explanations for what follows. Elements of the opening dream sequence recur and the scene concludes with astounding suddenness.

This story, like Darwīsh's *Phraim! Phraim!*, stands in contrast to the nostalgic tales of a safe and protected childhood. Ballas presents a nightmare of terror in which the protagonist suffers the loss of protection and control. The outside invades the house to the point where he is not safe even at home.

Several of the stories are narrated by a protagonist in his youth. He is somewhat politically active in the Communist underground, seemingly more out of boredom than ideological conviction. A mixture of ennui and uncertainty colors the mood.

In "Winds of February" a teenager with too much time on his hands becomes involved with politics because it is "the thing to do." His lack of commitment is demonstrated by his disinterest in reading the movement's pamphlets, his violation of its rules in the attempt to attract a girl he likes, and his belated visit to the coffeehouse for the Communists' weekly meeting. When he goes to the coffeehouse, the waiter tells him that the others haven't been there for days. His expendability has evidently been recognized by the leaders.

The story begins in the middle: "When Mahmoud told me, 'in the homes' and gave me the bundle I quickly nodded my head and said, 'I know'" (p. 20). It sets up the situation as if the narrator knows more than the reader. However, early on, the reader becomes aware that the reverse is true, as the narrator unwittingly reveals his ignorance. At every turn, he errs in trying to carry out the simple, straightforward distribution of pamphlets. He claims self-assurance ("I am different!"), but his hesitant actions reinforced by an arhythmic narrative style belie his claim. The story begins and ends with the winds of February bringing tears to his eyes. Despite the similarity, the winds of the ending are more biting, and the tears in the narrator's eyes are from disappointment as well as the cold.

"A Way of Parting" presents a series of episodes in which the twenty-one-year-old protagonist begins to say good-bye. He is due to report to the office of censorship the next day for receiving illegal publications from abroad. Conscious of an imminent departure, he passes his evening in a series of farewells. He parts from the Tigris, from his friend Sāmī, from the prostitute Salīmah. The narrative shifts between memories of the past and the present without clear markers. The reader's struggle to make sense of the fusion of time frames resulting from this technique echoes the protagonist's struggle to define his identity. He is similar to the character in the previous story who seeks relationships without commitment in politics and in romance. Again the mood is one of uncertainty; the protagonist is on the threshold of leaving without necessarily planning to leave.

"In Front of the Wall" plays with time to an even greater degree. The outer frame is set on a ship in the 1960s, but the other levels of the story take place in Iraq up through the 1940s. The story begins with the narrator-protagonist picking up a scrap of newspaper from the ship's deck and "recognizing" his boyhood friend Laṭīf. We find out later that Laṭīf was shot years ago in Iraq. The scrap brings back a rush of memories like a shuffled pile of old snapshots. Time is fractured and jumbled, lending an absurd air to the realistic fragments of memory. In quick succession, the narrative jumps from a walk with Laṭīf in front of the prison wall to visiting hours at the jail for political prisoners; from visits to his father in jail to visits with friends; from the conversation with a fellow passenger aboard ship to the shooting that killed Laṭīf. The dreamlike sequence of memories presents a dizzying challenge to the reader. The reader's need to unravel such a complex temporal web within the narrative mirrors the situation of the narrator-protagonist: Is it Laṭīf in the picture? The fellow passenger identifies the story that accompanies the photograph as an article about a ballet troupe, but finds no mention of the picture, whose solution remains a mystery.

The last story, which lends its title to the whole collection, invokes some of the elements from the previous stories, including the past made murky by the vagaries of memory. A middle-aged father of two, now living in Haifa, goes downtown to meet a long-lost friend from Iraq. The intensity of the rain is drawn in surrealistic terms; the taxi won't drive him close to the café because of the flooding; the situation prompts a torrent of memories. The narrator sees his friend in the window of the café, but when he gets there the host denies anyone else was there. The atmosphere of unreality is rooted in concrete tangible details.

"Aunt A'uni" is more of a portrait than a mood- or plot-oriented story. The title character is an Armenian woman from the narrator's old neighborhood. When he is four years old, the narrator is fascinated with her: the candy she gives him, her photographs, the mystery of her life, and her house that is often filled with company and strange-sounding singing.

At the age of six he moves from the old neighborhood and sees her on her way from church. "How much you've grown," she tells him. As the years pass, his world expands beyond the confines of the immediate neighborhood, and he becomes interested in other things. For her part, A'uni becomes less amazed by his growth. He begins to see her as fat and her husband as old; the narrator is clearly disenchanted.

As a high school student, he learns about Armenians and the "back to Armenia" movement. When he next sees her, he asks if she will go back. She asks how she can travel. She has no one left there (her family was murdered and her daughter taken to be a prostitute for the Turks before she was exiled with her husband). He carries her bundles back to her house for her and once again sees her photographs—a picture of her as a tiny, smiling cabaret singer, and a "new" photograph of her daughter. She acknowledges that he has grown up: "You're my son . . . when you first came you were a little boy . . . now you're a man."

The story might be interpreted as a relating to the plight of minorities in Iraq, or the tragedy of a people bereft of their own land, doomed to wander. Yet more than that it is a portrait of someone from his old neighborhood who was important to the narrator as a child,[15] as well as a story of growing up. The boy's maturing process is shown through his attitude toward A'uni. Unlike the works discussed above, the narrator offers a reevaluation of his childhood impressions, returning to the old neighborhood and encountering Aunt Aʿuni as he nears adulthood. The account is nonsentimental; it is devoid of nostalgic longings and coloration.

Most of the stories in this collection make subjective use of time, question the reliability of memory, and present reality as defined by one's perception of it. The dreamlike or nightmarish atmospheres are created from naturalistic details that accumulate and reach a level of surrealism. The emphasis in these stories is on conveying the mood of the Jewish community in Iraq on the eve of the exodus.

Home in these stories is a place that is not safe; it is a place where one has nightmares, a place that offers no safe haven for one's books or oneself. Outside of the home, where the majority of these stories take place, the streets are described as scary, cold, and forbidding. In one of the stories, the protagonist ends up *mul haḥomah* (in front of the wall), facing the prison, a grim inversion of home.

Political events lurk around the corners of these stories but are not directly confronted. The protagonists' participation in Communist activity—both a response to the changing political atmosphere and contributing factor to it—is limited to owning illicit publications and distributing pamphlets. Vaguely ominous signs, such as wintry weather, menacing beggars, displaced Armenians, and the prison, contribute to the sense of foreboding, but no specific incidents are mentioned. This is also true insofar as anti-Semitic acts or sentiments are concerned. While the protagonists are Jewish, this is indicated only by their names or other incidental details. By and large they are secular and seemingly unaffected by their Jewish identity. Other characters in these stories are Muslims and Christians; they too are identifiable by their names. No story in the collection, with the possible exception of "Aunt Aʿuni," focuses on the religious identity of its characters or religious differences among them.

The main characters suffer from alienation. They are shown alone, isolated, outside the family context, and with minimal interactions. There is no clear sense of the presence of a Jewish community nor of affiliation with it. The boy is chased by a beggar in "The Race"; the youth fails to connect with his "comrades" or communicate with the girl on whom he has a crush in "The Wind of February." The protagonist in "In Front of the Wall" loses contact with Laṭīf and others, just as the main character in "Baʿir HaTaḥtit" misses his reunion. Even in "Way of Parting," where the protagonist is intent on dissociating himself from his society, it does not seem to take much effort. His girlfriend stands him up. The most touching scene in the story is his encounter with a prostitute, and even then he spends most of the time alone on a bench waiting for her to finish with another client.

These stories are the beginning of a series of works in which Ballas explores exile as a metaphor for alienation. The next work he published, *Hitbaharut*[16] tells the story of an Iraqi Jew in Israel against the backdrop of war. His exclusion from participation in this war emphasizes his inability to fit into the society. The novel that followed, *Ḥeder Na'ul* (A locked room)[17] details the return of an Arab to Israel from Europe and his realization that he cannot make his home either in his village or in the city. Ballas's latest novels continue his examination of the alienation of the individual. *HaḤoref HaAḥaron* (The last winter)[18] is a roman à clef based on the life of Henri Curiel, a self-exiled Egyptian Jewish Communist. In *HaYoresh* (The heir)[19] Ballas constructs a complex multilayered mystery centering on the question of identity. The title of *LoBimkomah* (Not in her place)[20] summarizes the condition of the protagonist who moves between Tel Aviv and Paris, but has no real home, no place where she belongs. The first novella of *Otot HaStav*,[21] "Iyah" revisits the end of the Jewish community in Iraq. It retells the story from the perspective of a Muslim who served her Jewish employers long and well. Although facing an uprooting similar to that of the Jewish family, she remains an outsider even to the exodus.

### *SUFAH BEIN HADEKALIM*

Sāmī Michael's *Sufah Bein HaDekalim* (Storm among the palms)[22] and *Ḥofen Shel Arafel* (A handful of fog)[23] both deal with the changing atmosphere of Iraq in the 1940s. Like Ballas, Sāmī Michael moves the setting of his second book from the transit camp back to Iraq. Michael's novel for young adults,[24] *Sufah Bein HaDekalim*, describes the Farhūd, the 1941 riots against the Jews of Baghdad. The story is told in the third person from the perspective of Nūrī, a Jewish teenager living in Baghdad with his family. The narrative opens with the ominous sounds of drums in the night. The drums presage the overflowing of the Tigris and are played to warn people of imminent flooding. The drums also function on a symbolic level, warning our protagonist of impending doom. The warning signs become more literal and begin to pile up. Pro-Hitler slogans appear on the walls; Nūrī is mugged and cursed as a "bastard Jew," and his wristwatch is stolen; a Jewish peddler is trampled to death by crowds frenzied by the spurious rumor that he gave poisoned candy to non-Jewish children.

Not all of the warning signs come from impersonal or anonymous sources. Nūrī finds his Muslim friend Nā'if and his family on the verge of moving from the mixed neighborhood, so as not to be caught up in the expected violence. Their friendship cannot withstand the negative social pressures of the anti-Jewish environment. Soon after Nā'if moves, Nūrī and his friends encounter him at a local wedding celebration. Nā'if is now head of a gang of young thugs. Their fight moves from boyish play-fighting to an expression of hatred. "Take your Jews and go home," Nā'if orders his one-time friend, Nūrī. "Jewish dog," he shouts, "[S]ay 'I am a miserable dirty Jew' three times." (*Sufah Bein HaDekalim*, p.47–48). The atmosphere has not poisoned all such relationships. Nā'if's father is embarrassed by his son's behavior and apologizes to Nūrī. Nūrī stays friendly with the poor Muslim family who stay in the neighborhood.

The night the Farhūd begins, Nūrī and his younger sister are returning from a visit to their relatives (in honor of the Shavuot holiday). They find all the buses full and all the streets empty. As they start walking home, they run into a gang of barefoot youths brandishing knives. They escape by masquerading as fellow angry Muslims. Their neighbor, Nūrī's sweetheart Denise, is not so fortunate. She presumably meets her fate on the earlier bus that is attacked by the mob.

Several vignettes combine to present an impressionistic view of the ordeal: the young Asad, who dies sated and happy after feasting on laxatives and sugar-coated pills scavenged from a looted pharmacy; the resistance effort of the Jewish quarter (residents throwing furniture, bricks, and burning materials to repel the invasion); Nūrī's great-grandmother's heroic escape on a mule accepted as payment on her rental properties; Aunt Rachel seeking protection from her neighbor.[25] Rachel and her husband Haim turn to the biggest thug in the neighborhood, a man known for having murdered his first wife (among other crimes). Under his protection they pass the night and next day safely, and soon after they leave for Israel.

Nūrī and his family see them off.

> When the car [began to move away] Nūrī felt the earth move under his feet. He suddenly remembered his conversation with Jum'a, the guard . . . next to the railroad tracks the day after the flood. He had boasted then that the Jews had settled the land of Iraq even before the Arab tribes under the banner of Islam had burst forth from the

> desert and conquered the banks of the Euphrates and the Tigris. He believed that the Jews were set solid as a rock in the land of Iraq and that no force in the world could uproot them. And here the wheels of a truck leaving for the Land of Israel shook the land in which his fathers and forefathers had lived. He (suddenly) realized that the rock was not imbedded so deep. He felt the shaking of [the] truck. (P. 165)

The very fabric of society has changed. The norms of social order have broken down; looting and killing have become commonplace, acceptable behaviors during the chaos of those first two days in June 1941. Even more, anti-Jewish sentiment and hatred finds expression not only among the teeming masses of anonymous, hungry, barefoot youths but also divides Nūrī from his one time friend Nā'if.

Michael personalizes the Farhūd by showing it through the eyes of Nūrī, a very likable teenager who is both more engaged and more engaging than the characters in Ballas's stories. The tragic proportions of the event are conveyed in part by its juxtaposition with the more mundane concerns and interactions of Nūrī's daily life, such as the antics of his little sister. Focusing on the disappearance of Nūrī's friend Denise and her brother and on their father's search for them makes the many casualties more real.

Most of the story takes place outside, in the neighborhood and on the street. The neighborhood itself is mixed. Nūrī and Denise's families are both Jewish. The Jewish aspect of their identity is more explicit than in Ballas's stories and more of a factor than in Darwīsh's novella, but it is essentially an "ethnic" designation rather than expression of religious faith and practice. The Shavuot holiday celebration offers an opportunity for festive visits to relatives, but unlike Naqqāsh's narrative of Hoshana Raba no religious observances are mentioned. Because the story deals with characters more involved in the general Iraqi society, the anti-Semitic persecution is presented as incomprehensible and unjustified.

*Sufah Bein HaDekalim* displays an unusual choice of subject matter and tone for young adult readers. Michael's other book for younger readers, *Paḥonim VeḤalomot*,[26] treats the hardships of life in the *ma'abarah* in an optimistic manner, ending in an ode to the indomitable spirit of Grandmother Lulu. It is possible that Michael's softer tone in this depiction of life in the transit camp is due to a purging effect of having already written *Shavim VeShavim Yoter* rather than being influenced by its intended audience, whereas *Sufah Bein*

*HaDekalim* was Michael's first literary return to Iraq. It is true that Michael keeps the more horrific events at a distance; for example, he reports the death of the Jewish peddler by trampling but does not show it, and has the two neighbors disappear, rather than detailing their likely murder. Choosing to write about the Farhūd is a response to the growing body of literature on the Holocaust.[27] Without diminishing the horror of the Holocaust, Michael introduces the Israeli readership to the reality that Jewish suffering has not been limited to the Ashkenazim. The tragedies described in *Sufah Bein HaDekalim* are mitigated by episodes of humor and heroism, but the story ends on note of resignation. Members of Nūrī's family leave as the rich fabric woven by the Jewish community in Iraq begins to unravel.

### *ḤOFEN SHEL ARAFEL* (A HANDFUL OF FOG)

The second novel written by Sāmī Michael about life in Iraq before the exodus is directed to an adult audience.[28] The story takes place a few years after the Farhūd, on the eve of Israeli statehood. The novel focuses on Ramzī, a young Baghdadi Jew: his involvement in the Communist movement, his friendships with Jews and non-Jews, and his romantic involvements.

Ramzī's friendships cross religious and ethnic lines. His brother, Akram, asks him what will happen when his comrades in the movement discover that they are being led by a Jew to fight coreligionists. Ramzī shows him that they already know he is Jewish. It comes as no surprise to the reader, who has already encountered some of these Communists during the course of the narrative. Namīr, a Muslim, looks up to Ramzī as an older brother, his own brother having been killed when Namīr was only fourteen. George, a Christian, considers the question of religious identity irrelevant to his relationship with his Jewish friend. "I myself speak the Arabic of the Jews," he explains to his skeptical fiancée. "When I am with Ramzī he is not a Jew, I am not a Christian" (*Ḥofen Shel Arafel*, p. 172). He tells their mutual friend 'Alī: "He is Jewish just as I am Christian, only if you insist on sticking a cross on me" (p. 172).

George's family disagrees with him. His mother blames Ramzī ("a spoiled little Jew") for George's heresy and his arrest.[29] The prejudices of the older generation spill over to their children. George's wife calls him naïve for thinking that religion does not matter, saying, "It is good that there are Jews, it deflects [the Muslim's ill-will] from us" (p. 172).

His future brother-in-law dislikes Jews "because they will soon be despised" (p. 178). Even George's sister Suzanne, who has been in love with Ramzī for years, has realized the futility of such love because of the gap that exists between the different religious communities.

This is illustrated clearly in a short episode of innocent flirting. A young woman Ramzī meets on the bus cannot be dissuaded from continuing their nascent friendship despite Ramzī's best efforts. When he says it will never work, she asks is he married? a Sunni? mentally ill? She is even willing to entertain the idea of him being a Communist, but when he states that he is a Jew, she reluctantly concedes defeat. There is no hope for a romantic relationship between a Muslim and a Jew.

The narrative provides a realistic portrait of the diversity of the Iraqi Jewish community both in status and politics. Ramzī and his beloved Suhām come from middle-class Jewish families, living more or less comfortably. Suhām's uncle-turned-husband Sha'shū'a, a very successful businessman, represents the nouveaux riches. He buys solutions to his problems, paying a handsome dowry for a young attractive bride and financing his rival's escape from Iraq. Near the other end of the socioeconomic scale, Ramzī's grandparents and cousins still live in the traditional working-class quarters of the older Jewish neighborhood where the homes are built so close together that one can go the length of the alley by jumping from one rooftop to the next. Michael imbues the neighborhood with warmth and security. During the time when Ramzī hides in his aunt's house, the neighbors get together for Friday night (Shabbat) dinner on the rooftops. Hārūn, the lovesick neighbor whose cries rend the Sabbath quiet, is tolerated with gentle, teasing laughter. There is a place for everyone in the quarter, even a Communist seeking refuge from the authorities.

There is even a visit to Sha'shū'a's relatives who have moved to Teheran. Nazīm and Habība consider themselves superior to the local (Iranian) Jews and prefer to befriend the Bahai millionaires. Sha'shū'a, on the other hand, has difficulty with their abandonment of some of the traditional Sabbath observances.

The responses to the Farhūd and to the increasingly tense atmosphere of Iraq in the forties vary among the Jewish characters. Michael uses Ramzī's family to illustrate this diversity. While Ramzī's involvement in the Communist Party takes center stage in the novel, his two brothers represent alternative reactions to the changing texture of Iraqi society. Akram has joined the underground Zionist movement and is apparently involved with HaShurah, the defense branch of the illicit organization (rather than education, recruitment, or illegal immigration). The oldest of the three brothers, Baruch, works in his father's business, rejecting any political challenge to what he sees as merely a temporary setback in the two thousand-year-old history of the Babylonian Jewish community.

Ironically, it is the Communist brother who is the first to leave for the infant country of Israel. He is the only one who has predicted the end of the Jewish community: "Everything has changed. Once there is an Israel we will be hated aliens in the country where we have buried our ancestors" (p. 230).

Despite Ramzī's avowed secularism, his Jewish identity becomes more and more important to him and the novel as the story progresses. The inclusion of characters from other religious backgrounds serves to highlight that of Ramzī, as do the discussions mentioned above concerning these characters' differences and relationships. While Ramzī never tries to deny or hide his Jewishness, his primary identification is "Iraqi." In the end, he is forced to admit the failure of the Iraqi identity as a viable option for him. While he lives as a Communist, he seeks refuge as a Jew: first in the traditional Jewish quarter with his aunt, and ultimately in the newly established Jewish state of Israel.

While neither as definitively antinostalgic in tone as Darwīsh's *Phraim! Phraim!*, nor as nightmarish as Ballas's *Mul HaḤomah* or Michael's own *Sufah Bein HaDekalim*, the representation of home is far from idyllic. Home is not the safe, secure universe of the works by the Jewish authors who write in Arabic. Rather Ramzī must flee from home, from both the family house and his homeland.

*Ḥofen Shel Arafel* brings up many issues—of loyalty and friendship, commitment and fear—and presents a rich array of ethnographic details of life in Iraq before the mass emigration of the Jews. Ultimately, however, it is about leaving a place that one can no longer call home.

Like Ballas, Michael goes on to explore other forms of exile and marginalization in his later works. *Ḥasut*[30] describes a group of Arab and Jewish Communists in Haifa against the backdrop of the Yom Kippur War. The diversity of the characters' religious and ethnic backgrounds, as well as of their political viewpoints is similar to that in *Ḥofen Shel Arafel*. Mardukh, a character who comes to dominate the book in Ramzī's absence, comes from a past similar to Ramzī's and could indeed be an older version of him. His gratitude for the refuge offered him by Israel leads to a complex web of relationships and interdependencies. Michael's next novel, *Haẓoẓrah BaVadi,*[31] tells of the romance, with all its twists and ironies, between an Arab Israeli woman of Christian faith and a Russian Jewish immigrant. In these novels, he pursues his literary inquiry into the forms and flavors of the experience of exile and the process of belonging. His latest novel *Victoria*[32] spans the life of the title character from her childhood in the Jewish ghetto of Baghdad on the eve of modernization through her old age in Israel. While overlapping much material in his earlier novels and other writers' works discussed above, it is chiefly remarkable for its lack of nostalgia and the demythologization of the Mizraḥi Jewish family.[33]

## CONCLUSION

The portrayal of Iraq as presented in these works differs from the stories of childhood written in Arabic. The main characters are older—or, at least in Doris's case, cast in a more adult role. The balance of each work takes place outside, away from the secure shelter of home. Doris's story takes place inside to a greater extent, yet neither her parents' home (from which she has been married), nor her husband's (which is described as forbiddingly grand) offers the same warmth or security as the *sukkah* or the *bayt fī Baghdād*. Doris enjoys her happiest moments on the playground, and no indoor playroom, however opulent, can serve as a substitute. In *Ba'Ir HaTaḥtit* the first protagonist's nightmarish encounter with the beggar is realized in the streets and alleys on his way to school; the wanderings of the disaffected youths cover the streets of Baghdad; the middle-aged Iraqi journeys through the streets of Haifa to meet his friend from the past. Nūrī roams outside his neighborhood for his adventures in *Sufah Bein HaDekalim*; the political involvement of Ramzī in *Ḥofen Shel Arafel* takes him to Kurdistan and elsewhere, finally to seek refuge in another country.

In the short stories by Ballas and in Michael's novel *Ḥofen Shel Arafel* home is not safe, due in part to the characters' involvement in Communist activities and the changing political climate. This contrasts with the view Yiẓḥak Bar-Moshe presents in his autobiographical *Khurūj Min Al-'Iraq,*[34] covering the same time period in Iraq. In this work, the first-person narrator offers his home as a safe haven to a friend with Communist leanings. Home is not safe for Communist characters in Ballas and Michael's stories. Ultimately, however, the arrests and persecutions are not based on political views but religious affiliation.

The religious aspect of the characters' Jewish identity is of such little significance as to be nearly irrelevant. Their primary identification as Jews is imposed on these characters from the outside. As the story takes place further away from home the outside, the increasingly hostile political climate intrudes more and more. The characters themselves are forced by these external pressures to become more aware of what it means to be Jewish in relation to the outside (non-Jewish) world.

The Jewish dimension of the lives of these characters is mostly downplayed in these works, as is Jewish communal life, except for the inclusion of a wedding scene in several of the works. A wedding is generally a joyous shared event, celebrating the pinnacle of harmony and the continuation of the community. Like most rites celebrating major life-cycle transitions, weddings give opportunities for religious expression. In *Phraim! Phraim!* the wedding is a catalyst for the rest of the novella. Instead of welcoming a happy couple to a new life it is seen as a near-tragedy exiling the child bride from her childhood. In *Sufah Bein HaDekalim* the wedding takes place outside of the Jewish community. It shows both the past norm of those from different religious communities joining together to share celebrations and the new atmosphere that no longer fosters coexistence. The wedding that begins the narrative of *Ḥofen Shel Arafel* excludes the protagonist as his childhood sweetheart leaves him behind.[35] The weddings in these works are no more joyous than home is safe. These illusions are shattered.

The stability and permanence described by Bar-Moshe and Naqqāsh have given way in these narratives to change and uncertainty. The irrevocable change that occurs in Doris's life is imposed on her by her family. The protagonists in Ballas's collection of stories share feelings of fear and doubt. Michael's novels also present the world of their main characters on the threshold of change. Each book ends with leavetaking; Nūrī stays behind in *Sufah Bein Hadekalim,* while Ramzī finds himself leaving forever.

These non-nostalgic works were written by the same group of writers who first wrote the *ma'abarah* novels, those who chose Hebrew as their literary tongue. Those authors who chose not to hold on to Arabic are also less likely to hold on to the past or idealize it. Their departure from Arabic and from the past is a leavetaking similar to that of their characters. It is as if the decision to write in an acquired language precludes the nostalgic mood. Hebrew will be less evocative of a time experienced in an Arab context and thereby less prone to nostalgia. The audience too is less likely to participate in nostalgia for an unfamiliar past.

These writers write without nostalgia because they are looking at Iraq when it is no longer home. Their protagonists are only beginning to become aware of this, but the writers clearly show that it is the beginning of the end. They write about the recognition of the inability of Jews to keep Iraq as their home, returning to their past to understand how these roots became extirpated.

Darwīsh waited to write his story until he felt he had the tools with which to write. It is quite likely that he would not have written this story in Iraq or in Arabic. His novella deals with the society described by Bar-Moshe and Naqqāsh—insulated from outside forces—in a manner more similar to that adopted by Michael and Ballas.

The works by Ballas and Michael discussed in this chapter are not their first works in Hebrew. In writing about the *ma'abarah,* they mirrored their own transition. Only once they felt more at home in Hebrew and in Israel could they return to Iraq in their work.[36] This may also explain why they then could be so critical of what was once "home."

Michael and Ballas are also continuing their earlier agenda in writing the transit camp novel: to explain to the non-Iraqi Hebrew audience as well as to themselves from whence they came and why. This helps answer why they focus on the time when everything begins to disintegrate, and why Michael also wrote the book he did for young adults. Just as the *ma'abarah* novels are novels of transition, so these works set in Iraq mark another transition in the writers' continuing exploration of the meaning of exile and the question of identity.

While there is no room for nostalgia in these accounts of life in Iraq before the mass emigration there is, perhaps, a sense of wistfulness, an acknowledgment of the momentousness of the change. This change affects not only the individual but the history of an entire community.

# 8

# Conclusion

THIS BOOK HAS EXAMINED A GROUP OF WRITERS WHO MOVED FROM ONE culture to another—from Iraq to Israel—and their writing. After looking into the factors causing this move and the culture left behind, the study went on to explore the issues raised by this move and its expression in their writing. These issues—choices of language, genre, and topics; considerations of audience; and literary contributions—are inextricably linked with each other in parallel, complementary, and causal relations.

One of the first issues in deciding (to continue) to write in Israel was the choice of language: whether to write in the language of their former culture or their new culture. An author's reasons for choosing one language over another are complex and often highly individual; however, there are similarities among those writers who have made the same choice. While I use the word "choice" in discussing the issue of language, it implies more volition than may actually exist. The writers who have stayed with Arabic seem to have done so because of their attachments to their mother language and because of what the writers perceive as their inability to replicate these ties. For those writing in Hebrew, their relation to both the world around their source material and that of their target audience is dominant. In both cases, the "literary appropriateness" of the language chosen and its inherent qualities are overshadowed by the above-mentioned considerations. The writers' perceptions of the past and the transition to Israel influence what they choose to write about as well as in which language.

Intuitively, the language in which the work is written becomes an inherent quality of the work, inseparable from the form and content.

> For although we may, albeit reluctantly, accept the idea that a work, at least a work of prose, can be more or less adequately translated into another language, we balk at the notion that it could, indifferently, have been written in a language other than the original one.[1]

Shimon Ballas initially attempted to translate a work he had written in Arabic into Hebrew. After completing the first chapter, he abandoned the procedure and began again, writing what was to become *HaMaʿabarah* in Hebrew. Both Shalom Darwīsh and Sāmī Michael have addressed entirely different concerns in their Hebrew works than in their earlier Arabic stories. Michael left behind the buffoonery of his first pieces. Darwīsh became freer and more explicit in his social criticism.[2]

Samīr Naqqāsh and Yiẓḥak Bar-Moshe have taken very different approaches to adapting Arabic for writing in their new home. Bar-Moshe simplifies the idiom in a style approaching the journalistic. Naqqāsh takes advantage of the complexity of the language to add to the many layers of meaning in his dense and reference-laden narratives. However, the degree of linguistic sophistication in his writing is taken to an extreme, resulting in a failure of communication.

The choice of language also has a less direct role in shaping the literary work. I have suggested ways in which it may influence the content of the work. Those writers who chose to write in Hebrew wrote their first novels about the transit camp experience. They present the trials of the new immigrant to Israel in a direct manner, thus giving rise to a new subgenre: *sifrut hamaʿabarah*, a literature of transition. These writers show a willingness to bring issues raised by the *maʿabarah* experience to the attention of the Israeli readership. Through these novels they confront the reality of the present (or the more recent past). While the various crises are described as specific to the Iraqi-born newcomer in the early years of the state of Israel, they also represent the crises encountered by immigrants in general. These crises—economic, social, religious, moral, cultural—arise from the differences between the two societies (motherland/home and exile/refuge) and cause the crisis of identity. Adolescence is used as a central metaphor for the condition of the migrant; both teenagers and uprooted immigrants stand on the brink of a new identity that they themselves must synthesize from their past and present.

These narratives present characters who respond to the identity crisis in a variety of ways. The strategies range from rejecting the new or the old to attempting to merge the two. Only this last option meets with any degree of success. These are the characters—Shā'ūl in *Shavim VeShavim Yoter*, Yosef in *HaMa'abarah*, and, we are led to believe, Nūrī in *Tarnegol Kaparot*—who deny neither their Iraqi past nor their Israeli present. Their attempts to reconcile the conflict between the two lead to the formation of an integrated identity.

Israeli institutions central to the process of socialization—the *ma'abarah* (transit camp), army, and kibbutz—are both background for the stories and subjects for scrutiny. While the army appears to succeed as a means of integration where the kibbutz fails, all three institutions allow the characters to begin to formulate an Israeli identity and allow the readers to probe the nature of this identity.

*Sifrut hama'abarah* introduces a new kind of identity to Hebrew literature. Stories of the Generation of 1948 present the sabra hero, the native-born builder and defender of the land. The literature of the next generation, the New Wave, offers the hero's fictional son, the sabra antihero. The characters of the transit camp come from outside the Ashkenazi-based sabra model and lineage; their fathers were not there to build or to defend the land. Their exile is neither the national exile brought to an end by the heroes in the works from the War of Independence generation nor the existentialist exile suffered by their successors, but a very real and personal one.

Those choosing to continue writing in Arabic return to their lost childhood in an attempt to prolong the past. They travel back in time through their remembrances, recovering the past and bringing it to the present through narrative. The subjective reconstruction of the past—the nostalgia lurking in the shadows—is not denied. These are personal accounts of the lost Garden of Eden, of home. The description of home in these narratives defines exile, for home is everything exile is not. Home is childhood, while exile is adolescence; home is the past, exile the present; home is stability, rootedness, continuity, and order, while exile is discontinuity, transience, and chaos. Home is the memory and exile the reality.

The narratives of Iraq written in Hebrew describe the area between home and exile. They offer a different view of life in Iraq from the Arabic works: of home no longer safe, of a permanence unraveling.

The stories take place mostly outside of the actual home and tell of leave-taking. This in-between stage—of knowing one is on the verge of leaving—offers a view of home without the nostalgia. While Darwīsh describes a society at least as insulated and unchanging as that portrayed by Bar-Moshe and Naqqāsh, his depiction is with as critical a pen as that of Ballas and Michael. The authors write with the hindsight that these are the final days of the Jewish community in Iraq; their protagonists are only starting to become aware of this. Home is on the verge of becoming not-home, and the tone—realistic, critical, nightmarish—reflects the changing moods. The tone of these works speaks to the successful resocialization of the authors themselves in Israel. Their adaptation to Israeli society enables them to reject nostalgia for Iraqi and Jewish Iraqi society. This does not, of course, preclude Michael and Ballas from continuing to view Israeli society in the critical manner of their *ma'abarah* novels.

The language decision also contributes to the definition of audience, potential and actual, and consequently to the readings given these works. Considerations of audience also differ according to the language. The Hebrew author is encouraged by the publishing industry to be concerned with marketability; the author of a work in Arabic must find a sponsor for a vanity press and may target a more specific following.

The type of work written coincides with the language in which it is written. The language of the work correlates with its place on the autobiography—fiction continuum rather than in terms of length-identified narrative genres (short story, novella, novel). Yiẓḥak Bar-Moshe is alone in identifying his roughly chronological assortments of vignettes as memoir, although he also suggests categorizing it as either a collection of short stories or as a novel. Samīr Naqqāsh's work clearly has elements of autobiography, while Darwīsh crafts into a fictional mode an incident he establishes as personally experienced. Shimon Ballas writes stories about his childhood but then casts doubt on their authenticity by the afterword. Sāmī Michael, Eli Amir, and Shimon Ballas all write about the transit camp from a position of personal experience in the best tradition of "write about what you know," but they do not write these novels as memoirs or autobiography.[3] The works in Arabic are more closely based on real life, almost as if the exercise of writing is intended for the writer's self and for no other audience. The Hebrew authors exploit the distancing quality of fiction, reaching for an outside audience.

The Hebrew authors write, in part, to educate those who do not come from similar backgrounds. They write of the horrors that befell them before the exodus—tragedy was not a monopoly of the European Jews—and the indignities and hardships suffered upon their arrival in Israel. Their accounts of the early transition period as newcomers call the veteran settlers to task.

The contribution of the Iraqi Jewish writers to Hebrew literature is comparable to the contribution the Jews made to modern Iraqi literature before their departure. Like their predecessors they use the literary tools of the majority culture. Unlike them, however, they are not actively developing these tools but accept those developed in the previous generation. Their writing is less central to their contemporary literary scene than was that of the Jewish literati of Baghdad because of this more conservative style. Their importance lay in their presentation of perspectives alternative to the mainstream Ashkenazi voice in modern Israeli literature. At a time when the future of Zionism is being questioned, they ask about its present and its past. In a society based on the principle of the ingathering of the exiles, they explore the exiles of the ingathered. The greatest collective achievement of the Jewish writers from Iraq is the creation of a new literary subgenre that focuses on the experiences and issues at the core of Israeli society.

The contribution made by the Arabic-writing authors to both Arabic and Israeli literatures is considerably more limited due to the lack of readers and the subsequent marginality. Few readers have both the language skills and interest to read about the Iraqi Jewish experience in the Arabic language. Despite the paucity of readers, these works do add to the diversity in both literatures, and they document a world that no longer exists.

The Jewish writers made great contributions to the national literary renaissance in Iraq in the early part of the century. Now in Israel they and their literary descendants serve as an important cultural bridge between Arabic and Hebrew literatures, and between European and Middle Eastern Jews. Within this group of Israeli writers from Iraq, there are many voices. As a group, however, they have given expression to the thoughts and feelings of a generation of Israeli readers and have helped broaden the scope beyond cultural hegemony. They present another, less uniformly joyful reaction to the 1948 War of Independence. While the victory was a cause for celebration among the Jews in Palestine, the founding of the State of Israel had negative consequences for Jewish communities in other Middle Eastern countries.

Similarly, the realization of the Zionist dream of "ingathering the exiles" affects those dreaming and realizing. For some, moving to Israel (realizing) is not coming home but leaving home. The Zionist homeland is exile from their native lands and childhood memories—an exile from exile. It is not a negation of Zionism, but rather an acceptance of the personal experience.

In contrast to the Jewish conceptions of exile and redemption discussed in chapter 1, this literature has precedents within the tradition. Jews have used the language of exile *(galut)* to express forced separation not only from Zion but also from a homeland in the Diaspora to which they felt a strong emotional attachment, such as Spain.[4] So, too, the "return" to Israel was not necessarily redemption for the Jews of Iraq but—at least temporarily—a "Second Babylonian Exile."[5] The Jewish notion of exile is the context by which this literature realizes its irony and its power.

The literature of these writers comprises another chapter in exile literature. Many of the same themes, issues, and strategies of exile literature from around the world find expression in the works of the Israeli writers from Iraq. Exile may serve as a metaphor for life in the modern era, for alienation from oneself and others; but it is also a literal condition: alienation from one's roots. The literature of these writers has redefined the concept of exile, placing it between the Jewish notion of exile as a national condition and the modern metaphor of human alienation. Exile is a personal experience even when shared by a community.

Until recently the literature of the Iraqi Jewish writers in Israel has been all but ignored. This study has identified and examined a literature of exile within the Israeli Jewish context. It has looked at a group of writers and their works previously unexplored and unmentioned in the linear model of Israeli literature. Perhaps this study will contribute to revising this model to include voices from the margins.

The Iraqi-born writers are among the first to challenge the European bias of the Israeli canon. They are not an aberration but a beginning. It is to be hoped that their contributions will be appreciated in their own right, and will open the canon to the voices of other Middle Eastern Jews and of more recent immigrants.

# Notes

## CHAPTER 1. EXILE, LITERATURE, AND JEWISH WRITERS

1. Paul Tabori, *The Anatomy of Exile* (London: Harrap, 1972), p. 27. "What sets exile fundamentally apart from other types of migration with their possible permutations and developments is that departure is involuntary and return impossible." Leon Grinberg and Rebeca Grinberg, *Psychoanalytic Perspectives on Migration and Exile*, trans. Nancy Festinger (New Haven: Yale University Press, 1989), p. 2.

2. *The American Heritage Dictionary* (1973), s.v. "Exile."

3. Edward Said, "Reflections on Exile," 7 March 1984, University of Pennsylvania. Public lecture.

4. Mary McCarthy, "Exiles, Expatriates and Internal Emigres," *Listener* 86 (25 November 1971): 706.

5. "Exile is the noble and dignified term, while refugee is more hapless. At one point in your flight you may be a refugee and later, covered with honours, turn into an exile." Ibid.

6. Andrew Gurr, *The Writer in Exile: Creative Use of Home in Modern Literature* (Atlantic Highlands, N.J.: Humanities Press, 1981), p. 10. Tabori has suggested that the Spanish word for exile, *destierro* (deprived of one's land), be extended, by analogy, to *destiempo* (deprived of one's time). Tabori, *Anatomy*, p. 32.

7. Said, "Reflections on Exile."

8. Lloyd S. Kramer, "Exile and European Thought: Heine, Marx, and Mickiewicz in July Monarchy Paris," *Historical Reflections* 11, no. 1 (Spring 1984): 48.

9. Robert Edwards, "Exile, Self and Society," in *Exile in Literature*, ed. Maria-Ines Lagos-Pope (Lewisburg, Pa.: Bucknell University Press, 1988), pp. 15–31.

10. Tabori, *Anatomy*, p. 30. See also Mahnaz Afkhami, "Women, Revolution, and Exile: Oral History," University of Pennsylvania, Conference on Iranian Women's Studies, 11 November 1989: "You begin to translate yourself so you become comprehensible to the new culture . . . [by doing so you then] become unfamiliar to yourself."

11. Tabori, *Anatomy*, p. 31.

12. Dr. Wittlin as cited by Tabori, in ibid, p. 32.

13. See, for example, Robert Edwards, "Exile, Self," p. 20; Claudio Guillén. "On the Literature of Exile and Counter-Exile," *Books Abroad*, Spring 1976, 272.

14. E.g., Elias Canetti, Czeslaw Milosz, Isaac Bashevis Singer, Vladimir Nabokov, Samuel Beckett, Pablo Neruda, Juan Ramon Jimenez, Miguel Angel Asturias. Lagos-Pope, *Exile in Literature*, p. 7.

15. Ewa Thompson, "The Writer in Exile: Playing the Devil's Advocate," *Books Abroad*, Spring 1976, 326.

16. David Williams, "The Exile as Uncreator," *Mosaic* 8 (Spring 1985): p. 11.

17. See the discussion of Claudio Guillén's notion of the literature of counterexile below.

18. For example, Samīr Naqqāsh. See below, chapter 4.

19. An instance would be Joseph Conrad. He wrote of English adopting him in "A Personal Record," as quoted in Sanford Pinsker, *Languages of Joseph Conrad* (Amsterdam: Rodopi, 1978), p. 10.

20. Asher Z. Milbauer, *Transcending Exile: Conrad, Nabokov, I. B. Singer* (Gainesville: University Press of Florida, 1985), p. xii.

21. Manoucher Parvin, "Iranian Fiction Writers Writing in a Second Language," Middle East Studies Association Meeting, Toronto, Canada, 17 November 1989.

22. Thus Isaac Bashevis Singer has continued to write in Yiddish in order to remain faithful to the memory of millions of killed Yiddish speakers. His 1978 Nobel lecture, delivered in Yiddish, began with a tribute to the language: "The high honor bestowed upon me by the Swedish academy is also a recognition of the Yiddish language—a language of exile, without a land, without frontiers. . . . Yiddish is the wise and humble language of us all, the idiom of frightened and hopeful humanity." Cited in *The Jewish Almanac*, ed. Richard Siegel and Carl Rheins (New York: Bantam, 1980), p. 435.

23. For example, the Iranian novelist Mashid Amershah-i.

24. Ngugi wa Thiong'o, for instance, decided to return to his own tribal language (Kikuyu) after writing his well-acclaimed works in English, including *Petals of Blood*.

25. Ewa M. Thompson, "Writer in Exile," pp. 327–28: "[F]or a certain category of writers at least, exile can be a good thing. It can stimulate rather than lull the writer's sensibility." See also Walter Benjamin, "The Task of the Translator," in *Illuminations* (New York: Schocken, 1969), pp. 80–81.

26. Czeslaw Milosz, "Notes On Exile," *Books Abroad,* Spring 1976, 284.

27. Vladimir Nabokov, *Strong Opinions* (New York: Putnam, 1951), p. 54.

28. Taghi Modaressi, "Iranian Writers Writing in a Second Language," Middle East Studies Association, Toronto, Ontario, 17 November 1989.

29. Pinsker, *Languages of Joseph Conrad,* p. 11.

30. See the discussion on Shimon Ballas and Sāmī Michael below.

31. Milbauer, *Transcending Exile,* p. 8.

32. Milbauer points out the irony that Nabokov makes contact with a new audience through a novel, *Pnin* (Garden City, N.Y.: Doubleday, 1957), that is about the constant failures of an exiled intellectual to communicate. With this book he establishes contact with a new country as well as new countymen. Milbauer, *Transcending Exile,* p. 60.

33. Thomas A. Kamla, *Confrontation with Exile: Studies in the German Novel* (Frankfurt: Peter Lang, 1975), p. 14.

34. My definition clearly embraces both conditions; see p. 6.

35. Joseph Strelka, "The Novel in Exile: Types and Patterns," in *Exile: The Writer's Experience,* ed. John M. Spalek and Robert F. Bell (Chapel Hill, North Carolina: University of North Carolina Press, 1982).

36. Claudio Guillén, "On the Literature," pp. 271–80. "In the [literature of counterexile] . . . exile is the condition but not the visible cause of an imaginative response often characterized by a tendency toward integration, increasingly broad vistas or universalism" (p. 272).

37. See for example Michael Seidel's discussion in his book *Exile and the Narrative Imagination* (New Haven: Yale University Press, 1986).

38. Ibid., p. x.

39. Eva Hoffman, *Lost in Translation: A Life in a New Language* (New York: Penguin, 1989), pp. 115–16.

40. Arnold M. Eisen, *Galut: Modern Jewish Reflection on Homelessness and Homecoming* (Bloomington: Indiana University Press, 1986), p. xiv.

41. H. H. Ben-Sasson, "Galut," in *Encyclopedia Judaica* (1972), preceded by *Jewish Encyclopedia* (1904) and *Encyclopaedia Judaica* in German. See also pp. 162 (#14), 165 (#59), and 167 (#22).

42. The two words are not completely synonymous. *Diaspora* stresses the scattering of the Jewish people in different lands while *galut* emphasizes the banishment from Zion.

43. Eisen makes a similar point, perhaps with greater elegance and certainly in greater detail, in his discussion of the Genesis narratives. He emphasizes the word *dispersion* in relation to the story of the Tower of Babel. This is especially important in the context of Jewish exile. He adds expulsion, insecurity, homelessness, and estrangement from the land to the qualities I highlight in my interpretation. Eisen, *Galut,* pp. 4–7.

44. Gen. 11:7 (The Jerusalem Bible).

45. Ben-Sasson, "Galut."

46. For a discussion of the dimensions of time versus space in Judaism and Jewish exile, see Étan Levine's introduction, "The Jews in Time and Space," in Levine, *Diaspora: Exile and the Contemporary Jewish Condition* (New York: Shapolsky Books), pp. 1–14.

47. Ben-Sasson, "Galut."

48. Levine, *Diaspora*, p. 2.

49. See, for example, Eisen's discussion of the Mishnaic tractate *Avodah Zarah*, in *Galut*, chap. 3.

50. David Biale, *Power and Powerlessness in Jewish History* (New York: Schocken, 1986), pp. 37–38. Biale suggests that this view of exile as "ennobling punishment" may show the influence of Christianity.

51. Michael Selzer, *Wineskin and Wizard* (New York: Macmillan, 1970).

52. Jacob Klatzkin in Eisen, *Galut*, p. 97.

53. Marc Saperstein points out that this widely accepted formulation never appears in the Bible or anywhere in rabbinic literature; it is always *or goyim*. Personal communication, 3 July 1994, St. Louis, Missouri.

54. Gershom Scholem in Eisen, *Galut*, p. 53. See also Shalom Rosenberg, "Exile and Redemption in Jewish Thought in the Sixteenth Century: Contending Conceptions," in *Jewish Thought in the Sixteenth Century*, ed. Bernard Dov Cooperman (Cambridge: Harvard University Press, 1983), pp. 399–430. In addition to theories of mission, *tikkun*, and alienation, Rosenberg adds the later concept of "exile as sin." This last view resonates until today.

55. Rosenzweig in Eisen, *Galut*, pp. 107–8.

56. Moshe ben Maimon (Maimonides) in Yitzhak F. Baer, *Galut*, trans. Robert Warshow (New York: Schocken, 1947), p. 36.

57. Jacob Neusner, *Self-fulfilling Prophecy: Exile and Return in the History of Judaism* (Boston: Beacon Press, 1987).

58. Ibid., pp. 2–4ff. "To be Israel in a genealogical sense is to have gone into exile and returned to Zion" (p. 34).

59. Heckelmann in Levine, *Diaspora*, p. 67: "[E]xile serves as a special spur to creativity. . . . Indeed, exile is fundamental to the Jewish condition." See also Ben-Sasson, "Galut." For an interesting counterpoint, see Ross Brann, "Tavniyot Shel Galut BeKinot ʿIvriyot VeʿAraviyot BeSefarad," in *Sefer Yisrael Levine: Kovez̧ Meḥkarim BaSifrut HaʿIvrit LeDoroteiha*, ed. Reuven Tzur and Tovah Rosen (Jerusalem: Makhon Katz, 1994), pp. 45–61. In his article Brann discusses examples of the literature lamenting the exile from Spain in relation to the "infinite exile of the people Israel from the land of Israel" (p. 47). See also Brann, *The Compunctious Poet: Cultural Ambiguity and Hebrew Poetry in Muslim Spain* (Baltimore: Johns Hopkins University Press, 1991).

60. Ben Halpern, "Exile and Redemption: A Secular Zionist View," *Judaism* 29, no. 2 (Spring 1980): 180.

61. Eisen, *Galut*, p. 50. Eisen credits Spinoza and Mendelssohn with a radical transformation of the conception of *galut* (demystification and universal-

ization, respectively). Biale argues that Spinoza emphasizes the political aspect of Judaism and the need for a state in order to exist. Biale, *Power,* pp. 113–15. These ideas enabled the modern Zionist appropriation of the concept from the spiritual and its transfer to the political realm. Eisen, *Galut,* p. 64.

62. Shlomo Avineri, *The Making of Modern Zionism: The Intellectual Origins of the Jewish State* (New York: Basic Books, 1981), pp. 8–10.

63. The Haskalah movement worked to end the state of exile by making the place of exile into home; modern Zionism dismissed this as a viable option.

64. Simon Rawidowicz, "On the Concept of *Galut,*" in *Israel: The Ever Dying People* (Rutherford, N.J.: Fairleigh Dickinson University Press, 1986), p. 97.

65. See Deut. 28; Eisen, *Galut,* p. 29.

66. The negative image of the Diaspora Jew "bears the imprint of anti-Semitic stereotypes." Charles S. Liebman and Eliezer Don-Yehiya, *Civil Religion in Israel* (Los Angeles: University of California Press, 1983), p. 37.

67. Ibid., p. 139.

68. Paradoxically, the idea of Jewish nationalism was based on the desires to maintain uniqueness and attain normalization. Shmuel Almog, *Zionism and History: The Rise of a New Jewish Consciousness,* trans. Ina Friedman (New York: St. Martin's Press, 1987), pp. 157–65.

69. Thus the failure of the so-called Uganda plan and other suggested alternatives to Palestine. Shlomo Avineri defines the paradox of Zionism as the historical passivity of the Jews toward returning to Ereẓ Yisrael (the Land of Israel) despite their "deep feeling of attachment . . . becoming perhaps the most distinctive feature of Jewish self-identity." *Making of Modern Zionism,* p. 4.

70. For the non-Zionist Orthodox and the ultra-Orthodox the very idea of hastening the Messiah is heretical.

71. Sobel, *Migrants,* p. 17.

72. Nissim Kazzaz, "The Iraqi Orientation in the Iraqi Jewish Leadership and Its Failure" (Ph.D. diss., Hebrew University, 1985), p. 19.

73. Ibid., p. 136.

74. Said, "Reflection on Exile."

75. Leon Israel Yudkin, *Jewish Writing and Identity in the Twentieth Century* (New York: St. Martin's Press, 1982), p. 11.

76. Ibid., chap. 5.

77. See, for example, Yael Feldman, *Modernism and Cultural Transfer: Gabriel Preil and the Tradition of Jewish Literary Bilingualism* (Cincinnati: Hebrew Union College Press, 1986); Alan Mintz, "A Sanctuary in the Wilderness: The Beginning of the Hebrew Movement in America in the Pages of *HaToren,*" *Prooftexts* 10 (1990): 389–412; Gershon Shaked, *HaSipuret HaIvrit, 1880–1970* (Jerusalem and Tel Aviv: Keter and HaKibbutz HaMeuchad, 1977), pp. 40–42; Hana Wirth-Nesher, "Between Mother Tongue and Native Language," *Prooftexts* 10 (May 1990): 297–312.

78. Gurr, *The Writer in Exile,* pp. 141–42.

79. Hans Bernhard Moeller, *Latin America and the Literature of Exile* (Heidelberg: Carl Winter Universitätsverlag, 1983), p. 8.

CHAPTER 2. THE JEWISH COMMUNITY IN IRAQ

1. See, for example: Daniel Elazar, *The Other Jews: The Sepharadim Today* (New York: Basic Books, 1989); Howard Sachar, *Diaspora* (New York: Harper and Row, 1985); Heskel Haddad, *Jews of Arabic and Islamic Countries* (New York: Shengold Publishers, 1984).

2. Hanna Batatu, *The Old Social Classes and the Revolutionary Movements of Iraq* (Princeton: Princeton University Press, 1978), p. 258. Previous to that comment Batatu points out that at some point Arab nationalists considered the Jews among them to be "an indivisible part of the Arab 'race'" (p. 258).

3. Siegfried Landschut, *Jewish Communities in the Muslim Countries of the Middle East: A Survey* (London: The Jewish Chronicle Limited, [1950]), p. 43.

4. See, for example, Heskel Haddad's account in his book *Flight From Babylon* (New York: McGraw-Hill, 1986), pp. 4, 8.

5. Nissim Rejwan, *The Jews of Iraq* (Boulder, Colo.: Westview Press, 1985), chap. 2.

6. Bernard Lewis, *The Jews of Islam* (London: Routledge and Kegan Paul, 1984) p. 41.

7. Ibid., p. 14.

8. Ibid.

9. Ibid., pp. 45–46.

10. See, for example, Jacob Neusner, *There We Sat Down* (Nashville, Tenn.: Abingdon Press, 1972), pp. 46–51; Norman A. Stillman, *The Jews of Arab Lands* (Philadelphia: Jewish Publication Society, 1979), pp. 30–39.

11. Solomon Grayzel, *A History of the Jews* (Philadelphia: Jewish Publication Society, 1968), pp. 250–53.

12. A. Asher, trans. and ed., *The Itinerary of Rabbi Benjamin of Tudela* (New York: HaKesheth Publishing Co., 1840). Pages are referenced first by those of Asher's published translation and secondly by those of the manuscript (listed in the margins of the translation).

13. See, for example, Walter Fischel, *Jews in the Economic and Political Life of Mediaeval Islam* (New York: Ktav, 1969), pp. 1–44; Stillman, *Jews of Arab Lands,* pp. 34–39.

14. *Encyclopedia Judaica* 1972, s.v. "Iraq."

15. Abbas Shiblak, *The Lure of Zion: The Case of the Iraqi Jews* (London: Al-Saqi Books, 1986), p. 20. See also Stephen Helmsley Longrigg, *Iraq, 1900 to 1950: A Political, Social and Economic History* (London: Oxford University Press, 1953), p. 35.

16. Hayyim J. Cohen, "A Note on Social Change Among Iraqi Jews,

1917–1951," *Jewish Journal of Sociology,* no. 8 (1966): 204–8; Longrigg, *Iraq, 1900 to 1950,* p. 34.

17. Rejwan, *Jews,* chap. 24. Many of the Kurdish Jews were farmers in the north.

18. Hayyim J. Cohen, *The Jews Of The Middle East, 1860–1972* (New York: John Wiley and Sons, 1973), p. 89.

19. Shiblak, *Lure,* chap. 1; Reeva S. Simon, *Iraq Between the Two World Wars* (New York: Columbia University Press, 1986), p. 192.

20. Haddad, *Jews of Arabic,* chap. 2.

21. Cohen, "A Note," p. 207.

22. Landschut, *Jewish Communities,* p. 44.

23. Nissim Kazzaz, "The Iraqi Orientation in the Iraqi Jewish Leadership and Its Failure" (Ph.D. diss., Hebrew University, 1985), p. iv.

24. See, for example, Daniel Silverfarb, *Britain's Informal Empire in the Middle East: A Case Study of Iraq, 1929–1941* (Oxford: Oxford University Press, 1986), p. 4.

25. Rejwan, *Jews,* p. 210. This statistic differentiates between Sunni and Shiite Muslims.

26. Landschut, *Jewish Communities,* p. 42; Silverfarb, *Britain's Informal,* p. 16.

27. Cohen, *Middle East,* p. 159.

28. Cohen, "A Note," pp. 206–7.

29. Haddad, *Jews of Arabic,* chap. 2.

30. Cohen, *Middle East,* p. 161.

31. Rejwan, *Jews,* chaps. 24, 26.

32. Cohen, *Middle East,* p. 160.

33. In his study *HaYehudim Be'Irak BeMeah Ha'Esrim* (Jerusalem: Makhon Ben-Ẓvi, 1991), Nissim Kazzaz argues that the Jewish attempts to integrate fully into Iraqi society were shortsighted and doomed to failure. Leaders of the Jewish community failed to appreciate the power of Sharīʿa (Islamic Law) and Arab patriotism.

34. Including the grand mufti of Jerusalem, Amin al-Ḥusaynī. Landschut, *Jewish Communities,* p. 46.

35. Rejwan, *Jews,* chap. 27.

36. Cohen, *Middle East,* p. 27; Longrigg, *Iraq, 1900 to 1950,* pp. 253, 264, 273, 277; Simon, *Iraq Between the Two World Wars,* pp. 37–42. See also Stillman, *Jews of Arab Lands,* pp. 104–7.

37. See, for example, Cohen, *Middle East,* p. 26 and Rejwan, *Jews,* chap. 27. Simon describes Ghazi as a "pawn" in *Iraq Between the Two World Wars,* p. 60. Longrigg concurs: "[Ghazi's] lack of intellectual equipment and of interest in public affairs and his devotion to pleasure and to sport, forbade the hope that he would prove to be adequate. . . ." (*Iraq, 1900 to 1950,* p. 237).

38. Rejwan, *Jews,* chap. 27; Cohen, *Middle East,* p. 27.

39. Cohen, *Middle East,* p. 27; Landschut, *Jewish Communities,* p. 46.

40. Simon, *Iraq Between the Two World Wars,* p. 65.

41. See Stillman, *Modern,* p. 369: "The Iraqi Government Initiates Several Anti-Jewish Measures."

42. Rejwan, *Jews,* chap. 27; also see Itẓḥak Bar-Moshe, *Bayt Fī Baghdād* (Jerusalem: Association of Jewish Academics from Iraq, 1983), chap. 68; Simon, *Iraq Between the Two World Wars,* p. 70; Longrigg, *Iraq, 1900 to 1950,* p. 252.

43. Rejwan, *Jews,* chap. 27; Stillman, *Modern,* pp. 101–3. (See also pp. 331–33).

44. In his novel *'Ayin Ve 'ayn* David Rabeeya asserts that the word comes from the Turkish. I have not been able to find any corroborating evidence.

45. In addition to the sources cited elsewhere in this chapter, see Uri Shaharbani, "44 Shanim LaFarhud," *BaMa'arakhah* 25, no. 296 (June 1985): 5; Esther Glitzenshtein-Meyer, "Hapera'ot BeYehudei Baghdad," *Pe'amim* 8 (1981): 20–37; Majid Khadduri, *Independent Iraq, 1932–1958* (London: Oxford University Press, 1960); A. J. Cohen, "The Anti-Jewish *Farhūd* in Baghdad, 1941," *Middle East Studies,* October 1966, 2–18; Longrigg, *Iraq, 1900 to 1950,* pp. 296–97; Stillman, *Modern,* pp. 116–20. The Farhūd is touched upon in several fictional works and is central to at least one novel, which will be discussed below in chapter 7.

46. Khadduri, *Independent Iraq,* p. 53.

47. For "The Report of the Iraqi Commission of Inquiry on the Farhūd," see Stillman, *Modern,* pp. 405–17.

48. Shiblak, *Lure,* chap. 2.

49. Moshe Gat, "The Connection Between the Bombings in Baghdad and the Emigration of the Jews from Iraq: 1950–51," *Middle Eastern Studies* 24, no. 3 (July 1988): 313.

50. Shiblak, *Lure,* chap. 3; Longrigg, *Iraq, 1900 to 1950,* p. 353.

51. Shlomo Hillel, *Operation Babylon,* trans. Ina Friedman (London: Collins, 1988), p. 113; Longrigg, *Iraq, 1900 to 1950,* p. 354; Rejwan, *Jews,* chap. 29.

52. See Shiblak, *Lure,* chap. 3; Hillel, *Operation Babylon,* chap. 5; Rejwan, *Jews,* chap. 29. When the wave of arrests began, freedom could be bought through fines and bribes. The arrests were first viewed by the Iraqi officials as a means of revenue.

53. For more about Jewish participation in the Iraqi Communist Party, and especially Jewish leadership, see Yosef Meir, *Be'Ikar BaMaḥteret: Yehudim VePolitikah Be'Irak* (Tel Aviv: Naharayim, 1993), esp. pp. 83–106.

54. Shiblak, *Lure,* chap. 3; Longrigg, *Iraq, 1900 to 1950,* p. 338; Khadduri, *Independent Iraq,* p. 360; Meir, *Be'Ikar,* pp. 107–26.

55. Shiblak, *Lure,* chap. 3.

56. Rejwan, *Jews,* chap. 28; Shiblak, *Lure,* chap. 3; Bar-Moshe, *Khurūj Min al-'Iraq* (Jerusalem: Association for Jewish Academics from Iraq, 1975), p. 200.

57. Bar-Moshe, *Khurūj Min al-ʿIraq,* p. 200.

58. Hillel, *Operation Babylon,* p. 140.

59. Yosef (Yehoshpat) Me'ir, "HaẒiyonut Beʿlrak" in Stahl, ed., *ʿEdot Yisrael* (Tel Aviv: Am Oved, 1978), pp. 251–54; *Encyclopedia Judaica* 1972, s.v. "Iraq."

60. In 1914 three Iraqi Jewish emissaries to Istanbul were rebuffed in their attempts to join the Ottoman Zionist Association and the World Zionist Organiztion (WZO). Rejwan, *Jews,* chap. 25.

61. This compares quite favorably to those from European communities. See, for example, Haddad, *Jews of Arab,* chap. 4.

62. Me'ir gives the date July 1920. *Beʿlkar,* p. 124.

63. Me'ir, "HaẒiyonut," p. 252.

64. See "A Report on the Ban Upon Zionist Activities in Iraq (1929)," in Stillman, *Modern,* pp. 342–44.

65. Hillel, *Operation Babylon,* p. 17.

66. Ibid.

67. Joseph B. Schechtman, "The Repatriation of Iraqi Jewry," *Jewish Social Sciences* 15 (April 1953): 152.

68. Rejwan, *Jews,* chap. 29.

69. Schechtman, "Repatriation," p. 153.

70. Hillel, *Operation Babylon,* chap. 5; Haddad, *Flight.*

71. Exhibit, Museum of Babylonian Jewry, Or Yehuda, Israel.

72. Hillel, *Operation Babylon,* p. 186.

73. See Shiblak, *Lure,* chap. 3.

74. Schechtman, "Repatriation," p. 152.

75. This story is recounted in many of the works on this period. However, only Shiblak and Gat give the full name of the youth. See Haddad, *Flight,* p. 186; Bar-Moshe, *Khurūj Min Al-ʿIraq;* Moshe Gat, *Kehilah Yehudit BeMashber,* (Jerusalem: The Zalman Shazar Center for Jewish History, 1989), p. 43; Shiblak, *Lure,* p. 157.

76. Bar-Moshe, *Khurūj Min Al-ʿIraq,* pp. 287ff.

77. See Rejwan, Jews, chap. 29.

78. Shiblak, *Lure,* chap. 4.

79. Hillel, *Operation Babylon,* p. 229.

80. Ibid.

81. See Stillman, *Modern,* pp. 522–24 for the discussion concerning this law and pp. 525–26 for the text of the law.

82. Hillel, *Operation Babylon,* p. 243.

83. Schechtman, "Repatriation," p. 165.

84. Shiblak, *Lure,* chap. 5.

85. Bar-Moshe, *Khurūj Min Al-ʿIraq,* chaps. 18, 23.

86. Lorenzo Kent Kimball, *The Changing Pattern of Political Power* (New York: Robert Speller and Sons, 1972), p. 147.

87. Schechtman, "Repatriation," p. 168.

88. The most infamous of them were the January 1969 hangings of alleged spies. See Max Sawaydee, *All Waiting to Be Hanged* (Tel Aviv: Levanda Press, 1974).

## CHAPTER 3. JEWISH WRITERS OF MODERN IRAQI FICTION

1. H. J. Cohen, *The Jews of the Middle East, 1860–1972* (New York: John Wiley and Sons, 1973), p. 26.

2. Shmuel Moreh, *Short Stories by Jewish Writers from Iraq, 1924–1978* (Jerusalem: Magnes Press, 1978), p. 31 (Arabic introduction); also in Shmuel Moreh, "HaYeẓirah HaRuḥanit Shel Yehudei Irak BaSafah Ha'Aravit" in *Arabic and Islamic Studies,* ed. Jacob Mansour (Ramat Gan: Bar Ilan Press, 1978), 2:64–65.

3. Reuven Snir, "Temurah Tarbutit BeRe'i HaSifrut," *Peamim,* no. 36 (1988): 109.

4. 'Abd al-Ilāh Aḥmad, *Nash'at al-Qiṣṣa wa Taṭawwuruhā fī 'l'Irāq, 1908–1939* (Baghdad: Maṭba'at Shafīq, 1969), p. 85; Da'ūd Sallūm, *Tatawwur al-Fikrah wa-al-Uslūb Fī Al-Adab Al-'Irāqiyyah* (Baghdad: Matba'at al-Ma'arif, 1959), p. 109; Moreh, "Ha Yeẓirah HaRuḥanit, p. 65.

5. Moreh, *Short Stories*, p. 26.

6. Nissim Kazzaz, *HaYehudim Be'Irak BeMeah Ha'Esrim* (Jerusalem: Makhon Ben-Ẓvi, 1991) pp. 65–69.

7. Shuja' Musallam al-'Ānī, *Al-Mar'ah Fī al-Qiṣṣah al-'Irāqiyyah* (Baghdad: Dār Al-Shu'ūn al-Thaqāfiyyah al-'Āmma, 1986), p. 77.

8. Ibid.

9. Moreh, *Short Stories,* p. 16.

10. According to Moreh, "HaYeẓirah HaRuḥanit," pp. 61–62; also in *Short Stories,* p. 24 (Arabic introduction).

11. Shmuel Moreh and Lev Hakkak, "Yeẓiratam HaSifrutit V'HaMeḥkarim Shel Yoẓei 'Irak B''Irak U'B'Yisrael BeDoreinu" in *Meḥkarim beToldot Yehudei 'Irak VeTarbutam,* ed. Shmuel Moreh (Or Yehuda: Merkaz Moreshet Yahadut Bavel, 1981), p. 109.

12. See, for example, Matti Moosa, *The Origins of Modern Arabic Fiction* (Washington, D.C.: Three Continents Press, 1983); John A. Haywood, *Modern Arabic Literature, 1800–1970* (London: Lund Humphries, 1971); 'Abd al-Ilāh, *Nash'at al-Qiṣṣah;* Clement Huart, *A History of Arabic Literature* (Beirut: Khayats, 1966); 'Abd al-Muḥsin Ṭāhā Badr, *Taṭawwur al-riwāyah al'arabiyyah al-ḥadīthah fī Miṣr* (Cairo: Dār al-Ma'ārif, 1963).

13. "Shahīd al-Waṭan wa-Shahīdat al-Ḥubb" (Martyr of the homeland and martyr/ess of love), *Al-Mufīd* 1, no. 15 (April 1922).

14. "Al-Shābb al-Makhdū'" (The betrayed youth), *Al-Nāshi'ah* 1, no. 1 (27 December 1922).

15. Aḥmad 'Abd al-Ilāh, *Nash'at al-qiṣṣah wa-taṭawwuruha fī al-Irāq,*

*1908-1939* (Baghdad: Maṭba'at Shafīq, 1969) p. 85; Moreh, *Short Stories,* p. 32 (in Arabic).

16. Salmān Darwīsh, *Kull Shay' Hādi Fī Al-'Iyādah* (Jerusalem: Association of Jewish Academics from Iraq, 1981), p. 49

17. Me'īr Baṣrī, *'Ālam al-Yahūd fī al-'Irāq al-Ḥadīth* (Jerusalem: Association for Jewish Academics from Iraq, 1983), p. 79.

18. Shmuel Moreh, *Short Stories,* p. 81.

19. Baṣrī, *'Ālam,* p. 79.

20. Ibid.

21. Ibid.

22. *Encyclopedia Judaica* 1972, s.v. "Anwar Shaul."

23. Ibid.

24. Shmuel Moreh, "Rishon HaMeshorarim HaYehudim Be'Irak BaSafah HaAravit," in *Peamim,* no. 22 (1985): 130.

25. Moreh and Hakkak, "Yeẓiratam HaSifrutit," p. 109.

26. The fourth, according to Moreh, *Short Stories,* p. 26.

27. Secretary of the Zionist "Hebrew literary association"—according to Moreh, "Rishon haMeshorarim," p. 129.

28. Ibid.; *Encyclopedia Judaica,* s.v. "Anwar Shaul." The seeming contradiction of Shā'ul first working on a Zionist weekly and then signing the anti-Zionist declaration has several possible explanations, not the least of which is the passage of time and the change in official policy toward Zionist activities (see chapter 2). Also, one might distinguish between overtly political activities and other kinds of activities.

29. 'Abd al-Ilāh, *Nash'at al-Qiṣṣah,* p. 242.

30. "One of the best literary, social and political weeklies in Iraq" (Moreh, "Rishon HaMeshorarim," p. 129).

31. According to Baṣrī, publication began 14 February 1929, halted after sixteen issues, resumed 24 July 1930, and continued until the end of March 1938. Baṣrī, *'Ālam,* p. 80.

32. *Al-Ḥaṣīd* 3, no. 15 (November 1931): 5.

33. Emile Marmorstein, "Two Iraqi Jewish Short Story Writers: A Suggestion for Social Research," *Jewish Journal of Sociology* 1, no. 2 (December 1959): 190; Moreh, *Short Stories,* p. 85.

34. All of the stories—four originally from the Russian, five French, three English, one each Italian, Turkish, German and Yiddish are translated from the original or intermediary English and French language versions. Moreh, *Short Stories,* p. 82.

35. Baṣrī, *'Ālam,* p. 80.

36. Anwar Shā'ūl, *Al-Ḥiṣaād Al-Awwal* (Baghdad, 1930). Thirty-one Iraqi stories.

37. Anwar Shā'ūl, *Fī Ziḥām al-Madīnah* (Baghdad: Sharikat al-Tijārah wa-al-Ṭibā'a Al-Maḥdūdah, 1955). Eleven stories.

38. 'Abd al-Ilāh, *Nash'at al-Qiṣṣah,* p. 243.

39. Yūsuf ʿIzz al-Dīn, *Al-Qiṣṣah Fī Al-ʿIrāq Wa-taṭawwuruha* (Baghdad, Maṭbaʿat al-Baṣrī, 1974), p. 91.
40. Ibid.
41. Suhayl Idrīs, "Al-Qiṣṣah al-ʿIrāqiyyah al-Ḥadīthah," *Al-Ādāb*, no. 2 (February 1953): p. 24.
42. ʿIzz al-Dīn, *Al-Qiṣṣah Fī Al-ʿIrāq*, p. 90.
43. Idrīs, "Al-Qiṣṣah al-ʿIrāqiyyah," p. 24.
44. ʿAbd al-Ilāh, *Al-Adab Al-Qaṣaṣi Fī al-ʿIrāq* (Baghdad: Dār al-Ḥurriyya, 1977), p. 315.
45. Sallūm, *Taṭawwur al-Fikrah*, p. 128.
46. From the introduction of *Al-Ḥiṣād Al-ʿAwwal*, quoted by ʿIzz al-Dīn, *Al-Qiṣṣah Fī Al-ʿIrāq*, p. 88.
47. Moreh and Hakkak, "Yeẓiratam HaSifrutit," p. 108.
48. Snir, "Temurah Tarbutit," p. 121.
49. ʿIzz al-Dīn, *Al-Qiṣṣah Fī Al-ʿIrāq*, p. 90.
50. Ibid.
51. Ibid., p. 112.
52. ʿAbd al-Ilāh, *Nash'at Al-Qiṣṣah*, p. 238.
53. Ibid., p. 240.
54. Idrīs, "Al-Qiṣṣah al-ʿIrāqiyyah," pt. 1, p. 24.
55. Anwar Shaul left for Israel in 1971 and died in 1984. For more on his literary activity later in life, see Sasson Somekh, "Lost Voices: Jewish Authors in Modern Arabic Literature," in *Jews Among Arabs: Contacts and Boundaries*, ed. Mark R. Cohen and Abraham L. Udovitch (Princeton, N.J.: Darwin Press, 1989), esp. pp. 16–19.
56. Moreh, *Short Stories*, p. 97.
57. Ibid.
58. Interview with author, 15 May 1989 at Tel Aviv, under the auspices of the Conference to Document the Heritage of Babylonian Jewry.
59. Interview with author.
60. Moreh, *Short Stories*, p. 98, quotes ʿAbd Al-Husayn Al-Sankūr, *Al-Aqlām*, October 1976, 56: "[T]he importance of this collection comes from that the writer was aware of the devices of narrative art in some of the stories in addition to his critical awareness of the concept of story and its social role."
61. ʿIzz al-Dīn, *Al-Qiṣṣah Fī Al-ʿIrāq*, p. 120.
62. Idrīs, "Al-Qiṣṣah al-ʿIrāqiyyah," pt. 2, p. 49.
63. Sallūm, *Taṭawwur*, p. 134.
64. ʿIzz al-Dīn, *Al-Qiṣṣah Fī Al-ʿIrāq*, p. 123: "[G]ood narrative style despite homiletic, didactic tone . . . nears good artistic dialogue"; ʿAbd al-Ilāh, *Nash'at Al-Qiṣṣah*, p. 152: "good narrative style."
65. Sallūm, *Taṭawwur*, pp. 126–41.
66. Raoul Makarius and Laura Makarius, *Anthologie de la littérature arabe contemporaine* (Paris: Editions du Seuil, 1964), p. 234.

67. ʿAbd al-Ilāh, *Nash'at Al-Qiṣṣah,* pp. 153–54; John Thomas Hamel, "Jaʿfar Al-Khalili and the Modern Iraqi Story" (Ph.D. diss., University of Michigan, 1972), p. 14 lists Khalaf Shawqī al-Dawūdī and Muḥammad Ḥasan Al-Namrī al-Qatīfī; earlier he mentions Sulayman Fayḍī (p. 13). For discussion on the use of the colloquial, see chapter 4.

68. Nir Shoḥet, *Sipurah Shel HaGolah: Perakim BeToledot Yahadut Bavel LeDoroteiha* (Jerusalem: Association of Jewish Academics from Iraq, 1981), p. 28; Moreh, *Short Stories,* p. 111.

69. Interview with the author, Haifa, 4 June 1989.

70. Ibid.

71. Yosef Me'ir has Darwīsh as secretary of the Jewish community until 1946. Me'ir, *BeʿIkar BaMaḥteret: Yehudim VePolitikah BeʿIrak* (Tel Aviv: Naharayim, 1993), p. 77.

72. Moreh, *Short Stories,* p. 111. See also Me'ir, *BeʿIkar,* p. 73.

73. Moreh has 1928, but the weekly did not begin publication until 1929.

74. ʿIzz al-Dīn, *Al-Qiṣṣah Fī Al-ʿIrāq,* p. 84.

75. Sallūm, *Taṭawwur,* p. 136.

76. Including critics as diverse as Aḥmad ʿAbd al-Ilāh and Shmuel Moreh.

77. "His satiric style raised ugliness to the heights of artistic beauty" Shoḥet, *Sipurah,* p. 289.

78. Ibid.

79. Shalom Darwīsh, "Qafīlah Min al-Rīf," in *Ba'ḍ al-Nas* (Baghdad: Sharikat Al-Tijārah Wa-al-Ṭibāʿah Al-Maḥdūdah, 1938), pp. 1–29.

80. Idrīs, "Al-Qiṣṣah al-ʿIrāqiyyah," pt. 3, p. 35.

81. Ibid.

82. Hamel, "Jaʿfar al-Khalili," p. 28.

83. Marmorstein, "Two Iraqi Jewish Short Story Writers," p. 198.

84. Ya'qūb Bilbūl, *Al-Jumrah Al-'Ūlā* (Baghdad: Maktabat al-Maʿarif, 1938), foreword.

85. In fact one writer used the obvious pseudonym of *Fatā' 'Isrāil* (A youth of Israel).

86. Marmorstein, "Two Iraqi Jewish Short Story Writers," p. 198.

87. The critic seems more sensitive than other critics mentioned above to the issue of Anwar Shā'ūl's religious identity. In the same essay he goes on to say:

> The material struggle in its most miserable expression relates to the Jewishness of Anwar Shā'ūl. This is one of the most outstanding traits of Jews in the world. It possessed the psyche of the writer, [as is] reflected in his stories. This materialistic struggle is not merely implied by the stories but is stated clearly and frankly. It is there for us to read from the first page of the introduction when he [Anwar Shā'ūl] addresses the reader: "Whatever your approval of my harvest, or your disapproval, dear reader *(dear of course because you bought a copy)* the matter doesn't

> concern me as much as it concerns me that you paid a rabeeya to Maḥmud Efendi Ḥilmī, owner of al-Maktabah al-'Aṣriyyah (the Modern Library) . . . [for] spikes and chaff and thorns. 'Abd al-Ilāh, *Nash'at Al-Qiṣṣah,* pp. 244–45; (my italics).

The critic here seems to display his own lack of a sense of humor and ignores Anwar's struggle to make writing a noble venture. Shā'ūl paid other writers to encourage them, understanding that it had to have value in the marketplace if it was to have any value anywhere.

88. 'Izz al-Dīn, *Al-Qiṣṣah Fī Al-'Irāq,* p. 87. In Muslim custom the *mahr* is paid to the bride. Some (Muslim) Arab tribes even delight in having daughters because of the future payment. In other religious groups the bride pays *mahr* to the groom because he would not marry otherwise.

89. Ibid., p. 122.

90. Shoḥet, *Sipurah,* p. 291.

CHAPTER 4. THE CHOICE OF LANGUAGE

1. For example, Ya'qūb (Lev) Bilbūl.

2. Professors Sasson Somekh, David Semach, and Shmuel Moreh are instances.

3. See A. S. Halkin, "The Medieval Jewish Attitude Toward Hebrew," in Alexander Altmann, ed., *Biblical and Other Studies* (Cambridge: Harvard University Press, 1963), pp. 233–48.

4. For more in depth discussions, see Dan Miron, *A Traveler Disguised: The Rise of Modern Yiddish Fiction in the Nineteenth Century* (New York: Schocken, 1973); Yael Feldman, *Modernism and Cultural Transfer* (Cincinnati: Hebrew Union College Press, 1986); Shaked, *HaSiporet HaIvrit, 1880–1970* (Jerusalem and Tel Aviv: Keter and HaKibbutz HaMeuchad, 1977), pp. 40–48.

5. See Miron, *Traveler,* pp. 1–33.

6. Charles Ferguson, "Diglossia," *Word* 15, no. 2 (August 1959): 325. The actual situation of Iraqi Arabic is more complex, but this definition adequately describes the difference between the written or literary dialect and spoken dialects.

7. Ibid., p. 327.

8. Ibid.

9. "ACTFL Proficiency Guidelines," *Foreign Language Annals* 22, no. 4 (September 1989): 374. See also Benjamin Hary, "Middle Arabic: Proposals for New Terminology," *Al-'Arabiyya* 22, nos. 1–2 (1989): 21.

10. Haim Blanc, *Communal Dialects in Baghdad* (Cambridge: Harvard University Press, 1964), chap. 1.

11. Ibid.

12. David Rabi, "A Preliminary Study of Hebrew Forms in the Arabic

Dialect of the Jews of Baghdad," *Gratz College Annual of Jewish Studies* 7 (1978): 51.

13. Blanc, *Communal Dialects,* chap. 1. See also Rabi, "A Preliminary Study."

14. Blanc, *Communal Dialects,* chap. 1.

15. Ibid., chap. 5.

16. H. J. Cohen, *The Jews of the Middle East, 1860–1972* (New York: John Wiley and Sons, 1973), p. 37.

17. Ferguson, "Diglossia," p. 325.

18. Cohen, *Middle East,* p. 38.

19. Naim Kattan, *Farewell, Babylon,* translated from the French by Sheila Fischman (New York: Taplinger, 1980).

20. Ibid., pp. 6–7.

21. Ibid., p. 8.

22. Ibid.

23. Ibid., pp. 9–10.

24. Cohen, *Jews of the Middle East,* p. 38.

25. Sāmī Michael. *Ḥofen Shel Arafel* (Tel Aviv: Am Oved, 1979).

26. Ibid, p. 188.

27. Ibid, p. 172.

28. Cohen, "A Note on Social Change Among Iraqi Jews, 1917– 1951," *Journal of Jewish Sociology* 8 (1966): 207.

29. Yūsuf ʿIzz al-Dīn, *Poetry and Iraqi Society* (Baghdad: Maṭbaʿat al-ʿĀnī, 1962), p. 4. In English.

30. Kattan, *Farewell,* p. 46.

31. Shmuel Moreh, *Short Stories by Jewish Writers from Iraq* (Jerusalem: Misgav Yerushalayim, 1981), p. 24 (Arabic introduction).

32. "Were we [the Jews] not the best Arab grammarians?" (Kattan, *Farewell,* p. 51).

33. See chapter 3.

34. The literal meaning of the Arabic word comes from the word for "teacher" or "professor"; here it refers to the one-room schoolhouse type of education and has connotations of learning traditional religious texts by rote.

35. Cohen, *Middle East,* p. 113.

36. Nissim Rejwan, *The Jews of Iraq: Three Thousand Years of History and Culture* (Boulder, Colo.: Westview Press, 1985), p. 188.

37. The former term is used by Kattan, *Farewell,* p. 108; the latter was suggested by Dr. David Rabeeya (Rabi), interview, Elkins Park, Pa., 21 November 1989.

38. "Since the institution of the French-Jewish schools of the Alliance Israelite Universelle in the 1880's, Jews had access to western education and concentrated on language study, especially English and French, but later Turkish when the young Turks came to power, and Arabic with Iraqi independence. Their language proficiency plus their involvement in commerce made them a

natural middle class in the new state. Under the British many filled civil service jobs. . . ." (Cohen, *Middle East,* p. 115).

39. Yosef Me'ir, "Hitpatḥut HaHaskalah Bekerev HaYehudim Be'Irak BeShanim, 1830–1974," in *Hagut Ivrit Be'Arẓot Ha'Islam,* ed. Menakhem Zohori (Jerusalem: WHU and WJC, 1981), p. 430.

40. Abbas Shiblak, *The Lure of Zion: The Case of the Iraqi Jews* (London: Al-Saqi Books, 1986), p. 24.

41. Me'ir, "Hitpatḥut," p. 442.

42. Cohen, *Middle East,* p. 120.

43. Siegfried Landschut, *Jewish Communities in the Muslim Countries of the Middle East: A Survey* (London: The Jewish Chronicle Ltd, [1950]), p. 46. See also Cohen, *Jews of the Middle East,* p. 27.

44. Me'ir, "Hitpatḥut," p. 442.

45. Cohen, *Middle East,* p. 121.

46. Me'ir, "Hitpatḥut," p. 443.

47. Ibid.

48. For a literary illustration, see the character of Esther Bazaz in Ballas, *HaMa'abarah* (Tel Aviv: Am Oved, 1964).

49. Turkish was omitted after World War I with the defeat and departure of the Ottomans.

50. Cohen, *Middle East,* p. 119.

51. For example, Kattan, *Farewell,* chaps. 15, 18.

52. Cohen, *Middle East,* p. 119. See also Reeva S. Simon, *Iraq Between the Two World Wars* (New York: Columbia University Press, 1986), p. 192n.

53. Landschut, *Jewish Communities,* p. 43.

54. See chapter 3 above for a description of his early literary career in Iraq and his contribution to the development of modern Iraqi literature.

55. Yiẓḥak Bar-Moshe, *Bayt Fī Baghdad* (Jerusalem: Association for Jewish Academics from Iraq, 1983), pp. 138ff.

56. Interview with Samīr Naqqāsh, Petaḥ Tikva, 21 May 1989.

57. Shmuel Moreh, *Short Stories,* p. 111.

58. Shalom Darwīsh, "Neft Aleikha," *Iton 77,* 5, no. 28 (June–August 1981): 36–37.

59. Sāmī Michael, "The Language of Literary Creation," lecture given at The Israeli Academic Center in Cairo, March 1985.

60. Interview with Shimon Ballas, Tel Aviv, 9 May 1989.

61. In his book of essays, *After the Tradition* (New York: Dutton, 1971), p. 241, Robert Alter has suggested that "a printing of 3,000 in Israel looms as large as perhaps a million copies of a book published in America."

62. Interview with Yiẓḥak Bar-Moshe, Jerusalem, 18 May 1989.

63. Interview with Shmuel Moreh, Jerusalem, 11 May 1989; interview with Yiẓḥak Bar-Moshe, Jerusalem, 18 May 1989.

64. Interview with Samīr Naqqāsh, Petaḥ Tikva, 21 May 1989.

65. Interview with Eli Amir, Jerusalem, 30 May 1989.

66. Interview with David Rabeeya, Elkins Park, Pa., 21 November 1989.

67. "The Association for Academics from Iraq in Israel, established in 1980, is a scientific, social and literary association whose interest is to help Iraqi-born academics in Israel publish their scientific and literary works and research written about the Jews of Iraq, and to arrange conferences of science, literature and the arts." Explanatory note from the frontispiece of works published by the association.

68. Interview with Samīr Naqqāsh, Petaḥ Tikva, 18 May 1988. By comparison, the first printing of Sāmī Michael's second novel, *Ḥasut,* was twenty-five thousand copies.

69. E.g., Sasson Somekh, "Ḥavayot Abudot," *Iton 77,* nos. 78–79, (July–August 1986): 6, 50.

70. *Al-Jadīd* vol. 3, no. 1 (November 1954), unpaginated.

71. Yiẓḥak Bar-Moshe, *Khurūj Min al-'Irāq* (Jerusalem: The Association for Jewish Academics from Iraq, 1975), pp. 581–91.

72. Samīr Naqqāsh, "Ṭanṭal," in *Anā Wa-Ha'ulā'ī Wa-al-fiṣām* (Tel Aviv: Association for the Promotion of Research, Literature, and the Arts, 1978), pp. 67–90.

73. Al-Shārūnī, *Dirāsāt Adabiyyah,* p. 138.

74. Ibid., pp. 186, 188.

75. The Nobel laureate Naguib Mahfouz asserted, "What is important in characterization is nature, temperament, education and behavior. The last thing we see as important in this is the manner of speech, and proof of this is that we are moved by international characters even though they are (originally) written in a foreign language." Cited in ibid, p. 186.

76. Ibid., p. 142.

77. Aḥmad 'Abd al-Ilāh, *Al-Adab Al-Qaṣaṣā fī al-'Irāq* (Baghdad: Dār al-Ḥurriyah, 1977), p. 328.

78. Shalom Darwīsh, *Ba'ḍ al-Nās* (Baghdad: Sharikat al-tijārah wa-al-ṭiba'ah, 1948), pp. 1–29, 117–30.

79. Ya'qūb Bilbūl "Ṣūra Tibq al-Aṣl" in *Al-Jamrah Al-Ūlā* (Baghdad: Maktabat al-Ma'arif, 1938), pp. 97–103. For a short discussion, see Aḥmad 'Abd al-Ilah, *Nash'at Al-Qiṣṣah Wa-Tatawwuruhā fī-l'Irāq, 1908–1939* (Baghdad: Maṭba'at Shafiq, 1969), p. 154. See also John Thomas Hamel, "Ja'far al-Khalīlī and the Modern Iraqi Story" (Ph.D. diss., University of Michigan, 1972), p. 14.

80. Aḥmad 'Abd al-Ilāh, *Al-Adab,* p. 328.

81. Yūsuf 'Izz al-Dīn, *Fī al-Adab al-'Arabī al-Ḥadīth* (Baghdad: Maṭba'at al-Baṣrī, 1968), p. 123.

82. Shmuel Moreh and Lev Hakkak, "Yeẓiratam HaSifrutit VeHaMeḥkarim Shel Yoẓai 'Irak Be'Irak UBeYisrael BeDoranu," in Shmuel Moreh, ed. *Meḥkarim beToldot Yehudei 'Irak VeTarbutam* (Or Yehuda: Merkaz Moreshet Yahadut Bavel, 1981), p. 108.

83. Shmuel Moreh, *Short Stories,* p. 113.

84. Bilbūl changed the name of the midwife from Habiba to the more neutral-sounding Saida as a result of prepublication editing (see below, p. 62). On the last page of the story the midwife's name was inadvertently left uncorrected.

85. Ya'qūb Mansūr notes:

> [T]he Muslim dialect is put in the mouth of the Muslim, but also in the mouth of the Jew, when he turns to the Muslim. The reverse, that the Muslim who turns to the Jew speaks in the Jewish dialect, is not found.

Mansūr, "Lahag Muslimi BeSiporim SheBeAravit-Yehudit shel Baghdad," in Zohori, ed., *Hagut Ivrit BeArẓot HaIslam* (Jerusalem: WHU and WJC, 1981), p. 47.

86. Samīr Naqqāsh, *Anā Wa-Hā'ulā'i Wa-al-fiṣam* (Tel Aviv: Association for the Promotion of Research, Literature and the Arts, 1978).

87. Interview with Samīr Naqqāsh, Petaḥ Tikva, 21 May 1989.

88. Interview with Yiẓḥak Bar-Moshe, Jerusalem, 18 May 1989.

89. Interview with Shalom Darwīsh, Haifa, 22 May 1989.

90. Interview with Yiẓḥak Bar-Moshe, Jerusalem, 18 May 1989. The sentence quoted was spoken in English.

91. I do not want to get involved in the discussion of whether or not *fuṣḥā* has changed over time; like any language it has undergone various adjustments and modifications. Instead I refer to the generally accepted notion of *fuṣḥā* as a single language "fixed" by the Qur'ān, and *al-'āmmiyyah*, or more accurately *al-lahjah*, as a multiplicity of dialects unfixed by any sacred text and prone to change more quickly and more radically.

92. Mansūr, "Lahag," p. 56.

93. See also Reuven Snir, "'We Were Like Those Who Dream': Iraqi-Jewish Writers in Israel in the 1950s," *Prooftexts* 11 (1991): 153–73. Snir's article is invaluable for presenting the poetry of the Iraqi immigrants and offers more discussion of the choice between Hebrew and Arabic.

94. Interview with David Semach, Haifa, 4 June 1989.

95. *Al-Jadīd* 3, no. 1 (November 1954), unpaginated.

96. Ibid. It should be noted that this discussion was reported in Arabic.

97. Alex Zehavi, "Lignov et HaIvrit," *Yediot Aharonot* 15 (October 1985).

98. Interview with Shimon Ballas, Tel Aviv, 9 May 1989.

99. Interview with Shalom Darwīsh, Haifa, 22 May 1989.

100. Sāmī Michael, "The Language of Literary Creation," *Bulletin of the Israeli Academic Center in Cairo*, no. 6 (Fall 1985): 9. The short article is based on a lecture delivered at the center March 1985 (See note 59 above).

101. Interview with Shalom Darwīsh, Haifa, 22 May 1989.

102. Alex Zehavi, "Lignov et HaIvrit."

103. Shulamit Gingold-Gilboa, "Lehikara' Bein Shetei Tarbuyot," *Iton 77*, nos. 52–53 (April–May 1984): 40–41.

104. Yael Lotan, "Lehafrid Bein Yahadut LiYisraeliyut," *Yediot Aḥaronot,* 29 May 1987, 22, 26.

105. Sāmī Michael, "On Being an Iraqi-Jewish Writer in Israel," *Prooftexts* 4 (1984): 29.

106. Michael, "On Being an Iraqi-Jewish Writer," p. 28.

107. Ibid., p. 29.

108. Gingold-Gilboa, "Lehikara'," pp. 40–41.

109. Shimon Ballas, *HaMa'abarah* (Tel Aviv: Am Oved, 1964).

110. See also Shimon Ballas, *Ḥeder Na'ul* (Tel Aviv: Zmora-Bitan, Modan, 1980), p. 91.

111. Shimon Ballas, *Hitbaharut* (Tel Aviv: Sifriyat Po'alim, 1972), p. 131.

112. Ballas, *HaMa'abarah,* p. 60. The residents of the transit camp referred to the Ashkenazi Jews by the language they spoke (Yiddish).

113. Ibid., p. 7.

114. Interview with Shimon Ballas, Tel Aviv, 9 May 1989.

115. Sāmī Michael, *Shavim VeShavim Yoter* (Tel Aviv: Boostan, 1974).

116. In Arab countries, a man is often referred to as the father of his oldest son.

117. Eli Amir, *Tarnegol Kaparot* (Tel Aviv: Am Oved, 1983), p. 136.

118. David Rabi, "A Preliminary Study of Hebrew Forms in the Arabic Dialect of the Jews of Baghdad," *Gratz College Annual of Jewish Studies* 7 (1978): 52.

119. Ballas, *HaMa'abarah,* p. 67.

120. Ibid., pp. 67, 84.

121. Michael, *Shavim,* p. 40.

122. Ballas, *HaMa'abarah,* p. 114.

123. Sāmī Michael, *Paḥonim VeḤalomot* (Tel Aviv: Am Oved, 1979), pp. 11, 89. Compare, for example, "a living dog is better than a dead lion," and "a running dog and not [rather than] a lion tied." Āḥmad Taymur, *Al-Amthāl al-'Āmmiyyah* (Cairo: Maṭābi' al-ahrām, 1980), p. 409.

124. The following chapter examines this literature in detail.

125. Interview with Ya'qūb [Bilbūl] Lev, Tel Aviv, 16 May 1989.

126. Ya'qūb Bilbūl, *Al-Jamrah Al-'Ūlā* (Baghdad: Maktabat al-Ma'aref, 1938), pp. 97–103.

127. See p. 54.

128. Interview with Ya'qūb [BilBūl] Lev, Tel Aviv, 16 May 1989.

129. Interview with Yiẓḥak Bar-Moshe, Jerusalem, 18 May 1989.

130. See, for example, Ballas, "Sofer Yehudi Ba'al Zehut Kefulah," *Ha'Areẓ,* 25 July 1975. This article was also translated into Arabic and printed in *al-Anbā'.*

131. Selim al-Bassūn "Riḥlah Ma'a Al-Dubb Al-Quṭbi, *al-Anbā',* 8 March 1984. He points out spelling, grammar, and language errors.

132. For instance, Ibrāḥim al-Wardānī, "Ṣawarīkh," *Al-Jumhūriyyah,* 19 October 1983.

133. Personal communication with Alex Zehavi, December 1988 and May 1989.

134. Samīr Naqqāsh, *'Indama tasquṭ aḍla' al-muthallāt* (Shefaram: Dār al-Mashreq, 1984).

135. *Nuzūluhu WaKhīt Al-Shayṭan* (Jerusalem: Association for Jewish Academics from Iraq, 1986) presents a character who can only utter the syllable "da." This is intended as a reference to dadaism.

136. Personal communication with Alex Zehavi, December 1988. Reiterated 25 May 1989.

137. Interview with Shalom Darwīsh, Haifa, 22 May 1989. Darwīsh told this story about his first editor:

> He wanted to revise it according to his religious beliefs. Not only that, but why did I get rid of him? I said give me back the manuscript—I'll do it myself. I think that in *Phraim! Phraim!* when the girl went to find David in the playground and she didn't find him, I used a verse from the Song of Songs: "I searched for him and did not find him." He said it was forbidden. I said it was not. He said, "But it is a holy verse." Then I said ""Give it to me" and sent it to [Alex] Zehavi.

138. "I didn't agree about the editing. I sat with another editor and replaced almost everything that the first had deleted. But I learned from that." Interview with Shimon Ballas, Tel Aviv, 9 May 1989.

139. Yael Lotan, "Lehafrid Bein Yahadut LiYisraeliyut," *Yediot Aḥaronot,* 29 May 1987, 22, 26.

140. Interview with Shimon Ballas, Tel Aviv, 9 May 1989.

141. Ibid.

142. Ibid.

143. Michael's latest novel *Victoria* (Tel Aviv: Am Oved, 1993) at first seems to run counter to this argument. The very different approach and choice of materials in this novel, however, actually supports my argument and is the subject of a detailed discussion in a forthcoming study.

144. Interview with Yiẓḥak Bar-Moshe, Jerusalem, 18 May 1989.

145. Interview with Shimon Ballas, Tel Aviv, 9 May 1989.

CHAPTER 5. THE EXPERIENCE OF TRANSITION: FIRST NOVELS IN HEBREW

1. Ballas, *HaMa'abarah,* p. 51.

2. S. N. Eisenstadt, "Process of Absorption of Immigrants in Israel," in Carl Frankenstein, ed., *Between Past and Future* (Jerusalem: Henrietta Szold Foundation for Child and Youth Welfare, 1953), p. 54.

3. Shlomo Hillel, *Operation Babylon,* trans. Ina Friedman (London: Collins, 1988), p. 192. "The need to bring [the immigrants] to Israel as fast as possible took precedence over the preparation of optimal material conditions for their absorption. The quality of their treatment, once the immigrants

arrived, was thus unavoidably sacrificed to the need to absorb them as quickly as possible." Dan Horowitz and Moshe Lissak, *Trouble in Utopia: The Overburdened Polity of Israel.* Trans. Charles Hoffman. (Albany, N.Y.: SUNY, 1989), 3.

4. Eisenstadt, "Process," p. 54.

5. Ibid., p. 55.

6. Heskel Haddad, *Flight from Babylon* (New York: McGraw-Hill, 1986), chap. 36.

7. Shlomo Hillel, *Operation Babylon,* p. 287. For more description of the transit camps, see Tom Segev, *1949: The First Israelis,* trans. Arlen Neal Weinstein (New York: Macmillan, 1986), pp. 123, 137.

8. Haddad, *Flight,* p. 113.

9. In fact, the Jewish communities of the East were often seen as a source for cheap labor. See for example: Shlomo Swirski, *Israel: The Oriental Majority,* trans. Barbara Swirski (Atlantic Highlands, New Jersey: Zed Books, 1989), p. 134. See also Yiẕhak Bar-Moshe, *Khurūj Min al-ʿIrāq* (Jerusalem: Association for Jewish Academics from Iraq, 1983), p. 590; and as presented in novels: Rabeeya, *Tehom Shemesh,* pt. 3 chap. 1; Eli Amir, *Tarnegol Kaparot,* chap. 12.

10. Samuel Z. Klausner, "Immigrant Absorption and Social Tension in Israel," *Middle East Journal* 9, no. 3 (1955): 283.

11. "Sephardi" literally refers to the Jews of Moslem Spain and their descendents. As such it does not include members of the Iraqi Jewish community, whose origin predates that of the Sephardi by many years. Today the term "Sephardi" is used in opposition to "Ashkenazi" (literally: of German origin) or "European," and has been extended to include all Jews of Middle Eastern origin. "Sephardi tahor" (pure Spanish) now signifies literal Sephardim. I use the term "Mizraḥi" (Eastern or Oriental) to refer to Jews from Arab countries.

12. Sammy Smooha, *Israel: Pluralism and Conflict* (Berkeley: University of California Press, 1978), p. 91.

13. Segev, *1949,* pt. 2 "Between Veterans and Newcomers"; see especially p. 117. Segev notes the use of the terms "material" (as in "the material is easily transportable," p. 153) and *"avak adam"* (human debris) to refer to the immigrants, but points out that "[m]any of them, however, were ground into debris only after their arrival, as part of the process of migration and the hardship of resettlement" (p. 116).

14. Henry Toledano, "Time to Stir the Melting Pot," in Michael Curtis and Mordecai S. Cheroff, eds., *Israel: Social Structure and Change* (New Brunswick, N.J.: Transaction Books, 1973), p. 335.

15. Celia Heller, "The Emerging Consciousness of the Ethnic Problem Among the Jews," in ibid., p. 327.

16. Kalman Katzenelson, *HaMahapekhah HaAshkenazit* (Tel Aviv: Anakh), 1964.

17. "As one commentator [Nissim Rejwan] on the book wrote, 'the book has not been written and produced in a complete vacuum—no book of this kind ever is.'" Smooha, *Israel: Pluralism and Conflict,* p. 49.

18. Sammy Smooha, "Black Panthers: The Ethnic Dilemma," Society, March 1972, p. 36.

19. Samuel Z. Klausner, "Immigrant Absorption," p. 294. Compare to Naim Giladi's comment: "The culture will remain oriental . . . your son will eat hummus or falafel not borscht" (cited in Swirski, *Israel,* p. 119).

20. Interview with the author, Jerusalem, 30 May 1989. The novel he was then writing has since been published as *Mafriaḥ HaYonim* [The pigeon keeper] (Tel Aviv: Am Oved, 1992).

21. Shimon Ballas, *HaMaʿabarah* (Tel Aviv: Am Oved, April 1964).

22. Sāmī Michael, *Shavim VeShavim Yoter* (Tel Aviv: Boostan, 1974).

23. Eli Amir, *Tarnegol Kaparot* (Tel Aviv: Am Oved, 1983). It has been published in English translation under the title *Scapegoat* (London: Weidenfeld & Nicolson, 1987).

24. This also holds true for the protagonists in David Rabeeya's *Tehom Shemesh* (The abyss of the sun) (Tel Aviv: Alef, 1983), and Sāmī Michael's *Paḥonim VeḤalomot* (Shacks and dreams) (Tel Aviv: Am Oved, 1979), written for young adults.

25. As I have tried to show, not every Jew ending up in Israel necessarily chose to immigrate to Israel, some were emigrants with few options and/or considered Israel as a temporary stop. In chapter 1 I have suggested the possibility of "exile" as an earlier phase in the immigrant experience. I also indicated that these are not two discrete phases, but rather different aspects of the same situation. The word "exile" implies "from," whereas "immigrant" indicates "to." Both of these orientations can exist simultaneously, and do so in the characters under discussion. As for the volitional difference—whether one has the choice to leave home or is forced to—that has been treated in chapter 2 as regards the community in question.

26. See, for example: Samuel Z. Klausner, "Immigrant Absorption," pp. 281–94; Heskel Haddad, *Jews of Arab and Islamic Countries: History, Problems, Solutions* (New York: Shengold Publishers, 1984); S. N. Eisenstadt, *The Absorption of Immigrants* (1954; reprint, Westport, Conn.: Greenwood Press, 1975); Curtis and Cheroff, *Israel: Social Structure and Change.*

27. Eisenstadt, *Absorption of Immigrants,* pp. 5–6.

28. Rivka Weiss Bar-Yosef, "Desocialization and Resocialization: The Adjustment Process of Immigrants," in Ernst Krausz, ed., *Studies of Israeli Society* (New Brunswick, N.J.: Transaction Books, 1980), pp. 19–35.

29. Ibid., p. 20.

30. Ibid.

31. Erik Erikson, *Identity, Youth and Crisis* (New York: W. W. Norton and Company, 1968), p. 19.

32. Ibid., p. 22. His italics.

33. Ibid., p. 17.

34. Bar-Yosef, "Desocialization," pp. 27–28.

35. Erikson, *Identity,* p. 157.

36. Eva Hoffman, *Lost in Translation: A Life in a New Language* (New York: Penguin Books, 1989), p. 132.

37. Kurt Lewin, "Field Theory and Experiment in Social Psychology: Concepts and Methods," *American Journal of Sociology* 44 (1939): 868–97.

38. "Liminal entities are neither here nor there; they are betwixt and between the positions assigned and arrayed by law, custom, convention and ceremonial." Victor Turner, *Ritual Process* (Chicago: Aldine, 1969), p. 95.

39. Bar-Yosef, "Desocialization," pp. 27–28.

40. Eisenstadt, "Process of Absorption," p. 346.

41. Ibid., pp. 344–49.

42. Ibid., p. 346.

43. *Klita* was the dominant term in Hebrew and was translated as "absorption" in English (see Eisenstadt's article, for example). I have chosen to use this term because I believe that it accurately reflects the prevailing attitude of the day.

44. Klausner, "Immigrant Absorption," pp. 283–84.

45. See Wayne C. Booth, *The Rhetoric of Fiction,* 2d ed. (Chicago: University of Chicago, 1983), pp. 3–20.

46. Yosef Even, "HaDibur HaSamui," *HaSifrut* (Spring 1968):140–52.

47. Miriam Yaḥil-Wax also singles him out in her essay "HaEmdah HaShlishit," *Iton 77,* nos. 91–92 (August–September 1987): 18–21: "is not a psychological, ethnic, or ideological protagonist, but rather an existential [one]."

48. The pregnant woman and her husband are minor characters. She herself is never named and only appears twice (chap. 3, chap. 45). Her husband is first known as Na'im Ḥabaz (chap. 3) and when he reappears he is renamed as Moshe Ḥabaz (chap. 45). This is apparently an oversight but does indicate the relative insignificance of the Ḥabaz couple as characters. They are merely at the service of the plot.

49. In addition to the shacks set up by the government agency, there is an area of the camp taken over by illegal squatters who live in tents while waiting for shacks to become available.

50. Menashe Nazakh's wife Georgia leads a protest of women against Na'aman, blaming him for her husband's arrest after the first meeting.

51. In the story, "Sephardi" is used instead of "Mizraḥi."

52. Michael, *Shavim VeShavim Yoter,* pp. 31 and 33 respectively. They both use the word *gever*, man, which connotes both maturity and masculinity.

53. Michael, *Shavim VeShavim Yoter,* p. 21. His emphasis.

54. The additional siblings—Ze'ev and Ḥanina—only reappear at David's wedding. Their absence contributes to the sense of loss.

55. Ella Shohat, *Israeli Cinema: East/West and the Politics of Representa-*

*tion* (Austin: University of Texas Press, 1989), p. 134. The name of this film genre refers to a food typical to Mizraḥim. The genre was popular in the sixties and seventies in Israel. For more discussion on the "bourekas" films, and the "gefilte fish" films, see ibid., pp. 115–78.

56. The term "ethnic" takes on a different meaning in the context of Israeli society. As Swirski suggests: "When people in Israel talk about ethnicity, they refer to the Oriental Jews. . . . (Swirski, *Israel,* p. 60).

57. *Layālī* (derived from the word "night") are songs popular in the Arab world. They are elaborately improvised and often repeat the word "night."

58. "When we arrived here, I swore that I would root myself in Kiryat Oranim, that I would become a part of it." Amir, *Tarnegol Kaparot,* p. 118.

59. Ibid., p. 42. In the novel *Tehom Shemesh,* the author David Rabeeya goes one step further: the immigrants are assigned Yiddish rather than Hebrew names by veteran Israelis: "telling Salman that his new name would be Zelig, and his parents would be called Zalman and Zelda" (Rabeeya, *Tehom Shemesh,* p. 47). Also: "Ya'akov became Yankele, Yitsḥak became Yitsḥakele" (p. 50). This establishes a ironic connection between the Mizraḥi immigrants and the shtetl Jews left behind by the Ashkenazi Israelis. At the same time, it points to the cultural coercion implicit in these ready-made identities. Salman's attempts to be like "the Baltic"—he even recites the *kaddish* for his father in a Baltic accent, virtually denying his identity as Iraqi-born (p. 77)—begins with his acceptance of his new name and ends in insanity and a loss of identity: "What is my name?" (p. 107).

60. See above in chapter 2. The school was opened at the invitation of the Jewish community (Yosef Me'ir, "Hitpatḥut HaHaskalah BeKrav HaYehudim Be-'Iraq BaShanim, 1830–1974," in Menakhem Zohori, ed., *Hagut Ivrit Be-'Artzot Ha'Islam* [Jerusalem: WHU and WJC, 1981], p. 430).

61. Klausner, "Immigrant Absorption," pp. 282–83.

62. "'What? Jews without a synagogue?' growled 'Abd al-'Azīz, the son of the rabbi of the Kfar Ono *ma'abarah* [upon his arrival to the kibbutz]." Amir, *Tarnegol Kaparot,* p. 41.

63. Rabbi Nosson Scherman, ed., *The Complete ArtScroll Siddur* (Brooklyn, N.Y.: Mesorah, 1984), p. 775. Today money is often used instead, and then donated to charity.

64. Eli Amir, "Iraqi Jews in Israel," *Present Tense* 11, no. 2 (Winter 1984): 33–34.

65. Hayyim J. Cohen, *Jews of the Middle East,* p. 169.

66. See Haddad, *Flight From Babylon.*

67. Madeleine: "Mom and Dad have one bastard after another. They have energy for one thing only: sex. Mom doesn't have the strength to take care of all of them. . . . Dad can't even stand up in front of the window of [the employment office]." Michael, *Shavim VeShavim Yoter,* p. 31.

68. As in Vladimir Propp's theory, outlined in *Morphology of the Folktale* (Bloomington, Indiana University Press, 1958).

69. Ballas, *HaMa'abarah,* p. 128 and elsewhere. The term "Yiddish" is used by the Iraqis as a generic label despite the fact that the spoken language in Israel is Hebrew and not all Israelis of Ashkenazi descent know how to speak Yiddish.

70. See Gershon Shaked, "Literature and Its Audience: On the Reception of Israeli Fiction in the Forties and the Fifties," *Prooftexts* 7 (1987): 207–23.

71. George Orwell, *Animal Farm* (New York: Harcourt, Brace, 1954).

72. The narrative uses the term Sephardim for Mizraḥim.

73. Derived from "Francophone," originally in reference to the French-speaking Jews from North Africa, then extended to all non-Europeans; a derogatory term in Hebrew.

74. *Shavim VeShavim Yoter,* pp. 39, 61. The first term mocks the way Yiddish sounds to a non-speaker, the second is a typical last syllable of an East European (Ashkenazi) name.

75. This incident is also described by other Iraqi-born Israelis in their fictional accounts of the arrival. In one, none of the arrivals knew what to expect: "It was hard to know the nature of the material that sprayed out of the giant pipes." With their exaggerated, untiring optimism the arrivals think the airport officials approaching them are carrying food, flowers, and gifts, and that the spray is a cosmetic powder designed to refresh them after their long journey. It is only when a pharmacist asks the officials directly that they tell him in embarrassment that they are spraying DDT. Rahamin Rejwan, *'Al HaGeḥalim* (Tel Aviv: Sifriyat Tarmil, 1985), pp. 7–23.

76. Michael, *Shavim VeShavim Yoter,* p. 30.

77. Compare this to the comments about gefilte fish between Shlomo Ḥamra and Me'ir:

> —You can throw up just from the smell.
> —I'll tell you the truth. Once I tasted it. I was in the army and didn't know what it was. I just put it into my mouth and foo!

Ballas, *HaMa'abarah,* p. 60.

78. Holocaust survivors and Mizraẓi immigrants are assigned similar status in mainstream Israeli literature and literary history as well. See, for example, chapters 9 and 10 of Gershon Shaked's "Lashon HaMarot: Al Sifrut VeḤevrah," which appared on Israeli channel 2, 1993–94.

79. Michael, *Shavim VeShavim Yoter,* p. 245. Emphasis in the original.

80. As discussed above, p. 94: "Laziness . . . is a contemptible Arab trait . . . ." (Michael, *Shavim,* pp. 52–53).

81. There are several exceptions. The nice Ashkenazim who fall outside this scheme do not have red hair. The counselor Sonia has "silver threads interwoven in her black hair" (Amir, *Tarnegol Kaparot,* p. 34), while Dolek's hair

color is never described. In any event, Dolek has been "purified" by the Holocaust (chap. 14) as has the gray-haired Aunt Olga (chap. 2). See p. 95.

82. Ibid., p. 48. Here, too, as in *Shavim VeShavim Yoter,* the Holocaust survivors are omitted from the negative characterization of the Ashkenazim.

83. Hanoch Bartov, *Shesh Kenafaim LeEḥad* (Tel Aviv: Sifriyat Po'alim, 1954).

84. Azriel Ukhmani, "Gidulo Shel Mesaper," *'Al HaMishmar,* 18 February 1955.

85. P. Azai, "Shimon Ballas, MeḤaber *HaMa'abarah,*" *HaAreẓ,* 19 April 1964.

86. Interview with Shimon Ballas, Tel Aviv, 9 May 1989.

87. Ibid.

88. Mordekhai Avishai, "Yisrael HaSheniyah BeRoman Ḥiver," from the Bet HaSofer Tchernichovsky archives, Tel Aviv, 28 August 1964.

89. Aliza Levenberg, "Ḥayei HaMa'abarah MiBifnim," from the Bet HaSofer Tchernichovsky archives, Tel Aviv, 25 July 1964.

90. Aliza Levenberg, "Eshnav LaMa'abarah," *Ma'ariv,* 30 April 1964.

91. Ruth Cohen, "HaMa'abarah l'Shimon Ballas," from the Bet HaSofer Tchernichovsky archives, Tel Aviv, 29 May 1964.

92. T. Golovsky, "Tivo Shel Ha*'ani Ma'ashim'* BaMa'abarah," *Tarbut, Sifrut VeOmanut,* 6 May 1964.

93. Other critics support my assessment. See, for example, Lev Hakkak, "Terumatam Shel Yoẓei Irak LaSifrut HaIvrit Ba'Areẓ," *Iton 77,* nos. 5–6 (November–December 1977): 22–23, who characterizes the tone as muted.

94. Ballas, *HaMa'abarah,* p. 76.

95. Ibid.: "O dove cooing close by me; O Shekhinah [Divine Presence], if You only knew of my sorrow."

96. Miriam Yaḥil-Wax, "HaEmdah HaShlishit," *Iton 77,* nos. 91–92, (August–September 1987): 18–21.

97. See, for example, Hannan Hever, "Israeli Fiction of Early Sixties," *Prooftexts* 10 (1990): 129–47.

98. Levenberg, "Ḥayei."

99. Yaḥil-Wax notes "the attempt to integrate it in the canon as an ethnic novel were forced and failed anyway." Yaḥil-Wax, "HaEmdah," p. 19.

100. See Erik Cohen, "The Black Panthers and Israeli Society," in Ernest Krausz, ed., *Studies of Israeli Society* (New Brunswick, N.J.: Transaction, 1980), pp. 147–64.

101. Shlomo Deshen, "Political Ethnicity and Cultural Ethnicity in Israel During the 1960s," in ibid., p. 126.

102. Hypotheses for the dissolution of the Israeli Panthers vary. While lack of organizational strengths contributed to its demise, Erik Cohen suggests that the most profound reason was their inability to "create a new 'social myth' . . . [they] were still too much attached to the fundamental assumption of the 'unity

of the Jewish nation' and had too strong a stake in the survival of Israel as a 'Jewish state', to create a radically separatist Oriental ideology." Cohen, "The Black Panthers," p. 160.

103. See, for example, Charles Liebman and Eliezer Don-Yehiya, *Religion and Politics in Israel* (Bloomington: Indiana University Press, 1984), p. 117.

104. Iza Perliss, "Aflayah Adatit BaRoman," *Davar,* 23 August 1974.

105. Perliss, "Aflayah."

106. One of their demands was to increase their eligibility for army service. See, for example, Cohen, "The Black Panthers and Israeli Society," pp. 148–49.

107. Although most of the story is set in a kibbutz, I include this novel in our discussion of *ma'abarah* literature because the protagonist and many of the other characters are products of the camps. Also, it covers the same period as the other books and many of the same issues.

108. Amir, *Tarnegol Kaparot,* pp. 32–33.

109. See, for example, Ruti Tradler, "HaDekel Lo Meḥubar Tov LaAdamah, Kamoni," *Moznayim* 57, nos. 5–6 (October–November 1983): 88; Ya'akov Rabi, "HaSipur VeHaTe'udah," *'Al HaMishmar,* 16 March 1984; Yaron Elikayam, "Ma'aseh Ḥinukhi," *Ma'ariv,* 6 December 1988.

110. Philip Gillon, "Robbed of Dignity," *Jerusalem Post Magazine,* 11 March 1988.

111. See p. 85 above.

112. As in S. Yizhar, "Efrayim Ḥozer LaAspeset" (Ephraim returns to the alfalfa) (1938) or many of Amos Oz's kibbutz stories.

113. Ammiel Alcalay, *After Jews and Arabs: Remaking Levantine Culture* (Minneapolis: University of Minnesota Press, 1993), p. 232.

114. Terms used to label the writers of this literature include the generation of 1948; *dor hapalmaḥ* (the Palmach generation), *dor ba'aretz* (first generation of native Israelis), and native writers.

115. Gershon Shaked credits Dan Miron with formulating the term; Shaked has himself written about these works under the title "First Person Plural." Gershon Shaked, *The Shadows Within* (Philadelphia: Jewish Publication Society, 1987), pp. 145–63.

116. Shaked, *Gal Ḥadash BaSiporet HaIvrit* (Tel Aviv: Sifriyat Poalim, 1970), pp. 11–12.

117. Shaked, "Literature and Its Audience: On the Reception of Israeli Literature in the Forties and Fifties," *Prooftexts* 7, no. 3 (September 1987) 207–8.

118. Shaked, "Hebrew Prose Fiction After the War of Liberation," in *Modern Hebrew Literature* 5, no. 1–2 (Summer 1979), pp. 21–34.

119. Ibid., pp 23–24.

120. Nurit Gertz, "Temurot BaSifrut HaIvrit," *HaSifrut* 29 (December 1969): 71.

121. *HaGal HaḤadash*: Gershon Shaked's term has been widely adopted by scholars of Israeli literature.

122. Arnold J. Band, "The Evanescence of Nationalist Themes in Israeli Literature," in Michael C. Hillman, ed., *Literature East and West: Essays on Nationalism and Asian Literatures* 23 (1979), p. 115.

123. See, for example, Shimon Sandbank, "Contemporary Israeli Literature: The Withdrawal from Certainty," *Triquarterly* 39 (1977): pp. 3–18.

124. For a more detailed discussion, see Gertz, "Temurot," pp. 69–75.

125. Note, for example, the title character of A. B. Yehoshua's *Molkho* (Tel Aviv: HaSifriyah, 1987), and the popularity of Dan Benaya Seri's writing: *'Ugiyot HaMelaḥ Shel Savta Sultanah* (Jerusalem: Keter, 1980) and *Ẓiporei Ẓel* (Jerusalem: Keter, 1987).

126. Bartov, *Shesh Kenafaim LeEḥad* (Tel Aviv: Sifriyat Po'alim, 1954). In an article on the mass immigration as a topic in Israeli literature of the 1950s, Dan Laor also mentions the novels Shlomo Schwartz, *Makom She'ayn Lo Shem* (A place without a name) (Tel Aviv: HaKibbutz HaMeuchad, 1955); Milo Ohel, *Gesher* (Bridge) (Tel Aviv: Sifriyat Yalkut, 1955). Dan Laor, "Ha'Aliyah HaHamonit Ke'Tokhen VeNose' BaSifrut Ha'Ivrit BiSh'not HaMedinah HaRishonot," *HaẒiyonut* 14 (1989): 161–75.

127. Menashe is the name of the character in Bartov's novel who leaves his family to join a kibbutz.

128. Cited in Laor, "Ha'Aliyah," pp. 161–75.

129. Shimon Ballas in an interview with P. Azai, 19 April 1964.

## CHAPTER 6. CHILDHOOD AND HOME IN IRAQ: NARRATIVES IN ARABIC

1. Susan Slyomovics, "Rebbele Mordekhele's Pilgrimage in New York, Tel Aviv, and Carpathian Ruthenia," paper delivered at the Conference on Jewish Folklore: An American-Israeli Dialogue, University of Pennsylvania, 17 October 1989.

2. Yiẓḥak Bar-Moshe, *Bayt Fī Baghdād* (Jerusalem: Association of Academics from Iraq in Israel, 1983), p. 63.

3. Kalir Yaniv, "Baghdad Sheli," in Stahl's *Adot Yisrael* (Tel Aviv: Am Oved, 1978), p. 187. The Sambatyon is a mythical river that rests on the Sabbath; according to tradition the ten lost tribes went beyond this river.

4. Eva Hoffman, *Lost in Translation* (New York: Dutton, 1989), p. 5.

5. There is no word for its opposite. Fred Davis, *Yearning For Yesterday: A Sociology of Nostalgia* (New York: Macmillan, 1979), p. 14.

6. Malcolm Chase and Christopher Shaw, "The Dimensions of Nostalgia," in *The Imagined Past: History and Nostalgia* (New York: Manchester University Press, 1989), pp. 1–17.

7. Davis, *Yearning*, p. 73. His emphasis.

8. Ibid., p. 95.

9. Samīr Naqqāsh, "Laylat 'Urābā," in *Yawm Ḥabalat wa-Ajhaḍat al-Dunyā* (Jerusalem: Al-Sharq Al-'Arabiyya, 1980).

10. See chapter 4 for a discussion of the reasons these authors chose to write in Arabic.

11. Yiẓḥak Bar-Moshe, *Warā' al-Sūr* (Jerusalem: Al-Sharq, 1972).

12. Samīr Naqqāsh, *Ḥikāyah Kull Zamān wa-Makān* (Story of any time and place) (Tel Aviv: Association for the Promotion of Research, Literature and Art, 1978).

13. See, for example, the discussion on childhood in Susanna Egan, *Patterns of Experience in Autobiography* (Chapel Hill: University of North Carolina Press, 1984), chap. 2.

14. Pascal explains the success autobiographers enjoy in writing about their childhood (relative to their treatment of later stages) in part by noting "the strength of an established tradition." Roy Pascal, *Design and Truth in Autobiography,* (Cambridge: Harvard University Press, 1960), p. 84.

15. Ibid.

16. "The Garden of Eden provides so familiar an analogue for childhood that the merest allusions to it set off chain reactions of comprehension." Egan, *Patterns,* p. 68.

17. Likewise, history, as a genre, has been analyzed as narrative. Autobiography is personal history and thus subject to similar tools of analysis.

18. Pascal, *Design,* pp. 61–83.

19. Egan, *Patterns,* pp. 14–22.

20. William Zinsser, "Writing and Remembering: A Memoir and an Introduction," in William Zinsser, ed., *Inventing the Truth: The Art and Craft of Memoir* (Boston: Houghton Mifflin, 1987), p. 21.

21. Pascal, *Design,* p. 78.

22. Alfred Kazin, "The Self as History: Reflections on Autobiography," in Marc Pachter, ed., *Telling Lives: The Biographer's Art* (Washington, D.C.: New Republic Books, 1979), pp. 88–89.

23. Georges Gusdorf, "Conditions and Limits of Autobiography," trans. James Olney, in James Olney, ed., *Autobiography: Essays Theoretical and Critical* (Princeton: Princeton University Press, 1980), p. 42. His italics.

24. Yiẓḥak Bar-Moshe. *al-Khurūj min al-'Irāq* (Jerusalem: Association for Jewish Academics from Iraq, 1975), p. 20.

25. Shmuel Moreh, foreword to Bar-Moshe, *Bayt Fī Baghdād,* p. 7.

26. Pascal, *Design,* p. 163.

27. Interview with Samīr Naqqāsh, Petaḥ Tikva, 21 May 1989.

28. Andrew Gurr, *The Writer in Exile: Creative Use of Home in Modern Literature* (Atlantic Highlands, N.J.: Humanities Press, 1981), pp. 23–24.

29. Ibid., p. 11.

30. *Jinn* is the root for the English word "genie" and the Arabic *majnun* (crazy, possessed).

31. Shmuel Moreh, "Olamo HeMeyuḥad Shel Yitzḥak Bar-Moshe," *Shevet Ve'Am* 3, no. 8 (April 1978): 425–44.

32. Yiẓḥak Bar-Moshe, *Warā' al-Sūr* (Jerusalem, Al-Sharq, 1976), pp. 167–78.

33. Yaniv, "Baghdad Sheli," p. 188:

> I remember the rooftops of Baghdad as a special sight. They were, it seems, the source of my great love of looking over the gardens of the city, and the pattern from the various carpets. In the summer, the rooftops were noisy with activity. Fruits and vegetables were left to dry, chains of okra were hung everywhere, and most importantly, on days of unbearable heat, people would bring up the beds and sleep there. . . .

34. "In a typical extended family living in a *hosh murabba'* separate suites would be used by each generation though major domestic tasks would be shared." John Warren, "The Courtyard Houses of Baghdad: A Rich Heritage," *Literary Review Supplement,* 1982, pp. 87–94.

35. Ibrāhīm al-Wardānī, "Ṣawārīkh," *Al-Jumhūrīyyah,* 23 September 1983.

36. Naim Kattan, *Farewell to Babylon,* pp. 37–38.

37. Bar-Moshe, *Bayt Fī Baghdād,* chap. 67. Chapter 2 discusses the historical background to this fear and describes the worsening atmosphere for the Iraqi Jews.

38. For one reading of the *sukkah* as a symbol, see Herbert Levine, "The Symbolic Sukkah in Psalms," *Prooftexts* 7 (1987): 259–67.

39. Compare this to Rousseau's quotation cited by Egan: "I may omit or transpose facts, or make mistakes in dates; but I cannot go wrong about what I have felt." Egan, *Patterns,* p. 75.

40. For discussion of the criteria used in categorizing the novella, see Henry Steinhauer, "Towards a Definition of the Novella," *Seminar* 6 (1970): 154–72; Judith Liebowitz, *Narrative Purpose in the Novella* (The Hague: Mouton, 1974); A. F. Scott, *Current Literary Terms: A Concise Dictionary of Their Origin and Use* (London: Macmillan, 1980).

41. The *qaṣīda* is a poetic genre that often begins with the *nasib,* a section full of longing for the past, leading into a long description of the journey or battle.

42. For more discussion on the use of colloquial Arabic, see chapter 4.

43. His name, meaning "the Persian" or "the foreigner," shares a root with the word translated as "obscure, unintelligible."

44. Moreh, foreword to Bar-Moshe, *Bayt Fī Baghdād.*

45. Davis, *Yearning,* p. 85.

46. Ibid., p. 47.

47. See, for example, Gerard Genette's discussion of the pseudoiterative in

*Narrative Discourse: An Essay in Method,* trans. Jane E. Lewin (Ithaca, N.Y.: Cornell University Press, 1980), p. 121.

48. Egan, *Patterns,* pp. ix–x.

CHAPTER 7. DIFFERENT PERSPECTIVES ON LIFE IN IRAQ. NARRATIVES IN ARABIC

1. Shalom Darwīsh, *Phraim! Phraim!* (Tel Aviv: Kedem House Publications, 1986).

2. His short story "Neft Aleikha" was published in *Iton 77,* vol. 5, no. 28 (June–August 1981) 36–37.

3. Shalom Darwīsh, *Bayḍat al-Dīk* (Jerusalem: Al-Sharq, 1976).

4. Interview with Shalom Darwīsh, Haifa, 22 May 1989.

5. Darwīsh, *Bayḍat al-Dīk,* pp. 40–46, "Abū Liḥyah" (Bearded One).

6. Ibid., pp. 28–37.

7. Ibid., "Hadīth al-Nāqarah," pp. 72–83.

8. 'Aḥmad "Abd al-Ilāh, *Nash'at Al-Qiṣṣah Wa-Taṭawwuruhā fī al-'Irāq, 1908–1939* (Baghdad: Maṭba'āt Shafīq, 1969), p. 244. The Jews of Kurdistan followed the Muslim custom. See also Moshe Islan and Raḥel Nissim, *MiMinhageihem VeOraḥ Ḥayeihem shel Yehudei 'Irak* (Tel Aviv: Ofer, 1982), p. 44.

9. Interview with Shalom Darwīsh, Haifa, 22 May 1989.

10. Dina: "Doris, look who is here to see you. Your sister Mazal. This is a sign from heaven that you have luck *[mazal],* and everything will be good luck" (p. 33).

11. *Bulbul khakh* is a game played using a thick stick to bat a smaller stick as far as possible. Here the phallic symbolism of the stick is reinforced by the name of the game. *Bulbul* is a children's name for penis in Hebrew according to Dan Ben Amoẓ, *Milon Olami LeIvrit Meduberet* (Tel Aviv: Zmora-Bitan, 1980).

12. Shimon Ballas, *Ba'Ir HaTaḥtit* (Tel Aviv: Sifriyat Tarmil, 1979).

13. Shimon Ballas, *Mul HaḤomah* (Ramat Gan: Massada, 1969).

14. "Nof Yerushalmi" [Jerusalem landscape], "Zeir Ḥarẓiot" [Bouquet of chrysanthemums], and "Nim-Lo-Nim" [Half asleep]. The first deals with the Six Day War, and the second focuses on the artistic process; neither has any evident connections to Iraq. In the last an Iraqi-born Jew is described as defeated by his move to Israel. This character has greater affinity to many of the characters included in Ballas's novel *HaMa'abarah* than to the others in the collection. For the discussion of this work, see chapter 5.

15. The afterword establishes the autobiographical basis to the story.

16. Shimon Ballas, *Hitbaharut* (Clarification) (Tel Aviv: Sifriyat Po'alim, 1972).

17. Ballas, *Ḥeder Na'ul* (A locked room) (Tel Aviv: Zmora-Bitan, Modan, 1980).

18. Ballas, *HaḤoref HaAḥaron* (The last winter) (Jerusalem: Keter, 1984).

19. Ballas, *HaYoresh* (The heir) (Tel Aviv: Zmora-Bitan, 1987).

20. Ballas, *LoBimkomah* (Not in her place) (Tel Aviv: Zmora-Bitan, 1994).

21. Ballas, *Otot Stav* (Signs of autumn) (Tel Aviv: Zmora-Bitan, 1992).

22. Sāmī Michael, *Sufah Bein HaDekalim* (Tel Aviv: Am Oved, 1975).

23. Sāmī Michael, *Ḥofen Shel Arafel* (Tel Aviv: Am Oved, 1979).

24. While the work deals with a very sophisticated topic, it does so in a manner appropriate for younger readers. The style is simpler than in Michael's other works, paragraphs are shorter, and the chapters are episodic. "The junior novel is less lengthy and less complex than the adult novel and is concerned with adolescent characters and their problems." Geneva R. Hanna and Mariana K. McAllister, *Books, Young People, and Reading Guidance* (New York: Harper and Brothers, 1960), p. 22. Michael's novel is 158 pages long, including 20 pages of illustrations.

25. At the time the story takes place, the ancient Bedouin code of honor and sanctuary was still very much in force in the modern city of Baghdad. The code required the granting of protective asylum to any one who requested it, no matter how odious the person or difficult the task.

26. Sāmī Michael, *Paḥonim VeḤalomot* (Tel Aviv: Am Oved, 1979). See the discussion in chapter 5.

27. See, for example, Aharon Appelfeld, *Ashan* (Jerusalem: Marcus, 1969); Ben Ẓion Tomer, "Yaldei HaẒēl," premiered *Habimah* 1962, published 1963; Natan Gross, Itamar Yaov-Kest, and Rinah Klinov, eds., *HaShoah BaShirah Ha'Ivrit: Mivḥar*, introduced by Hillel Barzel (Tel Aviv: HaKibbutz HaMeuchad, 1974).

28. See note 24 above.

29. To be fair, the mother of Ramzī's Jewish friend Edward cannot understand why Ramzī went over to "that Christian's house." It is not clear whether or not she knows that George had betrayed Edward to the police.

30. Sāmī Michael, *Ḥasut* (Refuge) (Tel Aviv: Am Oved, 1977).

31. Sāmī Michael, *Ḥaẓoẓrah BaVadi* (Tel Aviv: Am Oved, 1987).

32. Sāmī Michael, *Victoria* (Tel Aviv: Am Oved, 1993).

33. This book is the subject of a forthcoming study.

34. Yiẓḥak Bar-Moshe, *Khurūj Min Al-'Iraq* (Jerusalem, 1975).

35. None of Ballas's stories depict weddings; his characters are too alienated to join in such a communal event.

36. Eli Amir intended to focus on the period in Iraq before the departure of the Jews; instead he found that he had to write his *ma'abarah* novel first. Interview with the author, Jerusalem, May 1989. He later fulfilled this intention in *Mafriaḥ HaYonim* (Tel Aviv: Am Oved, 1992).

## CHAPTER 8. CONCLUSION

1. Elizabeth Klosty Beaujour, *Alien Tongues: Bilingual Russian Writers of the "First" Emigration* (Ithaca: Cornell University Press, 1989), p. 39.

2. These differences may also be attributed to the maturing of the respective writers.

3. Sāmī Michael, for example, never lived in a transit camp.

4. See for example Moshe ibn Ezra's poem "Ad an begalut shulḥu shaloaḥ raglai," in Ḥaim Schirmann, *HaShirah HaIvrit BeSefarad UVeProvans* (Jerusalem: Mosad Bialik, 1959) 1:385–87, subtitled *sivlo hagoleh* (the exile's suffering) in which the poet's exile is from Andalusia and all his longing for return is directed toward Muslim Spain. See also Abravanel's description of the 1492 Expulsion in his introduction to his commentary on Deuteronomy. He speaks of God having "sent into exile" the Jews who had lived securely on Spanish soil, noting, "I was among the exiles."

5. See chapter 5, p. 99.

# Bibliography

PRIMARY SOURCES


Amir, Eli. *Mafriaḥ HaYonim*. Tel Aviv: Am Oved, 1992

———. *Tarnegol Kaparot*. Sifriyat Ofakim, no. 113. Tel Aviv: Am Oved, 1983.

Ballas, Shimon. *Ash'ab mi Baghdad*. Tel Aviv: Am Oved, 1970.

———. *Ba'Ir HaTaḥtit*. Tel Aviv: Sifriyat Tarmil, 1979.

———. *HaMa'abarah*. Tel Aviv: Am Oved, 1964.

———. *HaYoresh*. Tel Aviv: Zmora-Bitan, 1987.

———. *Ḥeder Na'ul*. Tel Aviv: Zmora-Bitan, Modan, 1980.

———. *Hitbaharut*. Tel Aviv: Sifriyat Po'alim, 1972.

———. *Ḥoref Aḥaron*. Jerusalem: Keter, 1984.

———. *Lo Bimkomah*. Tel Aviv: Zmora-Bitan, 1994.

———. *Mul HaḤomah*. Ramat Gan: Massada, 1969.

———. *Otot Stav*. Tel Aviv: Zmora-Bitan, 1992.

———. *Shoes of Tanboury*. New York: Sabra, 1970. In English.

———. *VeHu Aḥer*. Tel Aviv: Zmora-Bitan, 1991.

Bar-Moshe, Yiẓḥak. *al-Khurūj min al-'Iraq*. Jerusalem: Association for Jewish Academics from Iraq, 1975.

———. *Āyyam fī Baghdād*. Shefaram: Dār Al-Sharq, 1988.

———. *Aswār al-Quds*. Jerusalem: Al-Sharq, 1976.

———. *Bayt Fī Baghdād*. Jerusalem: Association for Jewish Academics from Iraq, 1983.

———. *Raqṣat al-Maṭar*. Jerusalem: Al-Sharq, 1974.

———. *Wara' al-Sur*. Jerusalem: Al-Sharq, 1972.

Bilbūl, Ya'qūb. *Al-Jamrah Al-Ūlā*. Baghdad: Maktabat al-Ma'arif, 1938.

Darwīsh, Shalom. *Ba'ḍ al-Nās*. Baghdad: Sharikat al-tijārah wa-al-ṭibā'a, 1948.

———. *Baydat al-Ḍīk*. Jerusalem: Al-Sharq, 1976.

Darwīsh, Shalom. "HaMartef," *Apirion* 9 (Spring 1988): 20–23.
———. *Phraim! Phraim!* Tel Aviv: Kedem, 1986.
———. "Neft Aleikha," *Iton 77*, vol. 5, no. 28 (June–August 1981), pp. 36–37.
Hakkak, Lev. *HaAsufim*. Tel Aviv: Tammuz, 1977.
———. *Im Eshkeḥekh*. Jerusalem: Kiryat-Sefer, 1981.
Michael, Sāmī. *Ḥasut*. Tel Aviv: Am Oved, May 1977.
———. *Ḥaẓoẓrah BeVadi*. Tel Aviv: Am Oved, 1987.
———. *Ḥofen Shel Arafel*. Tel Aviv: Am Oved, June 1979.
———. *Paḥomin VeḤalomot*. Tel Aviv: Am Oved, 1979.
———. *Shavim VeShavim Yoter*. Tel Aviv: Boostan, 1974.
———. *Sufah Bein HaDekalim*. Tel Aviv: Am Oved, 1975.
———. *Victoria*. Tel Aviv: Am Oved, 1993.
Naqqāsh, Samīr. *Al-Junūh wa-al-insiyāb*. Shefaram: Al-Mashrek, 1980 [1979?].
———. *Al-Khaṭa'*. Jerusalem: Al-Ma'ārif, n.d. [1971].
———. *Al-Rijs*. Israel: [n.p.], 1987.
———. *Anā Wa-Ha'ulā'i Wa-al-Fiṣām*. Tel Aviv: Association for the Promotion of Research, Literature and Art, 1978.
———. *Fī Ghiyābihi*. Shefaram: Al-Mashrik, 1981.
———. *Fuwwah Yā Dam!* Israel: [n.p.] 1987.
———. *Hikāyat Kull Zamān Wa-Makān*. Tel Aviv: Association for the Promotion of Research, Literature and Art, 1978.
———. *Nazūlahu Wakhīṭ al-Shayṭān*. Jerusalem: Association for Jewish Academics from Iraq, 1986.
———. *Yawm Ḥabalat wa-Ajhaḍat al-Dunyā*. Jerusalem: al-Sharq Al-'Arabiyya, Jan.1980.
Rabeeya, David. *Tehom Shemesh*. Tel Aviv: Alef, 1983.
Rabi [Rabeeya], David. *Kapak HaBagdadi*. Tel Aviv: Alef, 1975.
Rejwan, Raḥamin. *'Al Geḥalim*. Tel Aviv: Sifriyat Tarmil, 1985.
Shā'ūl, Anwar. *Al-Ḥiṣād Al-Awwal*. Baghdad: Al-Maktabah, 1930.

## SECONDARY SOURCES

'Abd al-Ilāh, Aḥmad. *Al-Adab Al-Qaṣaṣī fī al-'Irāq*. Baghdad: Dār al-Ḥurriyah, 1977.
———. *Nash'at Al-Qiṣṣah Wa-Taṭawwuruhā fī al-'Irāq: 1908–1939*. Baghdad: Maṭba'at Shafīq, 1969.
"ACTFL Proficiency Guidelines." *Foreign Language Annals* 22, no. 4 (September 1989).
Afkhami, Mahnaz. "Women, Revolution, and Exile: Oral History." Lecture at the University of Pennsylvania, 11 November 1989.
Al-'Anī, Shujā' Musallam. *Al-Mar'ah Fī Al-Qiṣṣah Al-'Iraqiyyah*. Baghdad: Dār Al-Shu'ūn Al-Thaqāfiyyah Al-'Āmma, 1986.

Alcalay, Ammiel. *After Jews and Arabs: Remaking Levantine Culture*. Minneapolis: University of Minnesota Press, 1993.
———. "Keys to the Garden: Israeli Culture in the Middle East." *The Literary Review*, Winter 1994.
Almog, Shmuel. *Zionism and History: The Rise of a New Jewish Consciousness*. Translated by Ina Friedman. New York: St. Martin's Press, 1987.
Amir, Eli. "HaMahapekhah BeḤayai," *'Al HaMishmar*, 10 January 1986.
———. "Iraqi Jews in Israel." *Present Tense* 11 no. 2 (Winter 1984): 33–34.
Amir, Eli, Sāmī Michael, and Nissim Rejwan. "Iraqi Jews In Israel." *Present Tense* 11, no. 2 (Winter 1984): 32–45.
Amir-Coffin, Edna. "Stam Aravim VeStam Yehudim." *HaDoar*. 25 August 1978.
Antonovsky, Aaron, and Alan Arian. *Hopes and Fears of Israelis*. Jerusalem: Academic Press, 1972.
Arad, Miriam. "Hebrew Bookshelf." *Jerusalem Post*, 15 May 1964.
Avineri, Shlomo. *The Making of Modern Zionism: The Intellectual Origins of the Jewish State*. New York: Basic Books, 1981.
Avishai, Mordekhai. "Yisrael HaSheniyah BeRoman Ḥiver," 28 August 1964. From the Bet HaSofer Tchernichovsky archives, Tel Aviv.
Aviv, Shlomo. "Arabeskah 'Al HaAhavah HaAvudah." *Ma'ariv*. 22 August 1986.
'Ayatim, Yariv. "Ḥasut Kevedah," *Ma'ariv*, 10 February 1978.
Azai, P. "Shimon Ballas, Meḥaber *HaMa'abarah*." *HaAreẓ*, 19 April 1964.
Baer, Yitzhak F. *Galut*. Translated by Robert Warshow. New York: Schocken, 1947.
Ballas, Shimon. "Sofer Yehudi Ba'al Zehut Kefulah." *HaAreẓ*, 25 July 1975.
———. "Al-Tawjih al-Wāqu'ī fī qiṣṣaṣ Shalom Darwīsh," *Al Karmīl* 10 (1989): 29-60.
Balswick, J. D., and C. Macrides. "Parental stimulus for adolescent rebellion." *Adolescence* 10 (1975): 253–66.
Band, Arnold J. "The Evanescence of Nationalist Themes in Israeli Literature." *Literature East and West* 23, 1987, 111–16.
Barrett, Charles Raymond. *Short Story Writing: A Practical Treatise on the Art of the Short Story*. New York: Baker and Taylor Company, 1898.
Barshan, Yehuda (Jūrjī). "Ḥiwar Mā'a Samīr Naqqāsh." *Al-Sharq* 11 no. 3 (August–September 1981): 53–59.
Bartov, Hanoch. *Shesh Kenafaim LeEḥad*. Tel Aviv: Sifriyat Po'alim, 1954.
Basri, Me'ir. *A'lām al-Yahūd fī al-'Irāq al-Ḥadīth*. Jerusalem: Association for Jewish Academics from Iraq, 1983.
Al-Bassoun. "Riḥla Ma'a Al-Dubb Al-Quṭī." *al-Anbā'*, 8 March 1984.
Batatu, Hanna. *The Old Social Classes and the Revolutionary Movements of Iraq*. Princeton: Princeton University Press, 1978.
Beaujour, Elizabeth Klosty. *Alien Tongues: Bilingual Russian Writers of the "First" Emigration*. Ithaca, N.Y.: Cornell University Press, 1989.

Beck, Lois, and Nikki Keddie, eds. *Women in the Muslim World*. Cambridge: Harvard University Press, 1978.
Ben Amoẓ, Dan. *Milon Olami LeIvrit Meduberet*. Tel Aviv: Zmora-Bitan, 1980.
Ben Ezer, Ehud. "Bein Yehudim La'Aravim." *'Al HaMishmar*, 22 July 1977.
———. "HaYaldut Hī 'al-Z'manit." *HaAreẓ*, 27 July 1979.
Benaya-Seri, Dan. *'Ugiyot HaMelaḥ Shel Savta Sultanah*. Jerusalem: Keter, 1980.
———. *Ẓiporei Ẓel*. Jerusalem: Keter, 1987.
Ben Sasson, H. H. "Galut." In vol. 7 of the *Encyclopedia Judaica* 1972.
Ben-Yosef, Yiẓḥak. "Sāmī Michael: Ḥasut," Madrikh LeḤinukh ULeHora'ah. September 1978.
Benjamin, Walter. "The Task of the Translator." In *Illuminations*, edited by Hannah Arendt, translated by Harry Zohn. New York: Schocken, 1969.
Beser, Ya'akov. "Terumah LaMahalakh HaSifruti HehḤadash." *Davar*, 15 July 1977.
———. "Tiskul 'Amok." *'Al HaMishmar*, 26 July 1974.
Bezalel, Yiẓḥak. *Kitvei Soferim Yehudim Sefaradiyim U-Mizraḥiyim BiLeshonot Yehudiyot VeZarot*. Tel Aviv: Merkaz LeShiluv Moreshet Yahadut HaMizraḥ, 1982.
———. *Levadam BiMivẓar HaKeẓ*. Tel Aviv: Sifriyat Ma'ariv, 1976.
Biale, David. *Power and Powerlessness in Jewish History*. New York: Schocken, 1986.
Blanc, Haim. *Communal Dialects in Baghdad*. Cambridge: Harvard University Press, 1964.
———. "Hebrew in Israel: Trends and Problems." *The Middle East Journal* 11, no. 4 (Autumn 1957): 397–409.
Blau, Joshua. *Renaissance of Modern Hebrew and Standard Arabic*. Near Eastern Studies no. 18. Berkeley: University of California, 1981.
Booth, Wayne C. *The Rhetoric of Fiction*. 2d ed. Chicago: University of Chicago Press, 1983.
Bouvard, Marguerite Guzman. *Landscape and Exile*. Boston: Rowan Tree Press, 1985.
Brann, Ross. *The Compunctious Poet: Cultural Ambiguity and Hebrew Poetry in Muslim Spain*. Baltimore: Johns Hopkins University Press, 1991.
———. "Tavniyot Shel Galut BeKinot 'Ivriyot Ve'Araviyot." In *Sefer Yisrael Levine: Koveẓ Meḥkarim BaSifrut HaIvrit LeDoroteiha*, edited by Reuven Tsur and Tovah Rosen, 45–61. Jerusalem: Makhon Katz, 1994.
Calvino, Italo. *The Literature Machine*. Translated by Patrick Creagh. London: Secker and Warburg, 1987.
Chase, Malcolm, and Christopher Shaw. *The Imagined Past: History and Nostalgia*. New York: Manchester University Press, 1989.
Chomsky, William. *Hebrew: The Eternal Language*. Philadelphia: The Jewish Publication Society of America, 1957.

Cohen, A. J. "The Anti-Jewish *Farhud* in Baghdad, 1941." *Middle Eastern Studies*, October 1966, 2–18.
Cohen, Hayyim L. *The Jews of the Middle East, 1860–1972*. New York: John Wiley and Sons, 1973.
———. "A Note on Social Change Among Iraqi Jews, 1917–1951." *The Jewish Journal of Sociology*, no. 8 (1966): 204–8.
———. "University Education Among Iraqi-Born Jews." *The Jewish Journal of Sociology*, no. 11 (1969): 59–66.
Cohen, Mark R., and Abraham L. Udovitch, eds. *Jews Among Arabs: Contacts and Boundaries*. Princeton, N.J.: The Darwin Press, 1989.
Cohen, Ruth. "HaMaʿabarah LeShimon Ballas," 29 May 1964. From the archives of Bet HaSofer Tchernichovsky, Tel Aviv.
Curtis, Michael, and Mordecai S. Cheroff, eds. *Israel: Social Structure and Change*. New Brunswick, N.J.: Transaction Books, 1973.
Darwīsh, Dr. Salman. *Kull Shay' Hādī Fī al-ʿIyādah*. Jerusalem: Association of Jewish Academics from Iraq, 1981.
Davis, Fred. *Yearning For Yesterday: A Sociology of Nostalgia*. New York: Macmillan, 1979.
Debi-Juri, Lillian. "Sifrut Mivudedet." *Mifgash* [*Liqā'*], nos. 4–5 [8–9] (Winter 1986): 124–25.
Deshen, Shlomo. "Baghdad Jewry in Late Ottoman Times: The Emergence of Social Classes and of Secularization." *AJS Review* 19, no. 1 (1994): 19–44.
Deshen, Shlomo, and Walter P. Zenner. *Jewish Societies in the Middle East*. New York: University Press of America, 1982.
Eagleton, Terry. *Exiles and Emigres*. New York: Schocken Books, 1970.
Egan, Susanna. *Patterns of Experience in Autobiography*. Chapel Hill: University of North Carolina Press, 1984.
Eickelman, Dale F. *The Middle East: An Anthropological Approach*. Englewood Cliffs, N.J.: Prentice-Hall, 1980.
Eisen, Arnold. *Galut: Modern Jewish Reflection on Homelessness and Homecoming*. Bloomington: Indiana University Press, 1986.
Eisenstadt, S. N. *The Absorption of Immigrants*. Westport, Conn: Greenwood Press, 1975. Original edition, London: Routledge and Kegan Paul, 1954.
Eisenstadt, S. N., Rivkah Bar Yosef, and Chaim Adler, eds. *Integration and Development in Israel*. New York: Praeger, 1970.
Elad, P. "Shetei Panim LeḤasut," *Moznayim*. From the archives of Bet HaSofer Tchernichovsky, Tel Aviv.
Elazar, Daniel. *The Other Jews: The Sepharadim Today*. New York: Basic Books, 1989.
Elikayam, Yaron. "Maʿaseh Ḥinukhi." *Maʿariv*, 6 December 1988.
Ellis, Harry B. *One Land, Two Peoples*. New York: Thomas Cromwell, 1972.
Erikson, Erik. *Identity, Youth and Crisis*. New York: Norton, 1968.
Even, Yosef. "HaDibur HaSamui." *HaSifrut* 1, no. 1 (Spring 1968): 140-152.

Even-Zohar, Itamar. "Language Written in a Language with a Defective Polysystem: Notes to Paul Wexler's Rebuttal." *HaSifrut* 3, no. 2 (November 1971): 339–40.

Feldman, Yael. *Modernism and Cultural Transfer: Gabriel Preil and the Tradition of Jewish Literary Bilingualism*. Cincinnati: Hebrew Union College Press, 1986.

Ferguson, Charles A. "Diglossia." *Word* 15 no. 2 (August 1959): 325–40.

Fischel, Walter. *Jews in the Economic and Political Life in Mediaeval Islam*. New York: Ktav, 1969.

Fisher, Sydney Nettleton. *The Middle East: A History*. New York: Knopf, 1959.

Fox, Sarit. "Mahapekhot Nil'agot." *HaDo'ar*, 19 December 1980.

Frankenstein, Carl, ed. *Between Past and Future: Essays and Studies on Aspects of Immigrant Absorption in Israel*. Jerusalem: The Henrietta Szold Foundation for Child and Youth Welfare, 1953.

Gallman, Waldeman. *Iraq Under General Nuri*. Baltimore: Johns Hopkins University Press, 1964.

Gat, Moshe. "The Connection Between the Bombings in Baghdad and the Emigration of the Jews from Iraq: 1950–51." *Middle Eastern Studies* 24, no. 3 (July 1988): 312–29.

———. "Iraq and the Legislation on Jewish Emigration: March 1950." *Asian and African Studies* 21, no. 3 (November 1987).

Genette, Gerard. *Narrative Discourse: An Essay in Method*. Translated by Jane E. Lewin. Ithaca, N.Y.: Cornell University Press, 1980.

Gertz, Nurit. "Temurot BaSifrut HaIvrit." *HaSifrut* 29 (December 1979): 69–75.

Gillon, Philip. "Robbed of Dignity." *Jerusalem Post Magazine*, 11 March 1988.

Gingold-Gilboa, Shulamit. "Lehikara' Bein Shetei Tarbuyot." *Iton 77*, nos. 52–53 (April–May 1984): 40–41.

Glitzenshtein-Meyer, Esther. "HaPra'ot BiYehudei Baghdad." *Pe'amim* 8 (1981): 20–37.

Golovsky, T. "Tivo Shel Ha'Ani Ma'ashim' BaMa'abarah." *Tarbut, Sifrut VeOmanut*, 6 May 1964.

Grayzel, Solomon. *A History of the Jews*. Philadelphia: Jewish Publication Society, 1968.

Grinberg, Leon, and Rebeca Grinberg. *Psychoanalytic Perspectives on Migration and Exile*. Translated by Nancy Festinger. New Haven: Yale University Press, 1989.

Guillén, Claudio. "On the Literature of Exile and Counter-Exile." *Books Abroad*, Spring 1976, 271–80.

Gurr, Andrew. *The Writer in Exile: Creative Use of Home in Modern Literature*. Atlantic Highlands, N.J.: Humanities Press, 1981.

Haddad, Heskel. *Flight From Babylon*. New York: McGraw-Hill, 1986.

———. *Jews of Arab and Islamic Countries: History, Problems, Solutions*. New York: Shengold Publishers, 1984.

Hagani, Amirah. "Mah Kedai." *HaShavu'a BaKibbutz HaArẓi*, 27 January 1978.
Hakkak, Herzl, and Balfour Hakkak. "Re'ayon Im HaSofer Sami Micha'el." *Turim*, May 1981, 42–46.
Hakkak, Lev. "Demut Yahadut HaMizraḥ BaSipur Ha'Ivri HaKaẓar." *Shevet Va'Am* 9 (1980): 149–58.
———. *Perakim BeSifrut Yehudei HaMizraḥ BiMedinat Yisrael*. Jerusalem: Kiryat Sefer, 1985.
———. "Terumatam Shel Yoẓei Irak LaSifrut HaIvrit BaAreẓ." In *Proceedings of Seventh World Congress on Jewish Studies*. Jerusalem: Magnes, 1977.
———. *Yerudim VeNa'alim*. Jerusalem: Kiryat Sefer, 1981.
———. "Yeẓiratam HaSifrutit Shel Yoẓei HaMizraḥ BeYisrael." Unpublished manuscript.
Halkin, A. S. "The Medieval Jewish Attitude Toward Hebrew." In *Biblical and Other Studies*, edited by Alexander Altmann, 233–48. Cambridge: Harvard University Press, 1963.
Halpern, Ben. "Exile and Redemption: A Secular Zionist View." *Judaism* 29, no. 2 (Spring 1980): 180.
Hamel, John Thomas. "Ja'far al-Khalili and the Modern Iraqi Story." Ph.D. diss., University of Michigan, 1972.
Ḥammūdī, Bāsim 'Abd al-Ḥamīd. *Riḥlah Ma'a Al-Qiṣṣah Al-'Irāqiyyah*. Manshūrāt wizārat al-thaqāfah wa-al-I'lām, 210. Baghdad: Dār al-Rāshid, 1980.
Hanna, Geneva R., and Mariana K. McAllister. *Books, Young People, and Reading Guidance*. New York: Harper, 1960.
Hary, Benjamin. "Middle Arabic: Proposals for New Terminology." *Al-'Arabiyya* 22, nos. 1–2 (1989):19–36.
"Ḥasut VeGiz'anut BaḤan HaYerushalmi." *HaAreẓ*, 16 October 1980.
Ḥazan, Ephraim, ed. *Misgav Yerushalayim Studies in Jewish Literature*. Jerusalem: Misgav Yerushalayim, Institute for Research and Oriental Jewish Heritage, 1987.
Hever, Hannan, "Israeli Fiction of the Early Sixties." *Prooftexts* 10 (1990): 129–47.
Hillel, Shlomo. *Operation Babylon: The Story of the Rescue of the Jews of Iraq*. Translated by Ina Friedman. New York: Doubleday, 1987.
Hoffman, Eva. *Lost in Translation: A Life in A New Language*. New York: Penguin, 1989.
Horowitz, Dan, and Moshe Lissak. *Trouble in Utopia: The Overburdened Polity of Israel*. Translated by Charles Hoffman. Albany, N.Y.: SUNY, 1989.
Idris, Suhayl. "Al-Qiṣṣah Al-'Irāqiyyah Al-Ḥadīthah, [part 1]." *Al-Ādāb* 2 (February 1953): 22–25.
———. "Al-Qiṣṣah Al-'Irāqiyyah Al-Ḥadīthah, [part 2]." *Al-Ādāb* 3 (March 1953): 46–50.

Idris, Suhayl. "Al-Qiṣṣah Al-ʿIrāqiyyah Al-Ḥadīthah, [part 3]." *Al-Ādāb* 4 (April 1953): 34–38.
Islan, Moshe, and Raḥel Nissim. *MiMinhageihem VeOraḥ Ḥayeihem Shel Yehudei 'Irak*. Tel Aviv: Ofer, 1982.
ʿIzz al-Dīn, Yūsuf. *Al-Qiṣṣah Fī Al-ʿIrāq Wa-Taṭawwuruhā*. Baghdad: Maṭbaʿat al-Baṣrī, 1974.
———. *Fi al-Adab al-ʿArabī al-Ḥadīth*. Baghdad: Maṭbaʿat al-Baṣrī, 1968.
———. *Poetry and Iraqi Society*. Baghdad: Maṭbaʿat al-Baṣrī, 1962. In English.
*Al-Jadīd* 3, no. 1 (November 1954).
Kamla, Thomas A. *Confrontation with Exile: Studies in the German Novel*. Frankfurt: Peter Lang, 1975.
Karpel, Dalia. "Baghdad, Ahuvati." *Ha'Ir*, 27 December 1985.
Kattan, Naim. *Farewell Babylon*. Translated from the French by Sheila Fischman. New York: Taplinger, 1980.
Katzenelson, Kalman. *HaMahapekhah HaAshkenazit*. Tel Aviv: Anakh, 1964.
Kazzaz, Nissim. "HaMarot Dat Bekrav Yehudei ʿIrak BeʿEt HaHadashah," *Pe'amim* (Winter 1990): 157-66.
———. *HaYehudim Be'Irak BeMeah Ha'Esrim*. Jerusalem: Makhon Ben-Ẓvi, 1991.
Kazzaz, Nessim. "The Iraqi Orientation in the Iraqi Jewish Leadership and Its Failure." Doctoral diss., Hebrew University, 1985.
Kedourie, Elie. "The Break Between Muslims and Jews in Iraq." In *Jews Among Arabs: Contacts and Boundaries*, edited by Mark R. Cohen and Abraham L. Udovitch. Princeton, N.J.: The Darwin Press, 1989.
"Keren Tel Aviv Ḥilkah 18 Maʿanakim LeSoferim." *Ma'ariv*, 21 June 1976.
Khadduri, Majid. *Independent Iraq: A Study in Iraqi Politics, 1932–58*. London: Oxford University Press, 1960.
Kimball, Lorenzo Kent. *The Changing Pattern of Political Power*. New York: Robert Speller and Sons, 1972.
Klausner, Samuel Z. "Immigrant Absorption and Social Tension in Israel: A Case Study of Iraqi Jewish Immigrants." *The Middle East Journal* 9, no. 3, (Summer 1955): 281–94.
Kramer, Lloyd S. "Exile and European Thought: Heine, Marx, and Mickiewicz in July Monarchy Paris." *Historical Reflections* 11, no. 1 (Spring 1984): 45–70.
Krausz, Ernest. *Studies of Israeli Society*. New Brunswick, N.J.: Transaction Books, 1980.
Lagos-Pope, Maria-Ines. *Exile in Literature*. Lewisburg, Pa.: Bucknell University Press, 1988.
Landschut, Siegfried. *Jewish Communities in the Muslim Countries of the Middle East: A Survey*. London: The Jewish Chronicles Ltd., [1950].
Laor, Dan. "Haʿaliyah HaHamonit KeʿTokhen VeNose' BaSifrut HaʿIvrit BiSh'not HaMedinah HaRishonot." *HaẒiyonut* 14 (1989): 161–75.
Levenberg, Aliza. "Eshnav LaMaʿabarah." *Ma'ariv*, 30 April 1964.

———. "Ḥayei HaMa'abarah MiBifnim," 25 July 1964. From the archives of Bet HaSofer Tchernichovsky, Tel Aviv.

Levine, Étan, ed. *Diaspora: Exile and the Contemporary Jewish Condition.* New York: Shapolsky Books, 1986.

Levine, Herbert. "The Symbolic Sukkah in the Psalms." *Prooftexts* 7 (1987): 259–67.

Lewin, Kurt. "Field Theory and Experiment in Social Psychology: Concepts and Methods." *American Journal of Sociology* no.44 (1939): 868–97.

Lewis, Bernard. *The Jews of Islam.* London: Routledge and Kegan Paul, 1984.

Liebman, Charles, and Eliezer Don-Yehiya. *Civil Religion in Israel.* Los Angeles: University of California Press, 1983.

———. *Religion and Politics in Israel.* Bloomington: Indiana University Press, 1984.

Liebowitz, Judith. *Narrative Purpose in the Novella.* The Hague: Mouton, 1974.

Longrigg, Stephen Hemsley. *Iraq, 1900 to 1950.* Beirut: Librairie du Liban, 1968.

Lotan, Yael. "Lehafrid Bein Yahadut LiYisraeliyut." *Yediot Aḥaronot,* 29 May 1987, 22, 26.

M. A. "Nigudim Bein Edot Yisrael VeYaḥasim Bein Yehudim Ve-'aravim." *Hedim,* December 1977. From the archives of Bet HaSofer Tchernichovsky, Tel Aviv.

Maerovitch, Dorit. "Meẓiyut Morkevet, Ketivah Funcẓionalit." *Siman Kriah,* April 1978.

Makarius, Raoul, and Laura Makarius. *Anthologie de la littérature arabe contemporaine.* Paris: Editions de Seuil, 1964.

Mandel, Neville J. *The Arabs and Zionism Before World War I.* Berkeley: University of California Press, 1976.

Marmorstein, Emile. "An Iraqi Jewish Writer in the Holy Land." *The Jewish Journal of Sociology* 6, no. 1 (July 1964): 91–102.

———. "Two Iraqi Jewish Short Story Writers: A Suggestion for Social Research" *The Jewish Journal of Sociology* 1, no. 2 (December 1959): 187–200.

Martin, B. "Parent-child relations." In vol. 4 of *Review of Child Development Research,* edited by F. D. Horowitz. Chicago: University of Chicago Press, 1975.

McCarthy, Mary. "Exiles, Expatriates and Internal Emigres." *The Listener* 86 (25 November 1971): 705–8.

Michael, Sami. "Lihiyot Sofer MiMoẓa 'Iraki." *Moznayim* 56 (February– March 1983): 8–11.

———. "On Being an Iraqi-Jewish Writer in Israel." Translated by Imre Goldstein. *Prooftexts* 4 (1984): 23–33.

Milbauer, Asher Z. *Transcending Exile: Conrad, Nabokov, I. B. Singer.* Gainesville: The University Press of Florida, 1985.

Milosz, Czeslaw. "Notes On Exile." *Books Abroad,* Spring 1976, 284–86.
Mintz, Alan. "A Sanctuary in the Wilderness: The Beginning of the Hebrew Movement in America in the Pages of 'HaToren.'" *Prooftexts* 10 (1990): 389–412.
Miron, Dan. *A Traveler Disguised: The Rise of Modern Yiddish Fiction in the Nineteenth Century.* New York: Schocken Books, 1973.
Modaressi, Taghi. "Iranian Writers Writing in a Second Language." Middle East Studies Association, Toronto, Ontario, 17 November 1989.
Moeller, Hans Bernhard. *Latin America and the Literature of Exile.* Heidelberg: Carl Winter Universitätsverlag, 1983.
Moreh, Shmuel. "Al-Adīb Samīr Naqqāsh Wa-Al-Qiṣṣah." *Al-Sharq* 8, no. 1. (January–March 1978): 63–81.
———. "Al-Shā'ir Wa-al-Qaṣṣāṣ al-Yahudi al-'Irāqi Me'ir Baṣrī." *Al-Sharq* 6, nos. 10–12 (March–April 1976): 29–33
———. "Anwar Shaul z"l: Rishon HaMeshorerim HaYehudim Be'Irak BaSafah Ha'Aravit." *Pe'amim,* no. 22 (1985): 46–69.
———. "HaYeẓirah HaRuḥanit Shel Yehudei Irak BaSafah Ha'Aravit." *Arabic and Islamic Studies* 2 (1978): 60–68.
———. "Jewish Poets and Writers of Modern Iraq." Jerusalem: Institute of Asian and African Studies, Ben-Zvi Institute, 1974. Unpublished manuscript.
______. "Olamo HaMeyuḥad Shel Yiẓḥak Bar-Moshe." *Shevet Va'Am* 3 [8] (April 1978): 425–44.
———. "Oriental Literature," In the *Encyclopedia Judaica* 1972.
———. "The Rise and Fall of Tantal the Demon in the Folk Literature of Iraqi Jewry." In *Researches on Oriental Jewry.* Jerusalem: World Jewish Union, 1981.
———. "Samīr Naqqāsh, Qiṣṣāṣ Ṣaghīr Min al-Irāq." *Al-Sharq* 8, no. 1 (January–March 1978): 63–81.
———. *Short Stories by Jewish Writers from Iraq, 1924–1978.* Jerusalem: The Magnes Press, 1978. In English, Hebrew, and Arabic.
———. "Ya'qub Bilbūl, Shā'ir Wa-Qaṣṣāṣ." *Al-Sharq* 7, nos. 5–7 (May–July 1977): 66–69.
Moreh, Shmuel, and Lev Hakkak. "Yeẓiratam HaSifrutit VeHaMeḥkarim Shel Yoẓei 'Irak Be'Irak UVeYisrael BeDorenu." In *Meḥkarim beToldot Yehudei 'Irak VeTarbutam,* edited by Shmuel Moreh. Or Yehuda: Merkaz Moreshet Yahadut Bavel, 1981.
Murad, Emil. *MeBavel BeMaḥteret.* Tel Aviv: Am Oved, 1972.
Nabokov, Vladimir. *Strong Opinions.* New York: Putnam, 1951.
Neusner, Jacob. *A History of The Jews in Babylonia.* 5 vols. Leiden: Brill, 1965–70.
———. *Self-fulfilling Prophecy: Exile and Return in the History of Judaism.* Boston: Beacon Press, 1987.
———. *There We Sat Down.* Nashville, Tenn.: Abingdon Press, 1972.

Nof, A. "Shavim VeShavim Yoter." *Zo HaDerekh,* 10 March 1976, 12.
Ohel, Milo. *Gesher.* Tel Aviv: Sifriyat Yalkut, 1955.
Olney, James, ed. *Autobiography: Essays Theoretical and Critical.* Princeton: Princeton University Press, 1980.
Pachter, Marc, ed. *Telling Lives: The Biographer's Art.* Washington, D.C.: New Republic Books, 1979.
Parvin, Manoucher. "Iranian Fiction Writers Writing in a Second Language." Middle East Studies Association Meeting, Toronto, Canada, 17 November 1989.
Pascal, Roy. *Design and Truth in Autobiography.* Cambridge: Harvard University Press, 1960.
Patai, Raphael. *The Arab Mind.* New York: Charles Scribner's Sons, 1983.
"Peras Ḥolon LeSifrut Yafah LeSami Michael VeYona Wollach." *Davar,* 17 January 1978.
Perliss, Iza. "Aflayah Edatit BeRoman." *Davar,* 23 August 1974.
Peters, Joan. *From Time Immemorial.* Philadelphia: Harper and Row, 1984.
Piamenta, Moshe. "Al Sifrut ʿAravit-Yisraelit VeʿAl Samīr Naqqāsh–Meḥadesh HaYeẓirah HaʿAravit–Yehudit B'Yisrael." *Ma'ariv,* 20 February 1981.
Pinsker, Sanford. *Languages of Joseph Conrad.* Amsterdam: Rodopi, 1978.
*Problems of the Oriental Jewry.* Jerusalem: Department for Jewish Affairs in the Middle East, Jewish Agency for Palestine [n.d.].
Propp, Vladimir. *The Morphology of the Folktale.* Bloomington: Indiana University Press, 1958.
Rabi [Rabeeya], David. "A Preliminary Study of Hebrew Forms in the Arabic Dialect of the Jews of Baghdad." *Gratz College Annual of Jewish Studies* 7 (1978): 51–64.
Rabi, Yaʿakov. "HaSipur VeHaTeʿudah." *ʿAl HaMishmar,* 16 March 1984.
Raphael, Chaim. *The Road From Babylon: The Story of Sephardi and Oriental Jews.* New York: Harper and Row, 1985.
Rappaport, A. "KaMaʿayan haMitgaber." *Kol Bo Ḥaifa,* 31 October 1978.
Rawidowicz, Simon. *Israel: The Ever Dying People.* Rutherford, N.J.: Fairleigh Dickinson University Press, 1986.
Rejwan, Nissim. *The Jews of Iraq: Three Thousand Years of History and Culture.* Boulder, Colo.: Westview Press, 1985.
———. "Lizkor Et HaZmanim," *Kesher* 17 (May 1995):110–13. Translated by Tali Barukh.
Ron, L. "Sin'ah VeRekhilut o 'Roman' shel Irak." *Zo Ha-Derekh,* 29 June 1977.
Rosenberg, Shalom. "Exile and Redemption in Jewish Thought in the Sixteenth Century: Contending Conceptions." In *Jewish Thought in the Sixteenth Century,* edited by Bernard Dov Cooperman, 399–430. Cambridge: Harvard University Press, 1983.
Sachar, Howard Morley. *The Course of Modern Jewish History.* New York: Dell, 1958.

Sachar, Howard Morley. *Diaspora: An Inquiry into the Contemporary Jewish World*. Philadelphia: Harper and Row, 1985.
Said, Edward. "Reflections on Exile." Lecture, Philadelphia, 7 March 1984.

Sallūm, Dā'ūd. *Taṭawwur Al-Fikrah Wa-Al-Uslūb Fī Al-Ādāb Al-'Irāqī*. Baghdad: Maṭba'at al-Ma'āref, 1959.
Sandbank, Shimon. "Contemporary Israeli Literature: The Withdrawal from Certainty." *Triquarterly* 39 (1977): 3–18.
Schechtman, Joseph B. "The Repatriation of Iraqi Jewry." *Jewish Social Sciences* 15 (April 1953): 151–72.
Scherman, Rabbi Nosson, ed. *The Complete Artscroll Siddur*. Brooklyn, N.Y.: Mesorah, 1984.
Schwartz, Shlomo. *Makom She'ain Lo Shem*. Tel Aviv: HaKibbutz HaMeuchad, 1955.
Scott, A. F. *Current Literary Terms: A Concise Dictionary of Their Origin and Use*. London: Macmillan, 1980.
Segev, Tom. *1949: The First Israelis*. Translated by Arlen Neal Weinstein. New York: Macmillan, 1986.
Seidel, Michael. *Exile and the Narrative Imagination*. New Haven: Yale University Press, 1986.
Selzer, Michael. *Wineskin and Wizard*. New York: Macmillan, 1970.
Shaharbani, Uri. "44 Shanim LaFarhud." *BaMa'arakhah* 25, no. 296 (June 1985): 5.
Shaked, Gershon. *Gal Ḥadash BaSiporet Ha'Ivrit*. Tel Aviv: Sifriyat Poalim, 1970.
———. *HaSiporet HaIvrit, 1880–1970: BaGolah*. Jerusalem and Tel Aviv: Keter and HaKibbutz HaMeuchad, 1977.
———. *HaSiporet HaIvrit, 1880–1980: BeḤevlai HaZ'man*. Keter and HaKibbutz HaMeuchad, 1993.
———. "Hebrew Prose Fiction After the War of Liberation." *Modern Hebrew Literature* 5, nos. 1–2 (Summer 1979): 21–34.
———. "Literature and Its Audience: On the Reception of Israeli Fiction in the Forties and the Fifties." *Prooftexts* 7 (1987): 207–23.
———. *The Shadows Within*. Philadelphia: Jewish Publication Society, 1987.
Shaked, Gershon, et al. "Lashon HaMarot: Al Sifrut VeḤevrah." Israeli Educational Television, November 1993–March 1994.
Shamir, Moshe. "Colloquial Language and Literary Language." *Sifrut* 3 (1957): 19–34.
Al-Shārūnī, Yūsuf. *Dirāsāt Adabiyyah*. Cairo: Maṭba'at al-ma'rifah, 1964.
Shā'ūl, Anwar. *Qiṣṣat Ḥayāti fī Wādī al-Rāfidayn* (My life in Iraq). Jerusalem: Association for Jewish Academics from Iraq, 1980.
Shiblak, Abbas. *The Lure of Zion: The Case of the Iraqi Jews*. London: Al-Saqi Books, 1986.
Shohat, Ella. *Israeli Cinema: East/West and the Politics of Representation*.

Austin: University of Texas Press, 1989.

Shoḥet, Nir. *Sipurah Shel Golah: Perakim BeToldot Yahadut Bavel LeDoroteiha*. Jerusalem: HaAgudah LiKidum HaMeḥkar VeHayeẓirah, 1981.

Siegel, Richard, and Carl Rheins, eds. *The Jewish Almanac*. New York: Bantam, 1980.

Silverfarb, Daniel. *Britain's Informal Empire in the Middle East: A Case Study of Iraq, 1929–1941*. Oxford: Oxford University Press, 1986.

Simon, Reeva S. *Iraq Between the Two World Wars*. New York: Columbia University Press, 1986.

Slyomovics, Susan. "Rebbele Mordekhele's Pilgrimage in New York, Tel Aviv and Carpathian Ruthenia." Lecture in conference entitled *Jewish Folklore: American-Israeli Dialogue*. University of Pennsylvania, 17 October 1989.

Smith, Jane I., ed. *Women in Contemporary Muslim Societies*. Lewisburg, Pa.: Bucknell University Press, 1980.

Smooha, Sammy. "Black Panthers: The Ethnic Dilemma." *Society* 9, no. 7 (May 1972): 31–36.

———. *Israel: Pluralism and Conflict*. Berkeley: University of California Press, 1978.

Snir, Reuven. "Hasifrut Ha'Aravit Shel Yehudei 'Irak: HaDinamikah HaPnimit Shel HaMa'arekhet HaTarbutit HaYehudit VeYaḥasei Gomlin 'Im HaMa'arekhet HaTarbutit Ha'Aravit." *MeKedem UMeYam*. Haifa: University of Haifa, 1995.

———. "Temurah Tarbutit BiRe'i HaSifrut: Reshit HaSipur Ha'Aravi HaKaẓar Me'et Yehudim Be'Irak." *Pe'amim*, no. 36 (1988): 108–29.

———. "We Were Like Those Who Dream': Iraqi-Jewish Writers in Israel in the 1950s." *Prooftexts* 11, no. 2 (May 1991): 153–73.

Sofer, A. "Likro: Sufah Bein HaDekalim." From the archives of Bet HaSofer Tchernichovsky, Tel Aviv.

Somekh, Sasson. "Ḥavayot Avudot." *Iton 77*, nos. 78–79 (July–August 1986): 6, 50.

———. "Lost Voices: Jewish Authors in Modern Arabic Literature." In *Jews Among Arabs: Contacts and Boundaries*, edited by Mark R. Cohen and Abraham L. Udovitch. Princeton, N.J.: The Darwin Press, 1989.

———. "Yehudim Be'Itonut Ha'Irakit, 1946–48," *Kesher* 17 (May 1995): 108-110.

Stahl, Avraham. *'Edot Yisrael*. Tel Aviv: Am Oved, 1978.

———. *Mizug Tarbuti BeYisrael*. Tel Aviv: Am Oved, 1976.

———. *Yehudei HaMizraḥ BeSifrutenu*. Jerusalem: Misrad HaHinukh VeHaTarbut, n.d.

Steinhauer, Henry. "Towards A Definition of the Novella." *Seminar* 6 (1970): 154–72.

Stetkyvetch, Jaroslav. *The Modern Arabic Literary Language*. Center for Middle Eastern Studies, no. 6. Chicago: University of Chicago Press, 1970.

Stillman, Norman A. *The Jews of Arab Lands: A History and Source Book.* Philadelphia: The Jewish Publication Society, 1979.
Stone, Russell A. *Social Change in Israel: Attitudes and Events, 1967–79.* New York: Praeger, 1982.
Strelka, Joseph. "Material Collectors, Political Rhetoricians and Amateurs: Current Methodological Problems in German Exile Literature Studies." In *Protest–Form–Tradition: Essays on German Exile Literature,* edited by Joseph Strelka, Robert F. Bell, and Eugene Dobson. Tuscaloosa: The University of Alabama Press, 1979.
———. "The Novel in Exile: Types and Patterns." In *Exile: The Writer's Experience,* edited by John M. Spalek and Robert F. Bell. Chapel Hill: University of North Carolina Press, 1982.
Swirski, Shlomo. *Israel: The Oriental Majority.* Translated by Barbara Swirski. Atlantic Highlands, N.J.: Zed Books, 1989.
Tabori, Paul. *The Anatomy of Exile.* London: Harrap, 1972.
Taymūr, Aḥmed. *Al-Amthāl al-ʿĀmmiyyah.* Cairo: Maṭābiʿ al-ahrām, 1980.
Thompson, Ewa. "The Writer in Exile: Playing the Devil's Advocate." *Books Abroad,* Spring 1976, p. 326–28.
Tradler, Ruti. "HaDekel Lo Meḥubar Tov LaAdamah, Kamoni." *Moznayim* 57, nos. 5–6 (October–November 1983): 88.
Tucker, Martin. "Exile and the Writer." In *Confrontation,* edited by Martin Tucker, 27–28. New York: Long Island University Press, 1984.
Turner, Victor. *The Ritual Process: Structure and Anti-Structure.* Chicago: Aldine, 1969.
Ukhmani, Azriel. "Gidulo Shel Mesaper." *ʿAl HaMishmar,* 18 Feburary 1955.
Al-Wardānī, Ibrāhīm. "Ṣawārīkh," *Al-Jumhūriyyah,* 23 September 1983.
———. "Ṣawārīkh." *Al-Jumhūriyyah,* 19 October 1983.
Warren, John. "The Courtyard Houses of Baghdad: A Rich Heritage." *The Literary Review Supplement,* 1982, 87–94.
Wexler, Paul. "Diglossia, Language Standardization, and Purism: Toward a Typology of Literary Languages." *HaSifrut* 3, no. 2 (November 1971): 326–38.
Williams, David. "The Exile as Uncreator." *Mosaic* 8 (Spring 1975): 1–15.
Wirth-Nesher, Hana. "Between Mother Tongue and Native Language: Multilingualism in Herman Roth's *Call It Sleep.*" *Prooftexts* 10 (May 1990): 297–312.
Yaḥil-Wax, Miriam. "HaEmdah HaShlishit." *Iton* 77, nos. 91–92 (August–September 1987): 18–21.
Yehoshua, A. B. *Molkho.* Tel Aviv: HaSifriyah, 1987.
Yudkin, Leon Israel. *Jewish Writing and Identity in the Twentieth Century.* New York: St. Martin's Press, 1982.
Zehavi, Alex. "'Anti-Gibor' Mul HaMeẓiut: 'Hitbaharut'–Roman Ḥadash Shel Shimon Ballas." *Yediot Aḥaronot,* 1 September 1972.
———. "Ashlayat HaShivyon." *Yediot Aḥaronot,* 16 August 1974.

———. "Lignov et Ha'Ivrit." *Yediot Aḥaronot*. From the archives of Bet HaSofer, Tel Aviv.
Zinsser, William, ed. *Inventing the Truth: The Art and Craft of Memoir*. Boston: Houghton Mifflin, 1987.
Zohori, Menahem, ed. *Hagut 'Ivrit BeArẓot Ha'Islam*. Jerusalem: World Hebrew Union and World Jewish Congress, 1981.

INTERVIEWS

Interview with Alex Zehavi, Jerusalem, 25 May 1989.
Interview with David Rabeeya [Rabi], Elkins Park, Pa., 21 November 1989.
Interview with David Semach, Haifa, 4 June 1989.
Interview with Eli Amir, Jerusalem, 30 May 1989.
Interview with Samīr Naqqāsh, Petach Tikva, 21 May 1989.
Interview with Shalom Darwīsh, Haifa, 22 May 1989.
Interview with Shimon Ballas, Tel Aviv, 9 May 1989.
Interview with Shmuel Moreh, Jerusalem, 11 May 1989.
Interview with Ya'qūb (Lev) Bilbūl, Tel Aviv, 16 May 1989.
Interview with Yiẓḥak Bar-Moshe, Jerusalem, 18 May 1989.

# Index